AF378326

ART
FOR CHILDREN

A STEP-BY-STEP GUIDE FOR THE YOUNG ARTIST

FENELLA BROWN · JO MOODY
TONY SMART

CHARTWELL
BOOKS, INC.

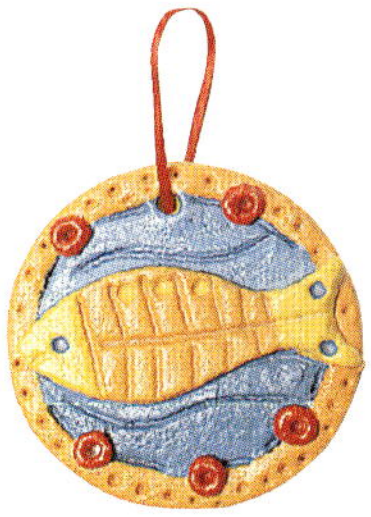

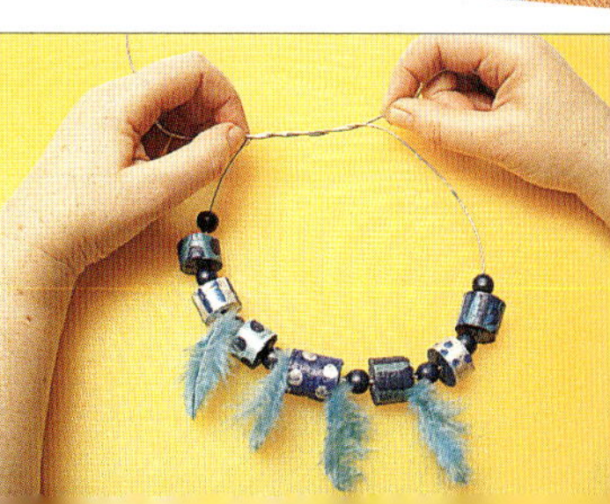

A QUARTO BOOK

Published by Chartwell Books Inc.
A Division of Book Sales, Inc.
114 Northfield Avenue
Edison, New Jersey 08837

This edition produced for sale in the U.S.A.,
its territories and dependencies only.

Hardback edition: ISBN: 0-7858-1046-3

Softback edition: ISBN: 0-7858–1031-5

This book was designed and produced by
Quintet Publishing Limited
6 Blundell Street
London N7 9BH

Creative Director: Richard Dewing
Designers: Ian Hunt and James Lawrence
Photographers: Colin Bowling and Paul Forrester

Typeset in Great Britain by
Central Southern Typesetters, Eastbourne
Manufactured by Bright Arts (Pte) Ltd, Singapore
Printed by Star Standard Industries (Pte) Ltd, Singapore

PUBLISHER'S NOTE

- Children should take great care when
completing these projects. Certain tools and
techniques, such as craft knives and using the
oven, can be dangerous and extreme care
must be exercised at all times.
- Adults should always supervise while children
work on these projects.
- As far as methods and techniques mentioned
n this book are concerned, all statements,
information, and advice given here are
believed to be true and accurate. However, the
author, copyright holder, and publisher cannot
accept any legal liability for errors or omissions.

Contents

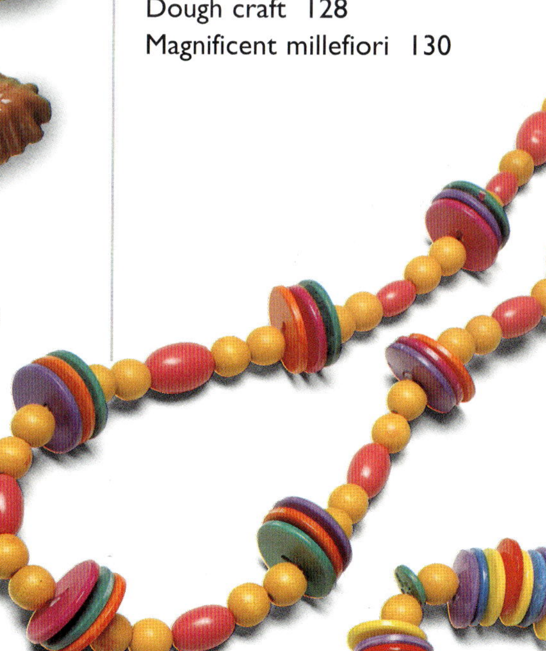

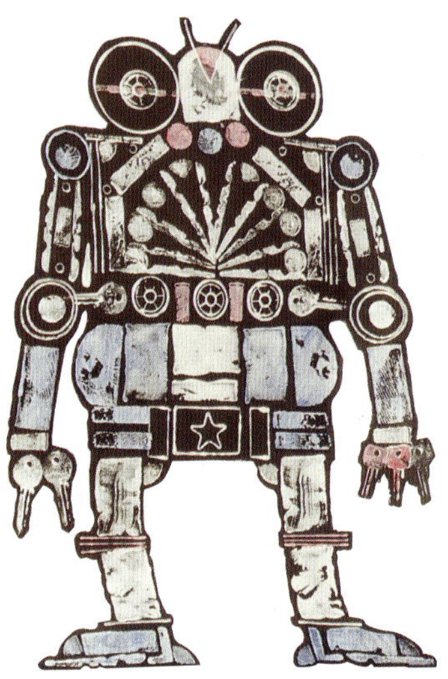

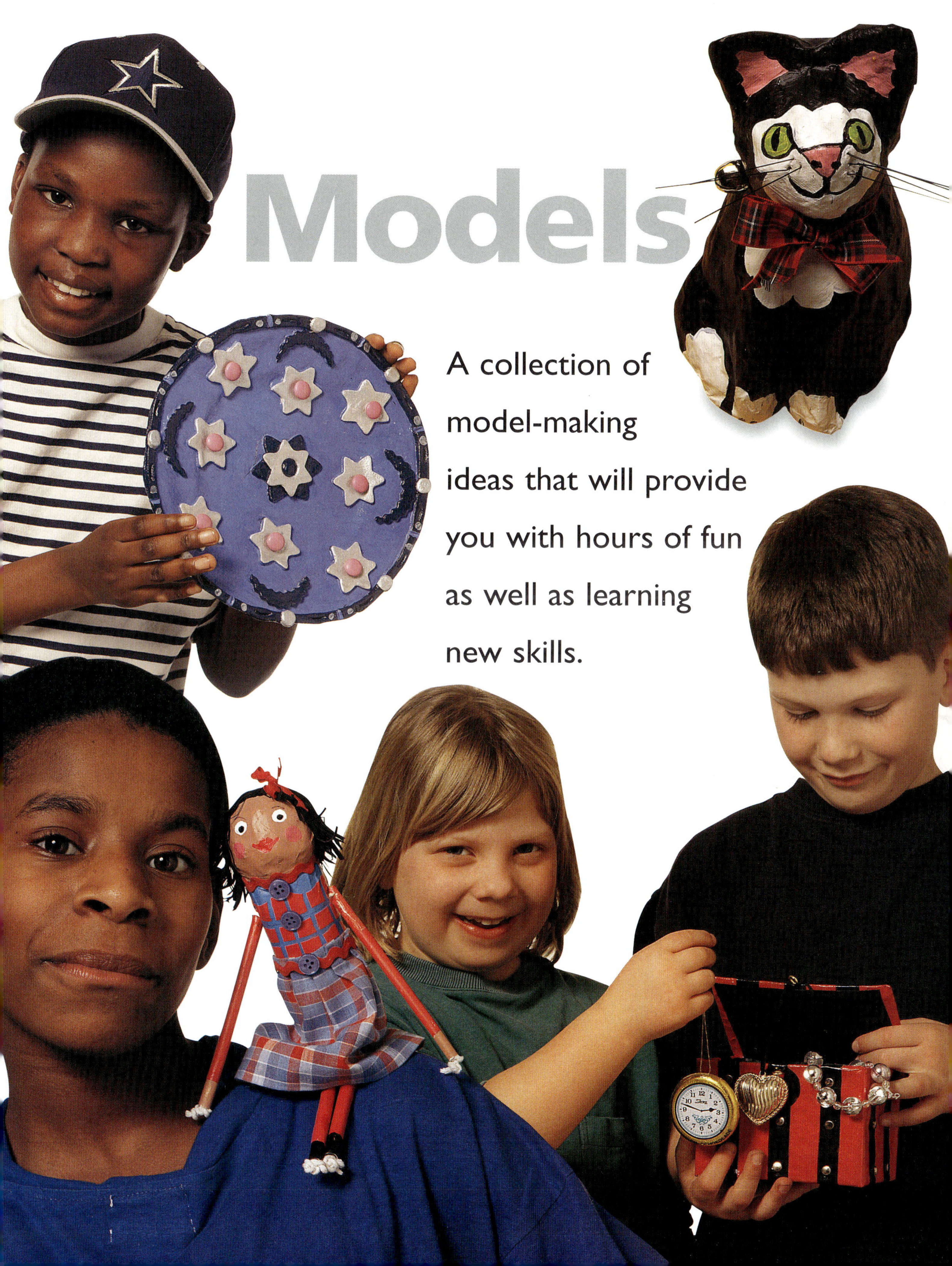

Models

A collection of
model-making
ideas that will provide
you with hours of fun
as well as learning
new skills.

Introduction

How often do you sit down on a cold, wet day or during school vacations and wonder what to do? This collection of model-making ideas will provide hours of interest and fun, as well as teaching you some new skills. If you do not want to make some of the models for yourself, you could make them as gifts for friends and relatives. Most of the materials you will need are inexpensive, and you will probably find the tools and equipment around the house. Colored clay, both the oven-bake and air-dried kind, is widely available in craft and art stores, and you will find the special light wood needed for some of the projects in craft and modeling stores.

It is a good idea to keep your own "inspirations" box. Collect pieces of colored construction paper, feathers, shells, scraps of fabric, dried flowers and seeds, buttons, and beads – anything, in fact, that you might want to incorporate into one of your designs to personalize it and make it unique to you.

It is also a good idea to keep a scrapbook in which you can stick illustrations cut out from magazines and newspapers. If you have a sketchpad or notebook, jot down ideas for colors and patterns as they come into your head – before they disappear. Artists always do this. Sometimes, just flicking through your sketchbook or rummaging in your inspirations box will give you an idea for something new to make. Use your scrapbook to inspire yourself to experiment with ideas and to adapt the models that are included in this book to suit your own likes and dislikes. Before you begin, it is a good idea to draw your idea quickly. Your sketch need not be accurate or beautiful, but you will find it helpful to have an idea of the overall shape and color of the model you are going to make as a guide while you work.

Each chapter in the book looks at a type of modeling material. The projects within each chapter are arranged in increasing order of difficulty – the first is the simplest, the last is the most complicated. However, if you want to make the dog pencil box, for example, look at the way it is made and see if you can find ways of making it less complicated – paint on the features instead of cutting them from wood. Don't worry if you want to make the salt dough plate but think that it looks too difficult. Try making it with fewer shapes or decorate it with shapes that you can quickly cut out freehand. Then, when it is dry, paint it with bright colors or add some glitter.

Some of the projects involve using templates, and these are given full size at the back of the book. Either photocopy or trace the outlines you need and transfer them to stiff cardboard. Cut out the cardboard and then use it to draw or cut around to make the appropriate shape. To highlight safety some of the photographs are bordered with red warning triangles and the instructions are written in bold underlined text.

SAFETY FIRST

The projects are fun to do, but as you work, keep the following in mind:

- Remember that you must always be very careful with sharp knives and pointed instruments. Ask an adult to help you when you need to cut out shapes with a craft knife.
- Be careful about leaving knives, scissors, and needles lying around when you are working – they could be dangerous to your younger brothers and sisters. Put a piece of cork on the end of your craft knife to protect you from cuts.
- If you have made a model that needs to be baked in the oven, ask for help. It is no fun being burned, so always use an oven mitt putting things in the oven and taking them out again.
- When you have finished for the day, clear away all the materials you have been using and put everything away, making sure that all your knives, scissors, needles, and materials are kept in a box, safely out of the way.
- At the end of the day, wash your paintbrushes and clean any brushes and containers that have been used for glue or varnish.
- Store any oven-bake and air-dried clay that you have not used in an airtight container so that it is ready for next time.

TOOLS AND EQUIPMENT

PAINT

For the projects shown in this book, we used poster paints and, occasionally, acrylic paints. Acrylic paints are useful because there is no need to varnish them to make them waterproof. Like poster paints, they are sold in art shops, and because they can be mixed to make almost any color you want, you need only buy red, blue, yellow, black, and white. Add a spot of black to make a color darker. A spot of white will make a color lighter. It is easier to make a light color dark than to make a dark color light.

GLUE

One of the easiest adhesives to use is craft glue, which is widely available and sticks nearly everything. It can be diluted with water to make a varnish. Although it looks milky as you apply it, it dries clear, so do not worry about using generous amounts to make surfaces stick together.

The papier mâché is made with wallpaper paste – granules that are mixed in water. These days, most wallpaper pastes contain chemicals to stop mold forming, so take care when you mix and use the paste. Wash your hands thoroughly when you have finished and mop up any spills.

If you need to stick a magnet or brooch back in place, you will need to use a strong, all-purpose household adhesive, of the kind used for mending broken china.

VARNISH

Poster paints are not waterproof, and when you have finished decorating a model you may want to protect it with a coat of varnish, which will give a smooth, glossy look to the surface. Art and craft stores sell varnish – remember to wash your brush thoroughly after use. Acrylic paint is waterproof when it is dry, so if you prefer a matte finish you can omit the varnish at the end.

PAINTBRUSHES

As in all arts and crafts it is far easier and more enjoyable to work with the right tools. There is nothing more annoying than trying to paint a fine, neat line with a fat paintbrush or trying to cover a large, flat area with a brush that has only a few hairs in it. To begin with, try to have a very fine brush (about size 11), a medium sized one (size 5 or 6), and a large one (size 1 or 2).

MODELING TOOLS

Some craft stores stock sets of modeling tools, like the ones illustrated in this book. You can, however, buy them one by one if you prefer. As with your paintbrushes, it is easier to work well if you have special tools to mark lines and textures rather than trying to use an old, blunt knife. Wooden toothpicks, used matches, and old ice-cream sticks can all be used, and you will find that old ballpoint pen cases are extremely useful. Build up a collection of tools that you like to use, and experiment until you know what you need for each effect you want to achieve.

KNIVES

You must be very careful if you use a knife. Unless you are using balsa wood, you can probably make all the models in this book with a blunt kitchen knife and a pair of scissors. Even so, do take care, because a blunt blade can cause a painful cut if it slips. Always cut away from you, and make sure you are working on a flat, stable surface. Place your work on a piece of thick cardboard to protect the worktop, or, better still, use one of the special non-slip cutting mats that you can buy in art stores. Make sure there is an adult around to help with any complicated cutting.

OVEN-BAKE CLAY

This is a great modeling material to use because it comes in so many beautiful colors. It is more expensive than some of the other modeling materials, so it is often used for small items, such as jewelry, little ornaments, or even dollhouse accessories. It needs to be softened in your hands before you can work with it, but when you have made your model and it has been baked in the oven, it becomes hard and quite strong. The colors can be mixed together to make new shades, so you will need only a few to begin with. There are several different brands available, so you must always read the manufacturer's instructions for baking times and temperatures.

SALT DOUGH

This is one of the cheapest of all modeling materials. You can either let your model dry out over a few days or you can bake it in the oven at a very low temperature for an hour or two. When you are mixing the dough, you must remember to use all-purpose flour. Self-rising flour will make your models rise like cakes. When you have mixed the dough you may find that, although you have carefully followed the instructions, the dough feels sticky and is difficult to work with. Simply add a little more flour and continue kneading. Repeat the process until the dough is firm and easy to model. Similarly, if it becomes too dry, dampen your fingers and smooth them over the dough. Remember to keep sprinkling flour over the work surface so that the dough does not stick to it.

AIR-DRIED CLAY

Traditionally, clay had to be hardened in a kiln at a very high temperature. This relatively new kind of clay, which is sometimes called self-hardening clay, contains fibers – so small you cannot see them – that make it strong as it dries out and eliminate the need for baking. If you smooth over any bumps and cracks with a damp finger before the clay is dry, and give it two or three coats of varnish when it has hardened, you will be surprised at how like china it looks. Take care, if you drop it, it will break.

EDIBLE MATERIALS

We have used two kinds for our models – marzipan and a store-bought mix based on icing sugar.

Marzipan is delicious, but, if you can resist eating it while you work, it can be used for fruits, people and animals. Vegetable food coloring can be added to create a rainbow of shades, so you could make a zoo full of exotic animals or an aviary full of colored birds.

We used ready-mixed icing, which is rolled out, to ice the cookies. If you add peppermint essence to the mixture, you will have peppermint creams, which can be made doubly delicious if you coat them in melted chocolate. You can add vegetable food coloring to the icing, or you could make a clown's face, for example, in white icing and then use food coloring to paint on the features and decorations.

PAPIER MACHE

This is one of those materials that is always popular, although at the moment it is enjoying something of a revival. It is not expensive to make, and it can be used for all kinds of things – from toys and masks to plates and jewelry. You can use it in one of two ways. The easier method is to build up layers of pasted strips of paper – the more layers you use, the stronger the finished object will be. If you want to make something very large, you can make a base shape from something like Plasticine and apply pasted strips to the surface, or you can use a plate or a box in the same way. The other way is to make a squashy pulp using torn pieces of newspaper, glue, and water in a bowl. The pulp can be used to make more solid objects, such as the cat on page 45.

NATURAL MATERIALS

When you come back from a hike in the country or along the seashore, what do you do with all the pebbles, seedheads, shells, and nuts that you collect? Keep them safe in your "inspirations" box for those rainy days when you are at loose ends, and then let them inspire you to use them in all kinds of ways. Use them on their own to create imaginary land and seascapes, or combine them with another material, such as Plasticine, to make animals and birds.

BALSA WOOD

All the projects in this chapter are made with a soft, light wood called balsa wood, which you will find in your neighborhood hobby store. It can be easily cut with a craft knife – but do be careful. Ask an adult to help you while cutting out the wood. The best way to cut is to use four or five gentler cuts instead of making one strong, deep cut. This not only stops the wood from splintering but, more importantly, makes it less likely that you will cut your fingers. Use special adhesive for balsa wood (available from your hobby store) and use plain dressmaking pins to hold pieces together while the glue dries. If you enjoy making models with balsa wood, try making some boats that really sail, or airplanes that really fly, or some furniture for a dollhouse, all to your own designs.

Oven-bake Clay

Busy Bee Key Ring

Oven-bake clay is ideal for key rings because it is quite strong when it has been baked. You could make a pin or a brooch in the same way by gluing a brooch pin to the back of the baked shape. Think of other insects – a butterfly or ladybug, perhaps – to make with different colors.

- Oven-bake clay: yellow, black, white
- Toothpick
- Rolling pin
- Blunt knife
- Modeling tools
- Cookie sheet
- Clear varnish and brush
- Narrow yellow ribbon
- Key ring

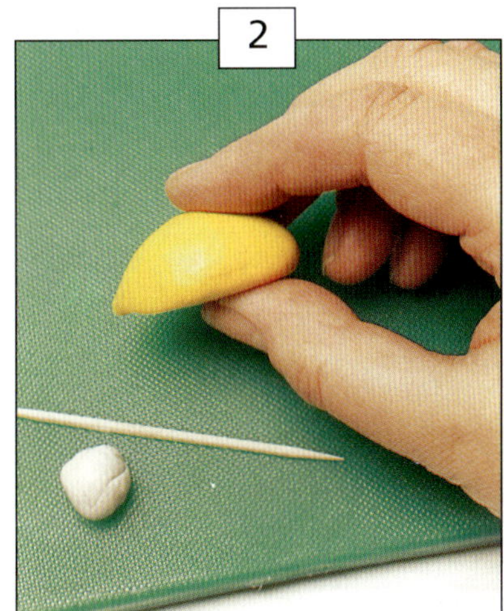

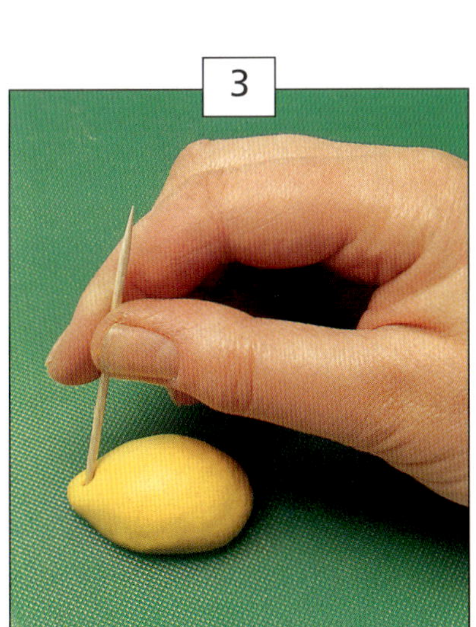

1 Take a piece of yellow clay and smaller pieces of black and white clay. Roll the pieces in your hands to warm and soften them.

2 Roll the yellow clay into an egg shape with a point at one end and flatten the base by pressing it on the worktop.

3 Use the toothpick to make a hole in the pointed end – the tail – through which the ribbon for the key will be threaded later.

4 Roll out the black clay until it is about ⅛ inch thick, and **cut three strips, each about ¼ inch wide.**

5 Carefully position the strips on the bee's body, pressing them gently in place.

6 Roll the bits of black clay that are left together and make two small balls for the bee's eyes. Flatten them with your finger and press them into position with the toothpick.

7 Divide the white clay into two equal pieces and roll each piece into a flattened oval for the wings.

8 Use a modeling tool to mark three lines on each wing.

9 Press the wings onto the sides of the bee's body.

10 **Carefully place the bee on a cookie sheet and put it in the oven. Leave it to bake for 20-30 minutes at 265°F.**

SAFETY FIRST

☛ Some makes of oven-bake clays contain chemicals that may come off on your hands as you model with them. Always wash your hands carefully when you have finished working with clay, and never, never try to eat it!

11 When the bee is cool, give it a coat of varnish. Remember to apply varnish to the base. Leave to dry.

12 Thread the ribbon through the hole in the tail and pull one end of the ribbon through the key ring.

13 Thread the ribbon through the hole again and tie a knot. Trim the ends of the ribbon.

Pirate Hat Magnet

This refrigerator magnet is in the shape of a pirate hat, but you could make a cowboy hat or a baseball cap in the same way. Some of the pieces used are very small, but if you use a toothpick or the end of a paper clip to help you, you should be able to move the little bits of clay around quite easily.

YOU WILL NEED

- Oven-bake clay: black, white
- Rolling pin
- White cardboard
- Pencil
- Scissors or craft knife
- Modeling tools
- Toothpick
- Cookie sheet
- Clear varnish and brush
- Small magnet
- Clear, all-purpose adhesive

1 Warm and soften the black clay by rolling it between your hands.

2 Roll out the clay on your work top so that it is about ¼ inch thick.

3 Copy the hat template on page 88 and transfer the outline to a piece of white cardboard. **Cut out the shape of the hat from the cardboard.**

4 Place the hat shape on the black clay and carefully **cut around the cardboard.**

5 Take about half the white clay and soften it in your hands. Roll it on your work top to make a long, thin strip.

6 Place the white strip around the edge of the hat shape so that it looks like piping. Gently press it in place.

7 Copy the skull template on page 88 and transfer the outline to white cardboard. Roll out the remaining white clay until it is ⅛ inch thick. **Place the skull template on the clay and cut out the shape.**

8 Roll the bits of white clay together and form the clay into four sticks and four small balls. Press a ball at one end of each stick and use a toothpick to position the "bones" around the hat.

9 From the scraps of black clay, cut four small, thin strips for teeth and two tiny circles for eyes. Use a toothpick to position these on the skull. Use the toothpick to smooth and tidy up all the edges.

10 **Carefully place the hat on a cookie sheet and put it in the oven. Leave it to bake for 20–30 minutes at 265°F, or according to the manufacturer's instructions.**

11 When the hat is completely cool, apply a coat of varnish. Leave to dry.

12 Glue a small magnet to the back of the hat.

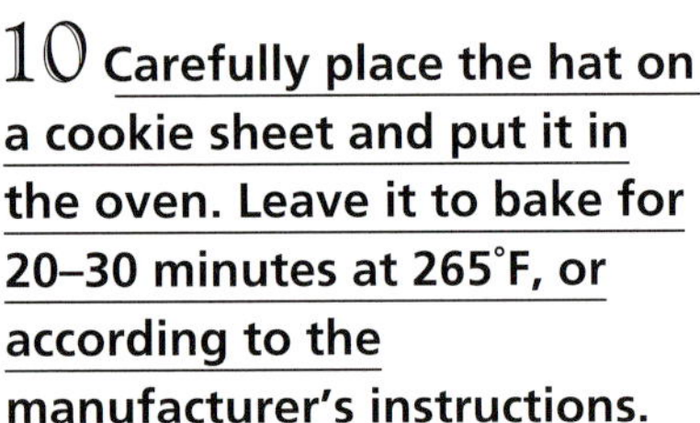

Pussycat Barrette

Hair clasps like this are easy to make and fun to wear. You could choose colors that will go with a favorite outfit or you could add some glitter for a party – some manufacturers of oven-bake clays also make glittery powders that can be added before baking. Metal barrettes are available from art and craft suppliers and beauty supply stores.

YOU WILL NEED

- Oven-bake clay: gray, white, black, yellow, pink
- Rolling pin
- Metal hair clasp
- Lipstick top
- Craft knife
- Toothpick
- Cookie sheet
- Clear varnish and brush

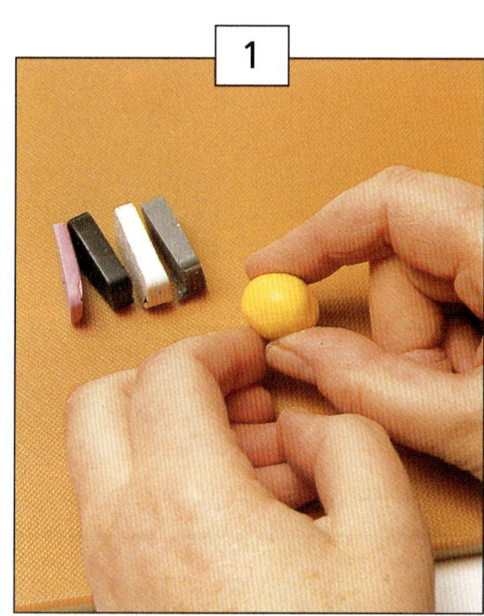

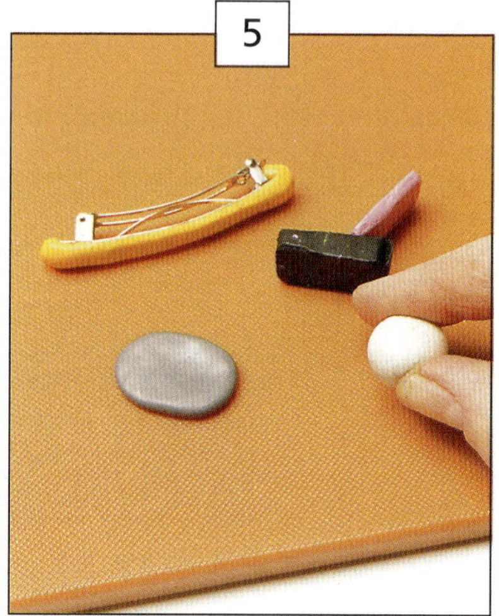

1 Soften the pieces of clay by rolling them in your hands. Roll the yellow clay into a ball.

2 Roll out the yellow clay into a long rectangle, about 2 x ½ inches.

3 Place the clasp face down on the yellow clay and **cut around the clasp so that the clay fits the top of the clasp.**

4 Press the clay to the top of the clasp. Make sure that the clay overlaps the ends of the clasp slightly.

5 Roll the gray, white, and black clay into balls and flatten each into a circle around 1⁄16 inch thick.

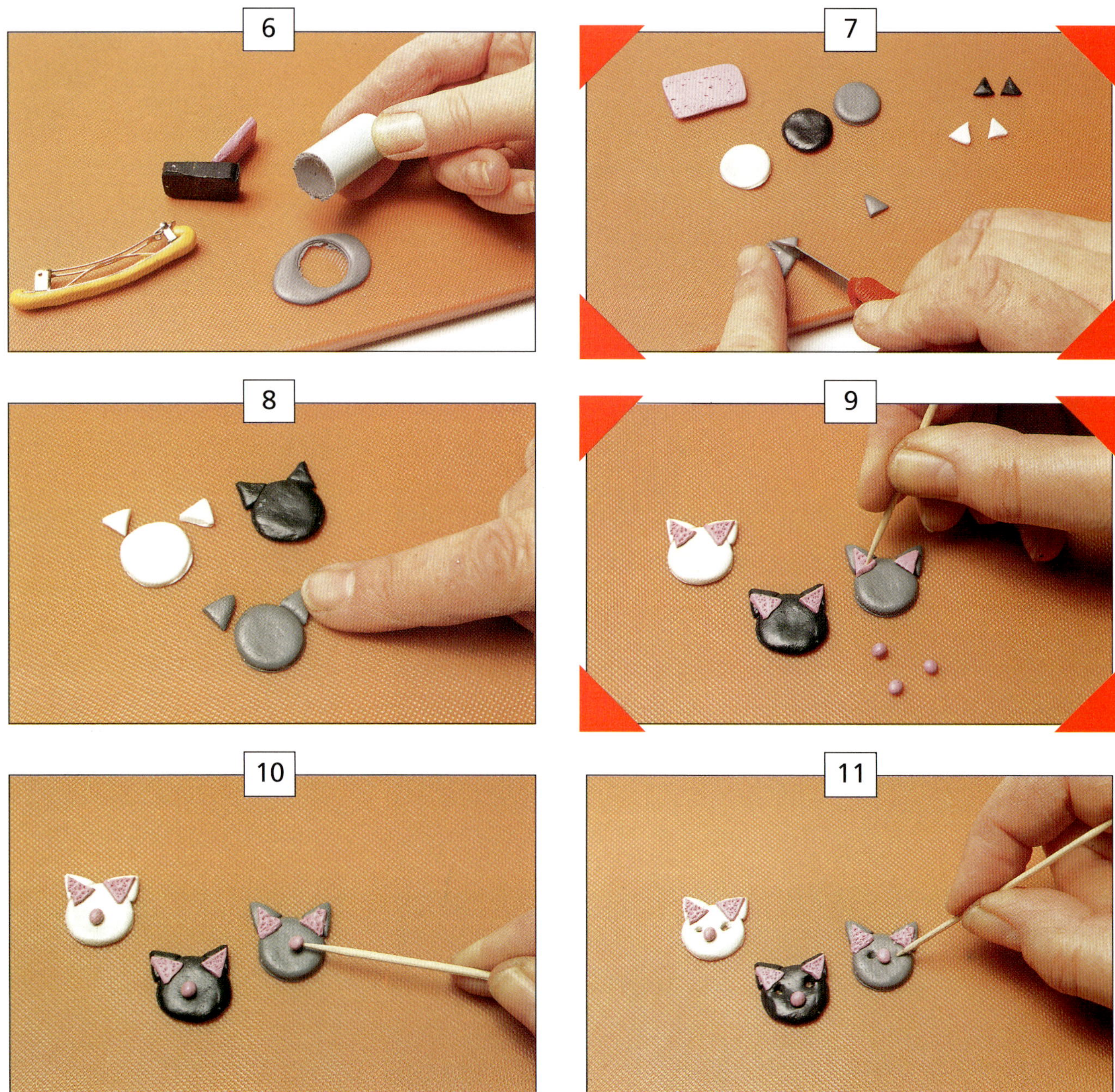

6 Use a small round object such as the top of a lipstick to press out neat circles for the cats' heads.

7 From the scraps of gray, white and black, **carefully cut two small triangles for the cats' ears – two gray, two white, and two black.**

8 Press the ears in place on the cats' heads.

9 Take a small piece of pink clay and soften it in your hands. Roll it out and **cut out six tiny triangles and three little balls.** Use a toothpick to make indentations in the ears, then carefully place the triangles in the ears.

10 Slightly flatten the balls and position them to form the cats' noses.

11 Blunt one end of a toothpick and use it to make indentations for the eyes on each face. Make sure that the hole goes all the way through so that the yellow background is visible.

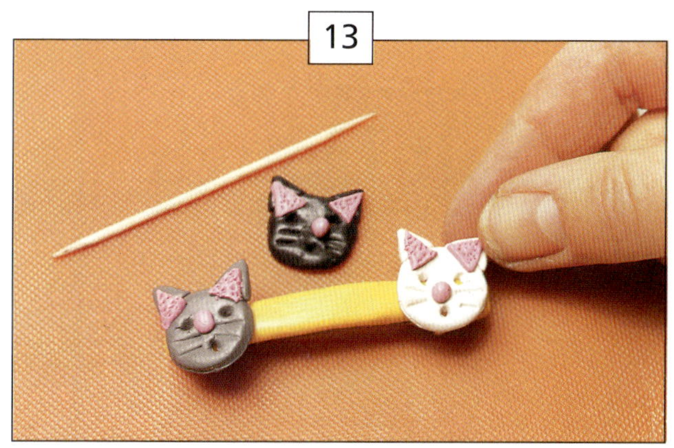

12 Use the sharp end of the toothpick to mark a hole for a mouth and lines for whiskers on each cat's face.

13 Place a cat at each end of the clasp and place one in the center, making sure that they are evenly spaced. Press them down very gently. The heat of the oven will make all the pieces stick together.

14 **Carefully place the clasp on a cookie sheet and put it in the oven. Leave it to bake for 20–30 minutes at 265°F or according to the manufacturer's instructions.**

15 When the clasp is cool, apply a coat of varnish. Leave to dry.

Blast-off!

These Christmas tree decorations can be as simple or as complex as you want. You can add patterns by painting more details or by using more colors, or you can leave them plain. We have made a space rocket, but you could use pastry cutters to make some interesting shapes, or you can create animals or flowers freehand.

YOU WILL NEED

- Large mixing bowl
- Mixing spoon
- 2 cups all-purpose flour
- 1 cup salt
- 1 cup water
- 1 tablespoon oil
- White cardboard
- Scissors and craft knife
- Rolling pin
- Modeling tools
- Toothpick
- Paints: white, red, blue, silver, black
- Paintbrushes
- Varnish and brush
- Cord or narrow ribbon

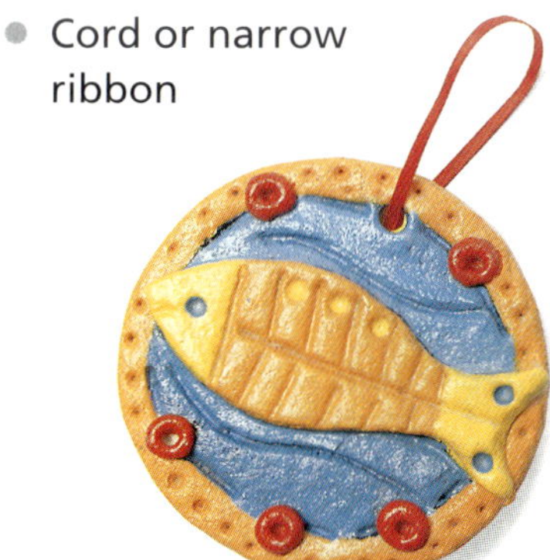

1 Add the flour to the salt in a large bowl.

2 Carefully pour in the water, adding a little at a time and stirring it with a large mixing spoon.

3 Add the oil and stir it in.

4 Knead the mixture with your fingers until the dough begins to hold together. Continue to knead until it becomes smooth.

5 Copy from the template on page 88 and transfer the outlines to white cardboard. Cut out the shapes.

6 Roll the dough until it is about ¼ inch thick. Place the templates on the dough and **cut out shapes.**

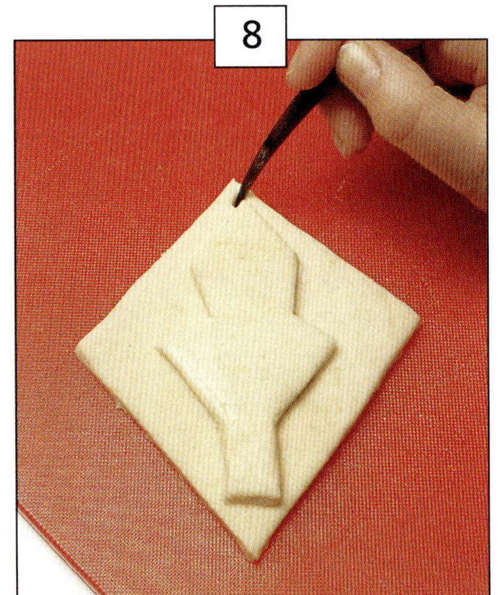

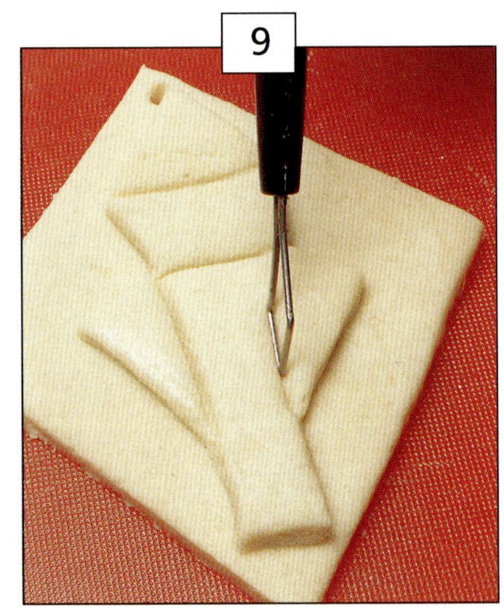

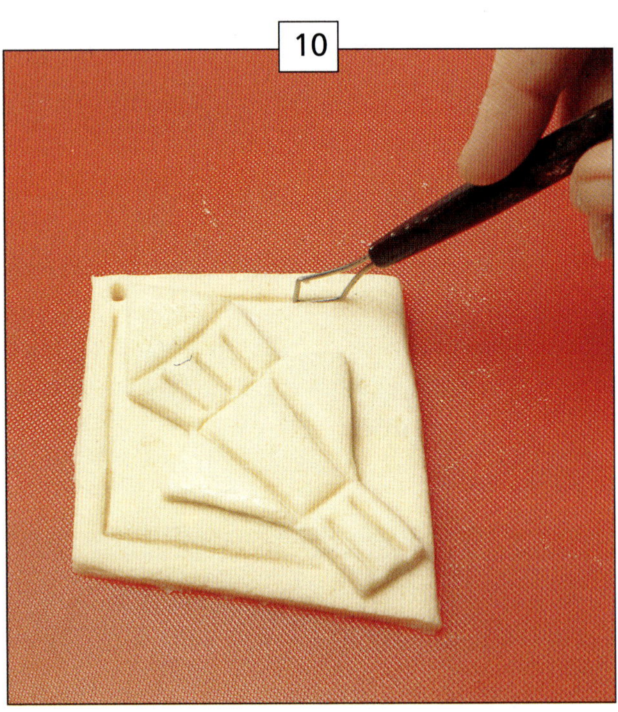

7 Brush a little water over the central part of the diamond shape and place the rocket shape on the diamond, making sure that there is an equal space all around.

8 Use a cocktail stick, modeling tool, or toothpick to make a hole in what will be the top of the diamond.

9 Use a modeling tool to mark the fins and tail of the rocket.

10 Mark a pattern of lines on the top and base of the rocket and use the modeling tool to impress a border around the edge of the diamond.

11 Allow the decoration to dry naturally **or ask an adult to help you bake it for about 8 hours at 250°F**. When it is completely dry or cool, apply a white undercoat all over the surface.

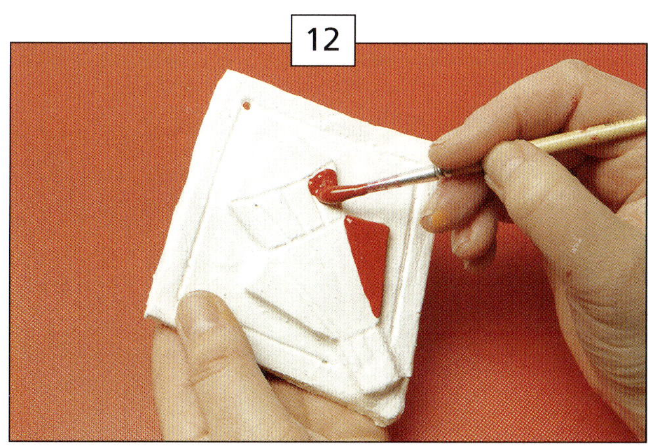

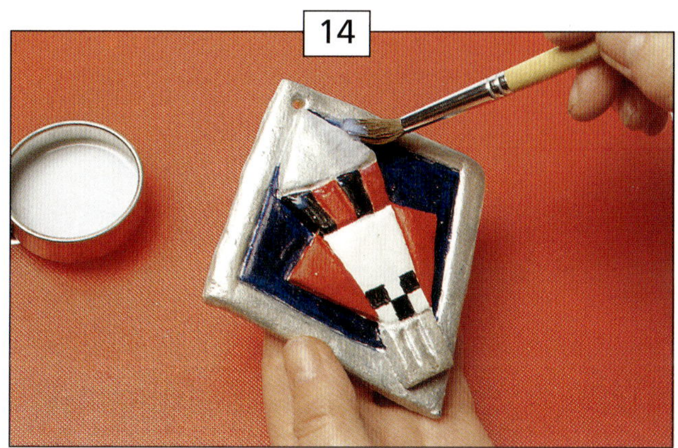

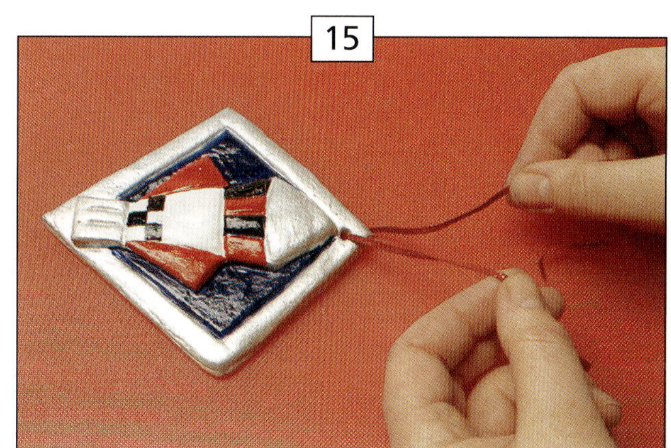

12 When the undercoat is dry, paint the fins and sections of the top red. Paint the background area inside the border dark blue. Use black paint to add details and patterns to the rocket. If necessary, go over the body of the rocket with white paint to cover all the smudges and uneven lines.

13 Paint the border of the diamond and the top and bottom of the rocket silver.

14 When the paint is completely dry, if you want, apply a coat or two of varnish to protect the paint and to give the decoration a good glossy finish.

15 When the varnish is dry, thread a piece of cord or narrow ribbon through the hole in the top so that you can hang up the decoration.

Clucking Egg Cup

This egg cup is made from a single piece of dough with the decoration added using modeling tools and paints. Use an egg to check the size of the cup – a hard-boiled one, preferably – and leave the egg in the cup for a day or two, because the dough will shrink slightly as it dries.

YOU WILL NEED

- Mixing bowl and spoon
- 2 cups all-purpose flour
- 1 cup salt
- 1 cup water
- 1 tablespoon oil
- Blunt knife
- Egg (hard-boiled)
- Modeling tools
- Paints: white, yellow, red, black
- Paintbrushes
- Varnish and brush

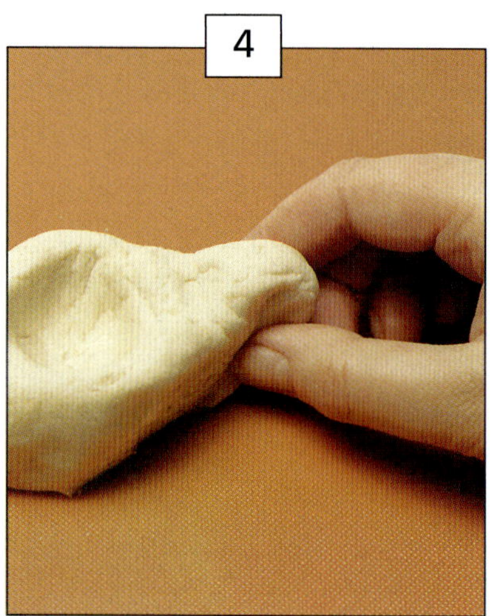

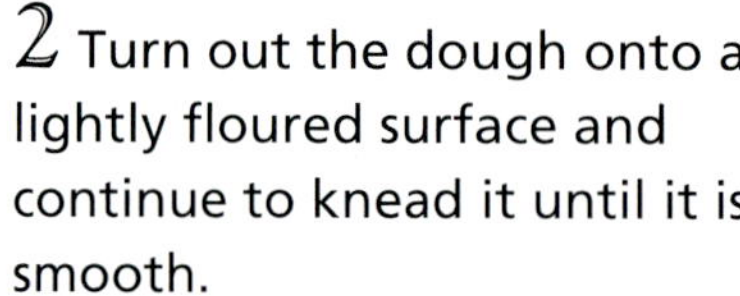

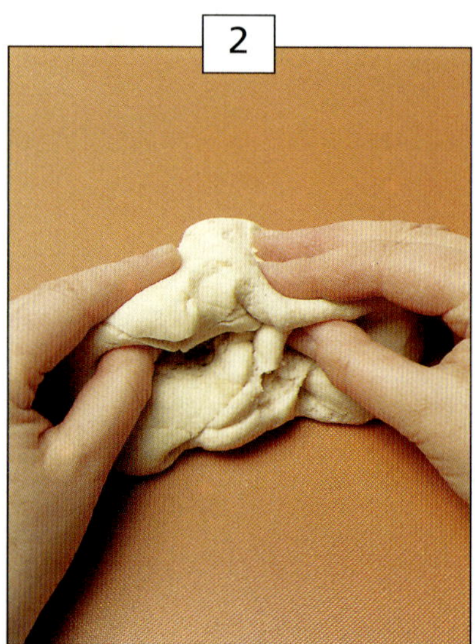

1 Add the flour to the salt in a large bowl. Carefully pour in the water, adding a little at a time and stirring it with a wooden spoon. Add the oil and stir it in. Knead the mixture with your fingers until the dough begins to hold together.

2 Turn out the dough onto a lightly floured surface and continue to knead it until it is smooth.

3 Use a blunt knife to cut off a piece about 3 x 2 inches and trim off the corners to make it into a rough diamond shape.

4 Begin to mold the dough with your fingers, pinching it at the head and tail ends and pressing a hole in the center for the egg.

5 Use a blunt knife to dig out a hole for the egg in the center.

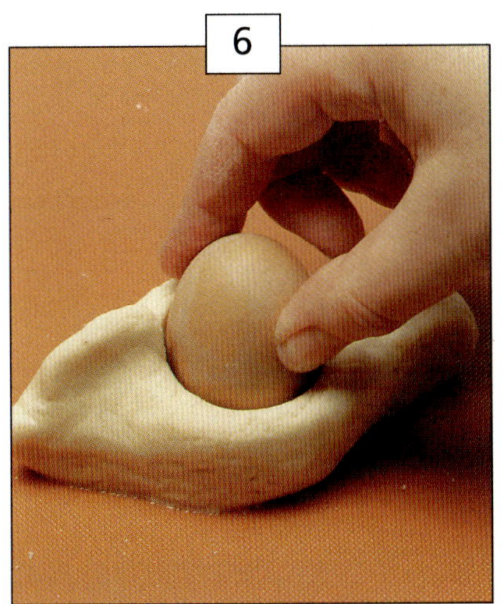

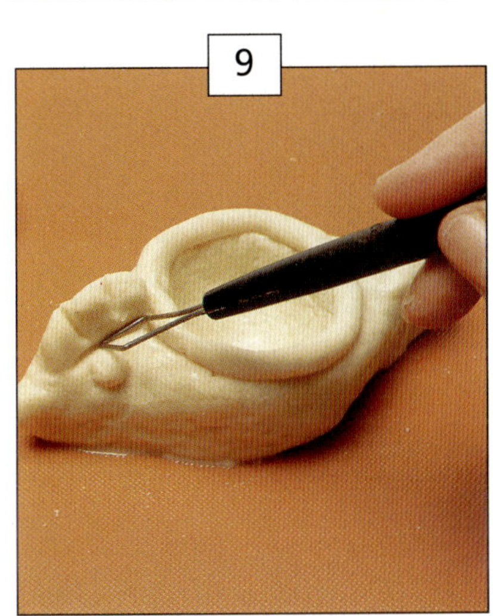

6 Check the size of the hole with an egg and smooth over the surface of the egg cup with your fingers.

7 Roll out a tube of dough and place it around the rim of the hole, using a little water to make the dough stick.

8 Take a little more dough and roll out two small balls. Press them to the sides of the chicken's head for the eyes.

9 Use a modeling tool to begin to mark the features on the chicken's face. Remember to mark a line along the beak to show where it would open. Add some marks to the tail to decorate the surface of the dough.

10 Use the handle of a paintbrush to indent a series of dots all over the surface of the dough, including the rim around the egg holder.

11 Allow the egg cup to dry naturally **or ask an adult to help you bake it for about 8 hours at 250°F**. When the egg cup is completely dry or cool, apply a white undercoat all over the surface.

TIP

☛ While you are working, check from time to time that the egg still fits inside the hole. Put the egg into the egg cup and gently move it back and forth to increase the hole size.

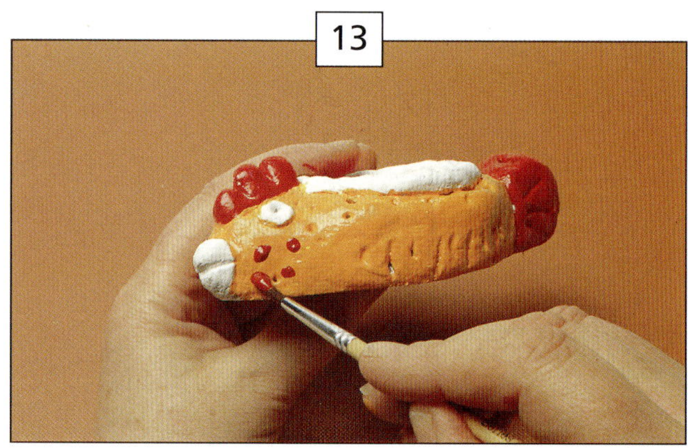

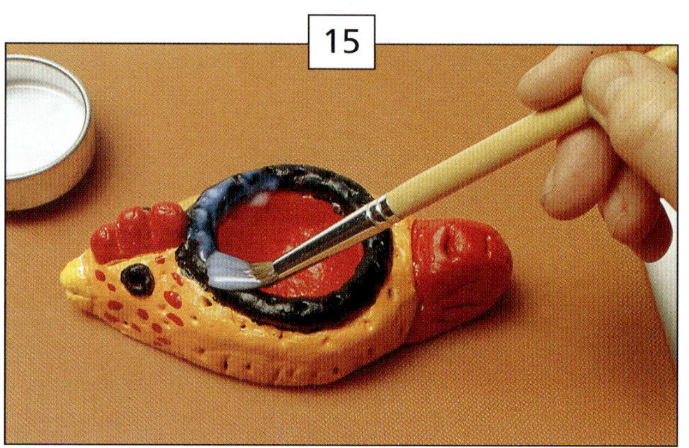

12 Mix some orange paint (red and yellow) and paint the chicken's body.

13 Paint the comb and tail red and add some red dots on the sides of the face. Paint the inside of the egg cup red.

14 Paint the rim around the top of the egg cup black. Paint the beak yellow and leave all the paint to dry.

15 Apply at least two coats of varnish, allowing the first coat to dry before you apply the next. You must also remember to apply varnish to the base of the egg cup.

TIP

☞ The more coats of varnish you apply, the more waterproof the egg cup will be. However, it is probably not a good idea to immerse it in water, so when you have used it, wipe it gently with a damp cloth.

Dish of Moon and Stars

This highly decorated plate is the most difficult of the salt dough projects because it is delicate to handle. Although the decoration looks complex, it is quite simple to apply. It would look attractive hanging on a wall, so you could make a hanger from a paper clip, glued securely to the back of the plate when you have finished.

YOU WILL NEED

- Mixing bowl and spoon
- 2 cups all-purpose flour
- 1 cup salt
- 1 cup water
- 1 tablespoon oil
- Large mixing bowl
- Large rolling pin
- Petroleum jelly
- Ovenproof plate
- Blunt knife
- Ruler
- Pastry brush
- Cookie cutters (star-shaped and round)
- Pen top
- Modeling tools
- Paints: white, blue, black, silver
- Paintbrushes
- Varnish and brush

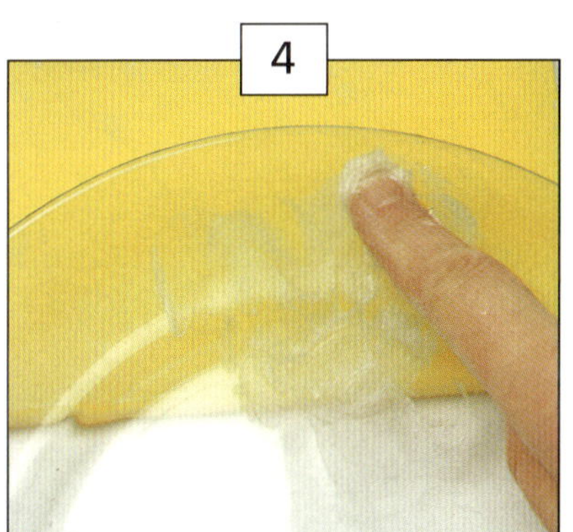

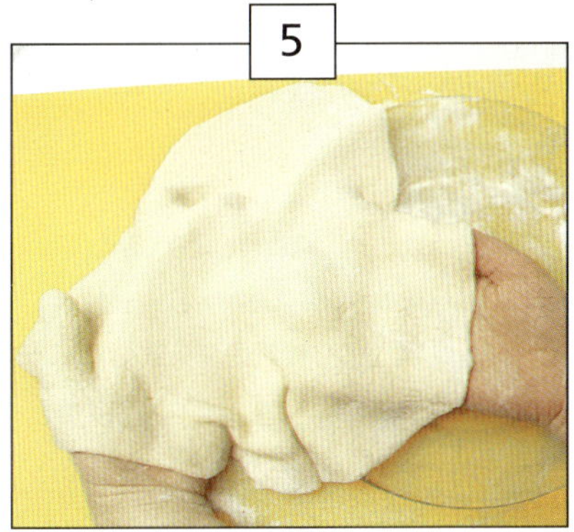

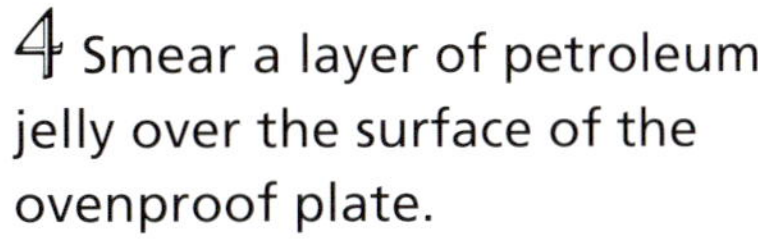

1 Add the flour to the salt in a large bowl. Carefully pour in the water, adding a little at a time and stirring it with a mixing spoon. Add the oil and stir it in.

2 Knead the mixture with your fingers until the dough begins to hold together. Continue to knead until smooth.

3 Lightly flour your worktop and roll out the dough until it is about ¼ inch thick.

4 Smear a layer of petroleum jelly over the surface of the ovenproof plate.

5 Carefully lift the dough and place it over the plate.

6 Press the dough gently down over the plate, taking care that you do not flatten it too much. Trim off the edge neatly all round with a blunt knife.

7 Roll out the scraps of dough again and use a ruler to cut strips about ½ inch wide.

8 Use a brush to dampen the edge of the dough and press the border in place all the way round. Use your fingers to smooth the joins in the dough strips.

9 Roll out some more dough so that it is less than ¼ inch thick. Use a small star-shaped cookie cutter to cut out nine stars. Cut one star with a larger cutter.

10 Use the side of a round cookie cutter to cut out some crescent moon shapes.

11 Brush the surface of the dough lightly with water so that the decorations will stick in place, then put the large star in the center of the plate. Arrange eight of the small stars and the moons around the edge of the plate, and place the last small star in the center of the large one.

12 Use the top of a large pen or something similar to cut out eight small circles from the dough and arrange them evenly around the rim of the plate. Use the pen top to impress a circle in the middle of the central star. Use a modeling tool to make a pattern of indentations between each circle. Pressing the edging down will also help make it stick to the dough underneath.

13 Ask an adult to help you bake the plate for about 8 hours at 250°F. When the plate is cool, apply a white undercoat all over the surface.

14 Leave the dough plate on the ovenproof plate while you decorate it so that it does not crack. Paint the background blue and paint the stars and circles silver. Mix dark blue (blue and black) to paint the edge, the moons, and the large star in the center and the circle in the center. Apply two coats of paint to give a really deep blue.

15 When the paint is dry, carefully remove the plate from the ovenproof plate and apply at least two coats of varnish, remembering to allow the first coat to dry before you apply the next.

CHAPTER THREE

Air-dried Clay

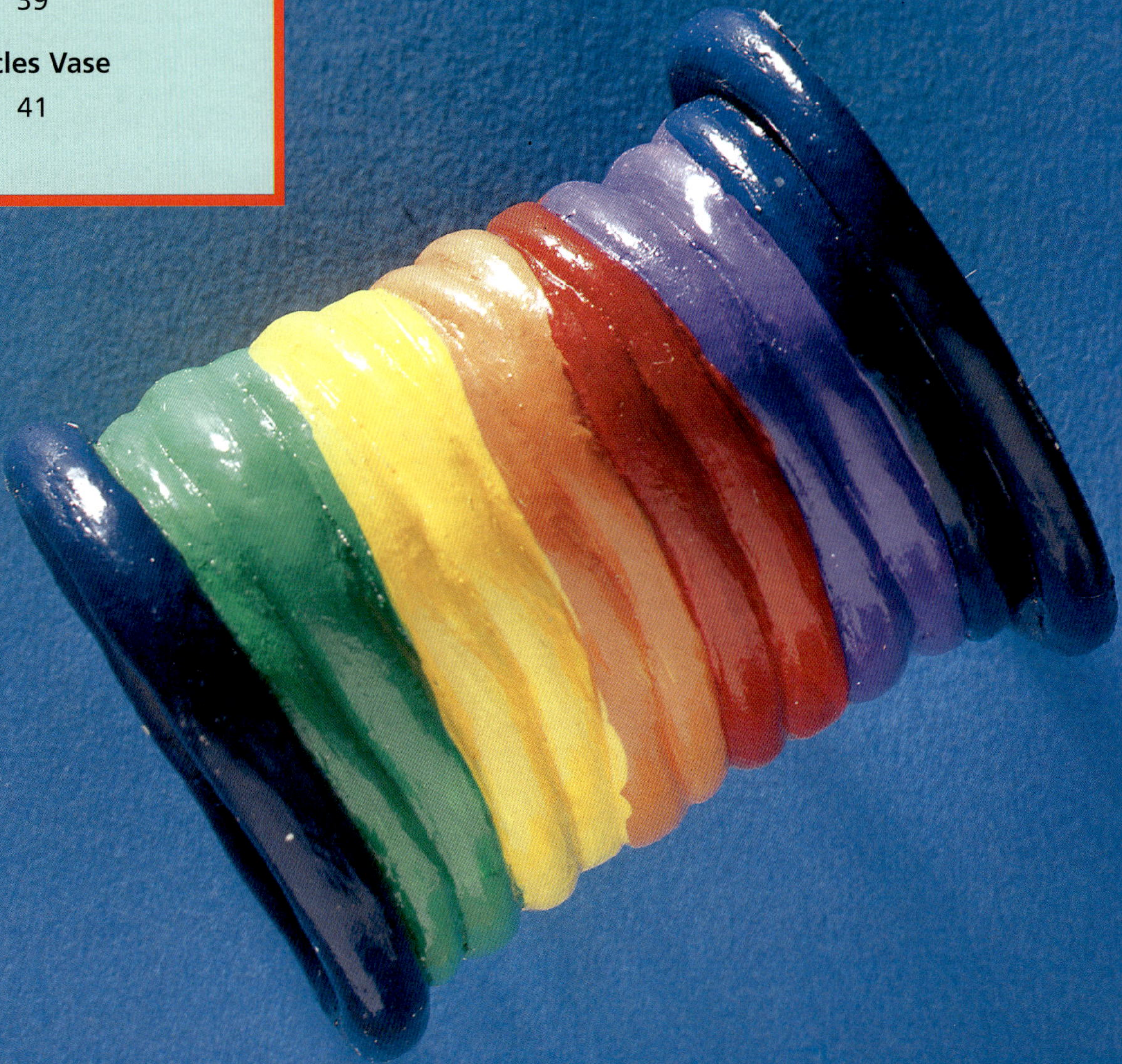

Rainbow Pencil Holder

It is possible to use this method to make all kinds of shapes and sizes. If you prefer, you can make a shallow pot with a matching lid. Because this is designed as a pencil holder, it is pretty tall. You could paint it to match other things on your desk or you could decorate it with a pattern of spots or stripes.

YOU WILL NEED

- Air-dried clay
- Rolling pin
- Jam jar or mug
- Blunt knife
- Paints: white and colors of your choice
- Paintbrushes
- Varnish and brushes

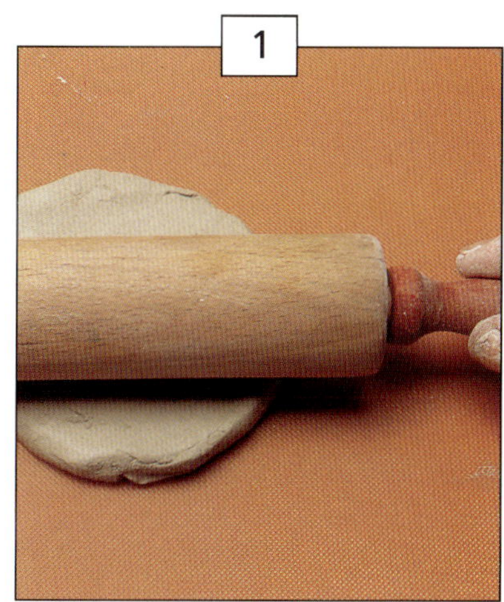

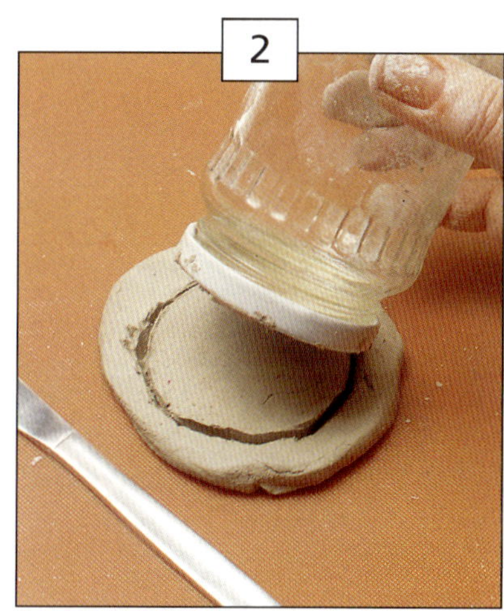

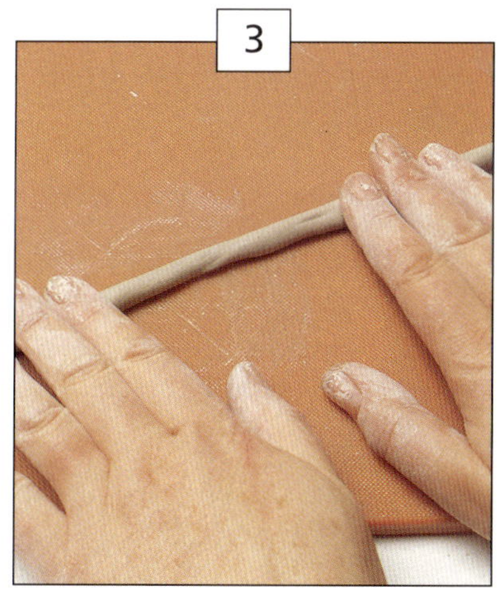

1 Take a piece of clay about 3 x 2 inches and roll it in your hands to soften it. Then roll it out on your worktop until it is about ¼ inch thick.

2 Find a jar or mug that is about the size you want the finished pot to be. Press it on the clay and cut around it to make the base of the pot.

3 Take pieces of clay and roll them into lengths just over ¼ inch thick. Make sure they are smooth and even.

4 Using some wet clay as a kind of glue, begin to coil the strips on the base. The wet clay will help the clay coils to stick together.

5 Keep adding spirals of clay until the pot is the height you want. Do not worry if it does not look very even – when it is painted no one will notice. Roll two thicker pieces of clay. Coil one of these thick pieces around the base of the pot. As well as making the pot look more interesting, it will help to make it more stable.

6 Coil the other thick piece around the rim of the pot, placing it so that it sticks out a little and balances the coil around the base. Check that the pot is straight and leave to dry

7 When the pot is completely dry, paint it white all over.

Leave to dry. This pot is painted in a rainbow of colors, but you could use just one or two colors if preferred. If you want to use purple, mix blue and red together.

8 Mix some dark blue (blue and black) to paint the inside of the pot.

9 When the paint is completely dry, apply a coat of varnish to the inside and outside of the pot. Leave to dry.

TIP

☞ If the clay gets too dry while you are working with it, dampen it with a little water and smooth over the cracks.

Bluebird Candlestick

This kind of clay is excellent for making the kinds of objects you would normally see made from ceramics, because when it has hardened it looks as if it has been baked in a kiln. This candlestick is easy to make. It is mostly cut from one piece of clay and then molded into shape. Try making a matching pair of candlesticks.

YOU WILL NEED

- White cardboard
- Pencil
- Scissors
- Air-dried clay
- Blunt knife
- Candle
- Modeling tools
- Paints: white, blue, orange, black, turquoise
- Paintbrushes
- Varnish and brush

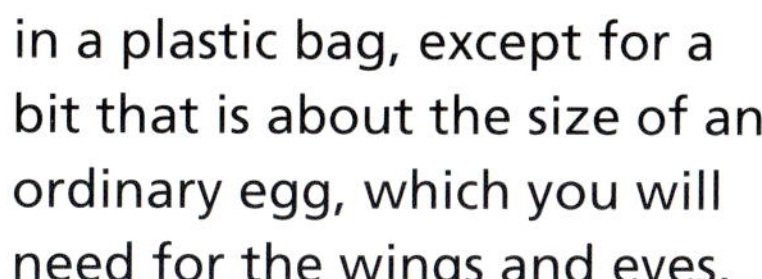

1 Copy the template from page 88 and transfer the outline to white cardboard. Cut out the shape of the bird from the cardboard.

2 Take a piece of clay, about 9 x 5 x 1¼ inches, and place the template on it. Cut around the outline of the bird. Put the remnants of clay in a plastic bag, except for a bit that is about the size of an ordinary egg, which you will need for the wings and eyes.

3 Smooth the edges of the clay with your fingers.

4 Trim the edges from the beak and tail of the bird so that they form points. Smooth the edges again.

5 With the bird sitting on your worktop, use a candle to mark the position of the hole in the back. Use a blunt knife to make the hole deeper, then smooth the surface neatly with your fingers.

6 Roll out a piece of clay about ¼ inch thick and place it around the hole.

7 Place another piece of rolled-out clay around the beak. Smooth the joins with your fingers.

8 Flatten some of the remaining clay until it is about ⅛ inch thick and cut two triangles, each about ½ inch along each side, for the eyes. Press them in position on the sides of the head, sticking them down with a little water.

9 Cut two large triangles from the remaining clay, each triangle about 1½ inch along each side. Make a template from cardboard to help you.

10 Apply a little water to the side of the bird where the wings will go. You may find that scratching the surface of the clay helps makes the wings stick to the body more easily.

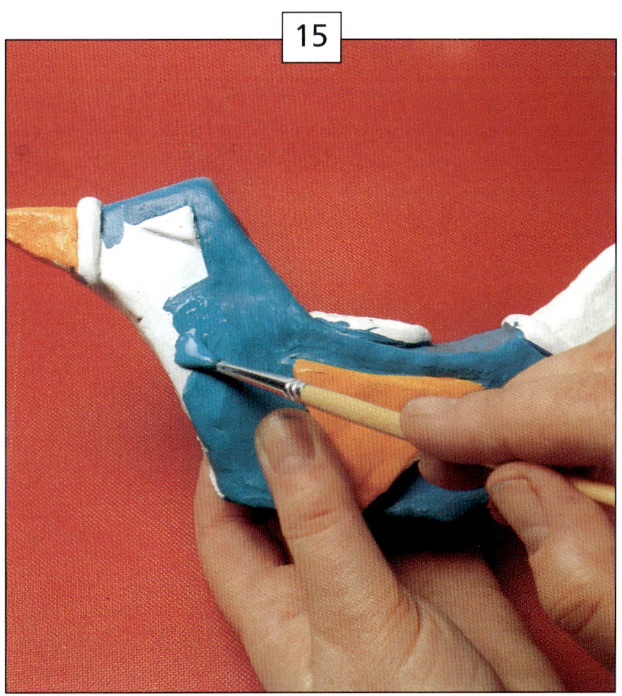

11 Press the wings into place, arranging them so that both sides match. Smooth over the top edges carefully with your fingers.

12 Use the remaining clay to make a little roll to go around the tail, matching the roll you put around the beak.

13 Smooth over the hole surface with a modeling tool, then leave the clay to dry.

14 Apply a coat of white paint all over the candlestick and leave to dry.

15 Paint the wings and beak orange and the body blue or turquoise. Leave the eyes white.

16 Use dark blue (blue and black) for the tail, the hole for the candle, and the rings around the beak and tail. Add blue stripes on the wings, and add some white decoration around the tail.

17 When the paint is dry, apply at least two coats of varnish to the whole surface, making sure that the first coat is dry before you apply the second.

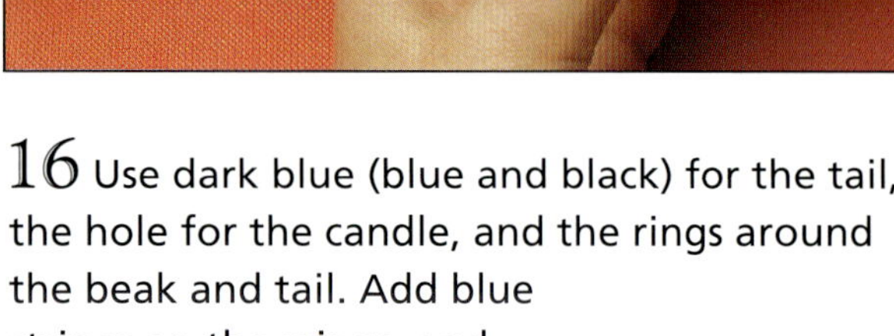

Metallic Marine Brooch

Although this is much smaller than the candlestick and the pencil holder, it is not difficult to make, as long as you have nimble fingers and use modeling tools to decorate the surface. Jewelry is always fun to make, because you can decorate it with all kinds of small stones and beads.

YOU WILL NEED

- Air-dried clay
- Rolling pin
- White cardboard
- Pencil
- Scissors
- Blunt knife
- Modeling tools
- Toothpick
- Paints: white, light blue, dark blue, silver
- Paintbrushes
- Varnish and brush
- Brooch back
- Clear, all-purpose adhesive

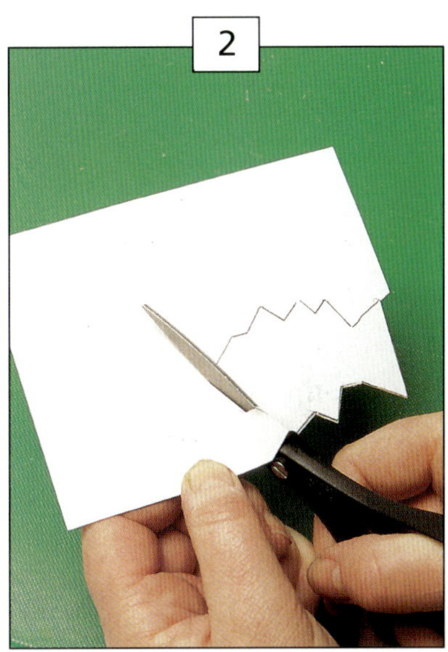

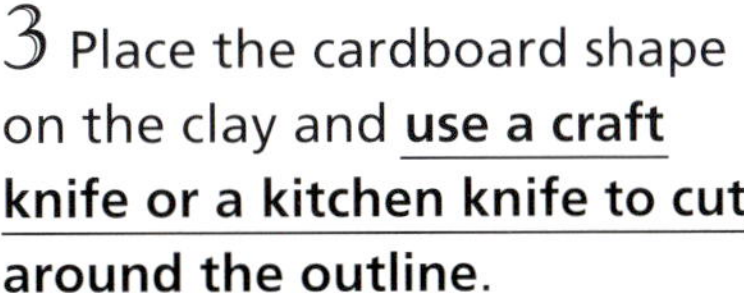

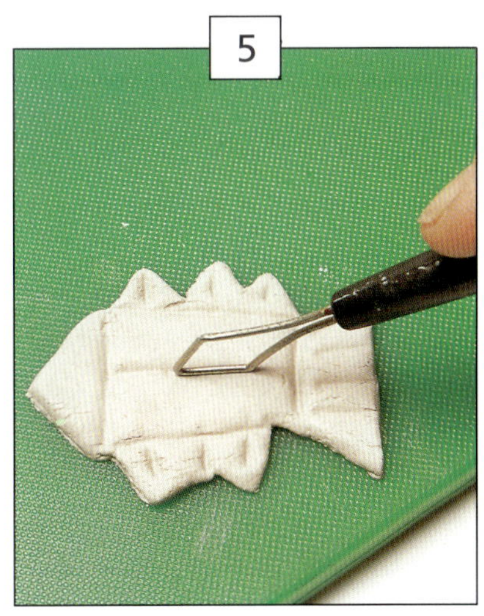

1 Roll out a piece of clay so that it is about ¼ inch thick.

2 Copy the fish template from page 88 and transfer the outline to white cardboard. Cut it out.

3 Place the cardboard shape on the clay and **use a craft knife or a kitchen knife to cut around the outline**.

4 Use a blade of a knife or your fingers to smooth the edge of the fish.

5 Use a modeling tool to draw lines to represent the fish's fins and add other decoration as you wish. Make a hole for the fish's eye with a wooden toothpick.

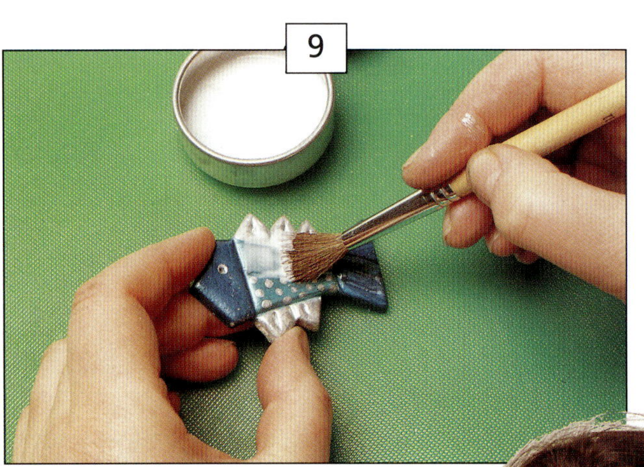

6 Leave the fish to dry, then turn it over so that the back can dry. If necessary, fill any holes by running wet clay over the surface and carefully smoothing it over to give a good finish.

7 Paint the fish, beginning with a light blue. If you mix silver with the blue, you will get lovely metallic, shimmery colors. Use darker blue for the head and tail.

8 Paint the fins silver and paint the back of the fish pale blue.

9 When the paint is dry, apply a coat of varnish all over the fish. Allow the varnish to dry.

10 Glue the brooch pin to the back of the fish and leave the glue to set hard before wearing the brooch.

Circles Vase

This vase is more highly decorated than the pencil holder, and it is more complicated to make. Unlike clay that is fired in a kiln, air-dried clay is not waterproof, and if you want to make a vase in which you can place flowers, you need to put a glass jar, slightly smaller than the vase, inside for the water. Alternatively, use it to hold a pretty display of dried flowers and grasses.

YOU WILL NEED

- Glass jar and plastic bag
- Petroleum jelly
- Air-dried clay
- Rolling pin
- Blunt knife
- Cookie cutter or similar, about 1¼ inch across
- Pen top or smaller circular object
- Paints: white, yellow, blue (or turquoise), red, black
- Paintbrushes
- Varnish and brush

TIP

☛ If you do not succeed in finishing the vase in one day, keep the clay soft and workable by covering it with a damp cloth.

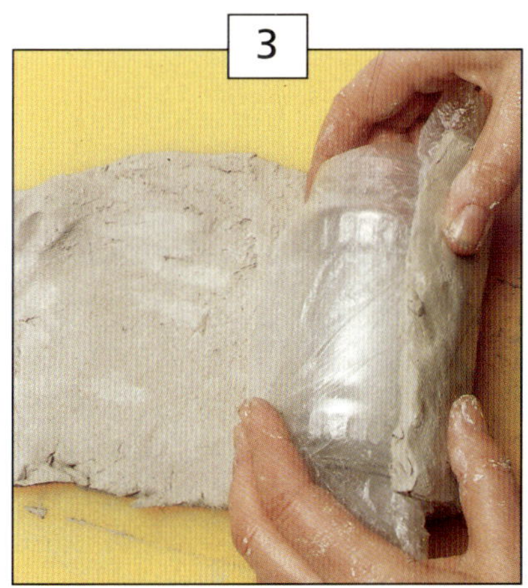

1 Place the glass jar inside a plastic bag.

2 Cover the bag with a layer of petroleum jelly.

3 Roll out the clay until it is about ¼ inch thick and long enough to go right round the jar. Wrap the clay around the jar.

4 Trim away any excess clay.

5 Smooth the join with your fingers.

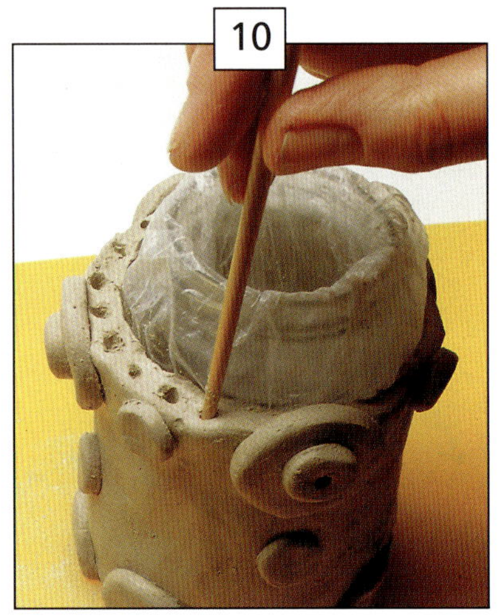

6 Stand the jar on a piece of the remaining rolled-out clay and with a knife cut around the bottom edge. Smooth the join with your fingers to give a neat finish.

7 Measure up about 4½ inches from the bottom and use a ruler to mark a line right around the vase. Cut off the top.

8 Roll out some of the trimmings of clay that are left until they are about ⅛ inch thick. Use the cookie cutter to cut out 10 circles. Use the pen top or a similar object to cut out 12 circles.

9 Use a piece of wet clay to stick larger circles around the top and bottom of the vase. Stick small circles in the center and put some small circles around the center. Cut two of the larger circles in half and position them between the circles around the bottom of the vase.

10 Place some small circles between the large circles around the top of the vase. Use the handle of a paintbrush to make indentations in the centers of some of the circles and to make a series of evenly spaced holes around the top edge of the vase.

11 Allow the vase to dry. When it is completely dry, remove the glass jar from the inside by pulling on the plastic bag.

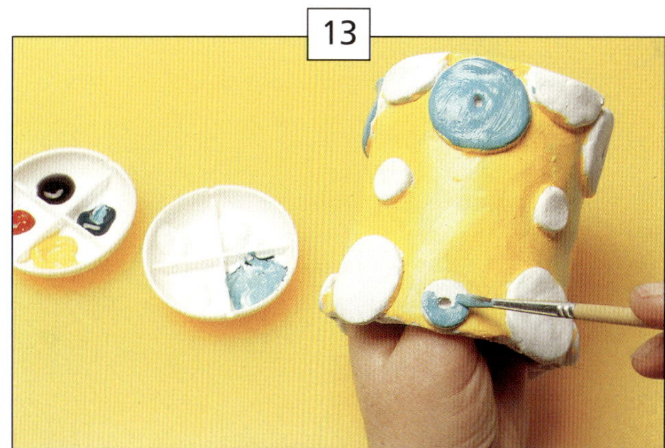

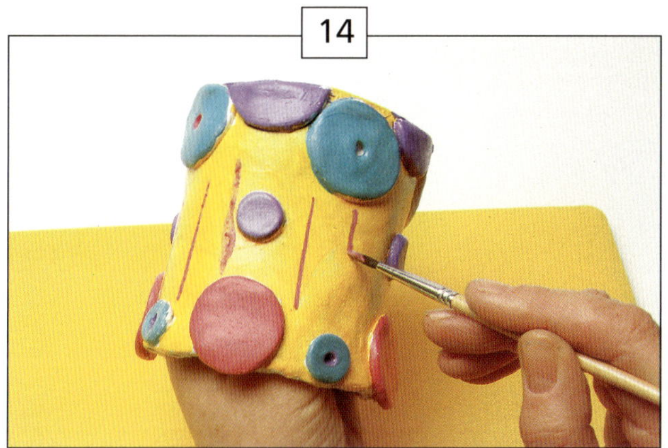

12 Apply a coat of white paint to the whole surface of the vase. Leave it to dry.

13 Paint the vase yellow all over. Allow the yellow to dry before using a pale blue (dark blue and white) or turquoise to paint some of the circles

14 Mix pink (red and white) and use it to paint some stripes down the vase, then use purple (red and blue) to paint some of the other circles. Leave the paint to dry.

15 Apply varnish all over the vase, inside and out and leave to dry.

Papier Mâché

Good-luck Cat

Papier mâché is French for "mashed paper" and it is made very simply from newspaper mixed with water and wallpaper paste. Strips of paper can be used, but for this project we are going to use a paper pulp, which is quick to make but takes quite a long time to dry out. The whiskers give the cat a wonderfully life-like look – almost as if it is about to catch a mouse.

YOU WILL NEED

- 2–3 newspapers
- 1 cup water and 1 rounded tablespoon wallpaper paste
- Large mixing bowl
- Modeling tools
- Paints: white, black, red, green
- Paintbrushes
- Pencil
- Toothpick
- 6 whiskers (from a broom or brush)
- Clear, all-purpose adhesive
- Plaid ribbon and bell

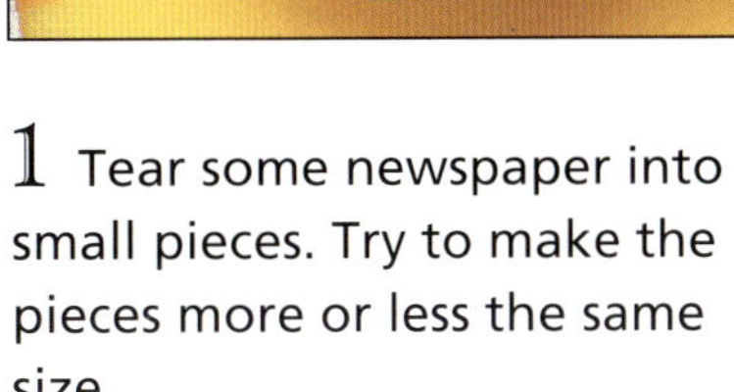

1 Tear some newspaper into small pieces. Try to make the pieces more or less the same size.

2 Add the wallpaper paste to the water in a large bowl and mix them together well. Leave the paste to stand for a while until the paste begins to thicken.

3 Add the pieces of paper to the paste, mixing them well. Keep on adding paper until the paste has all been soaked up.

4 Squeeze the paper and paste mix in your hands to remove excess water. then place it on your worktop. You need a lump that is about 6 inches thick and 4½ inches wide.

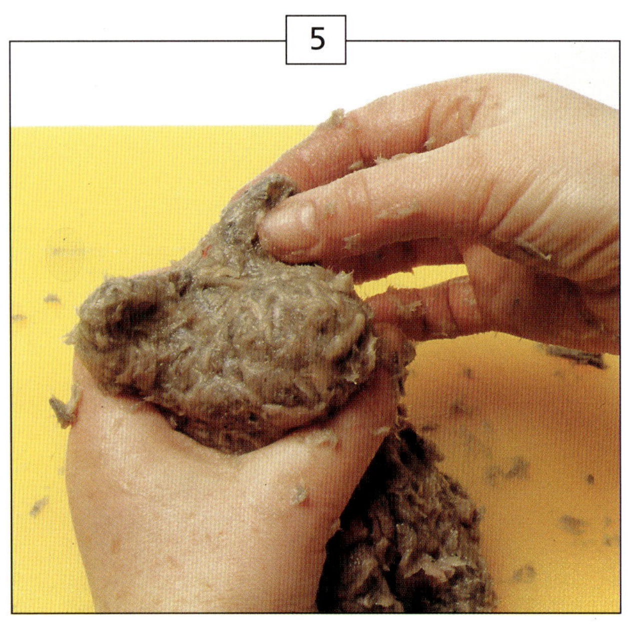

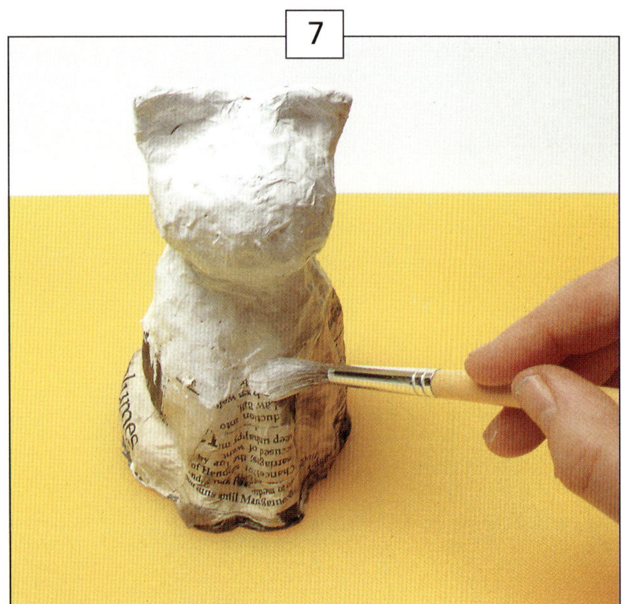

5 Begin to model the pulp into the shape of a cat, modeling the head and ears. If the pulp is too wet, add a little more paper or leave it to dry for a while in a warm, dry room.

6 Squeeze the pulp between your fingers to create the details and use a modeling tool to define the front legs and the tail. Apply little pieces of paper to the surface to give a smooth finish.

7 Place the cat in a warm, dry place – near a radiator, for example – and leave it to dry. When it is completely dry, apply a coat of white paint to cover the newsprint completely.

8 Use a pencil to draw the eyes, nose, paws, and chest on the cat. Paint the body and top of the head black. Use pink (red and white) for inside the ears and the nose, and paint the eyes green.

11 Finish off your cat by fastening a ribbon and bell around its neck.

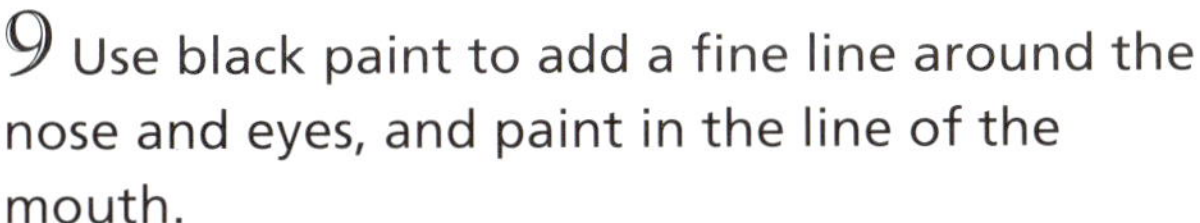

9 Use black paint to add a fine line around the nose and eyes, and paint in the line of the mouth.

10 Use a toothpick to make three holes at each side of the cat's face. Dip the end of each bristle into glue and insert it into a hole to form a whisker.

Dinosaur Mobile

These dinosaurs are made from pieces of card that have been covered with strips of paper to give texture so that they look as if they have thick, scaly, dinosaur-type skin. You can cover both sides of each dinosaur or, for speed, just decorate one side. The string is attached to each shape by a colored paper clip.

YOU WILL NEED

- White card
- Pencil
- Scissors
- Cardboard
- Craft knife (optional)
- Newspaper
- 1 rounded tablespoon wallpaper paste and 1 cup water
- Paintbrushes
- Paints: white, black, and colors of your choice
- Toothpick
- Colored paper clips
- Clear, all-purpose adhesive
- Varnish and brush
- Strong black thread

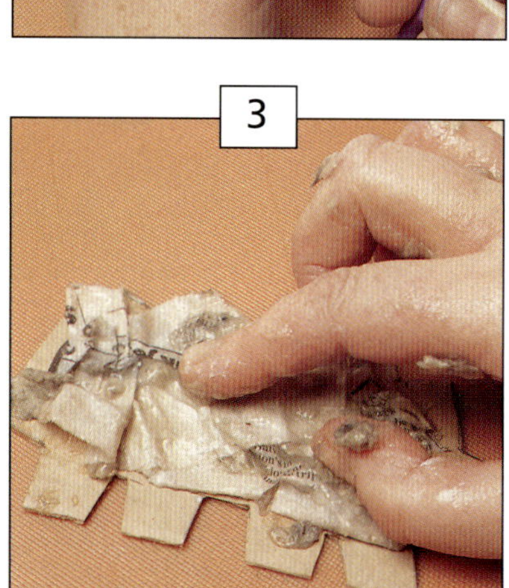

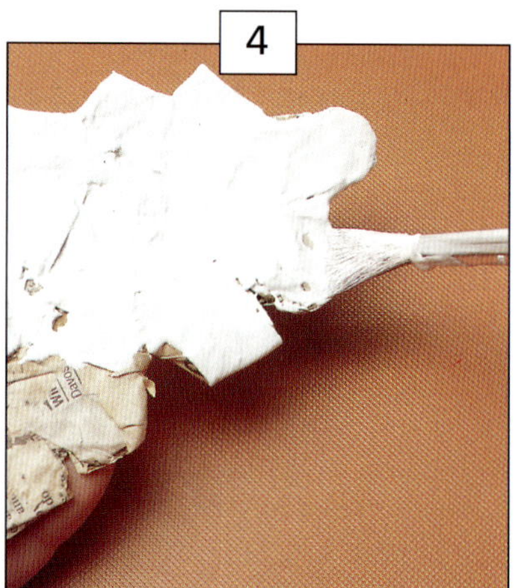

1 Transfer the templates on pages 90–91 to white card and cut around the outlines.

2 Place the templates on the cardboard and draw around the outlines. **Cut out the shapes of the dinosaurs.** If you **use a craft knife, ask an adult to help, because the cardboard can be difficult to cut through.**

3 Tear small rectangles from the newspaper and soak them in mixed wallpaper paste. Cover the cardboard shapes with pieces of paper. You only need apply one layer to each side and there is no need to be too neat because you want to give a rough look to the finished dinosaur.

4 Leave the paste to dry, then decide if you want to decorate the other side. If so, repeat the previous step. When the dinosaur is completely dry, apply a coat of white paint to cover all the newsprint.

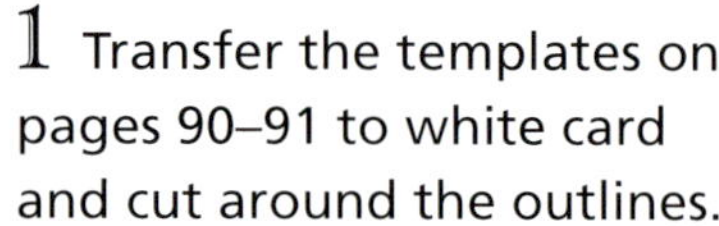

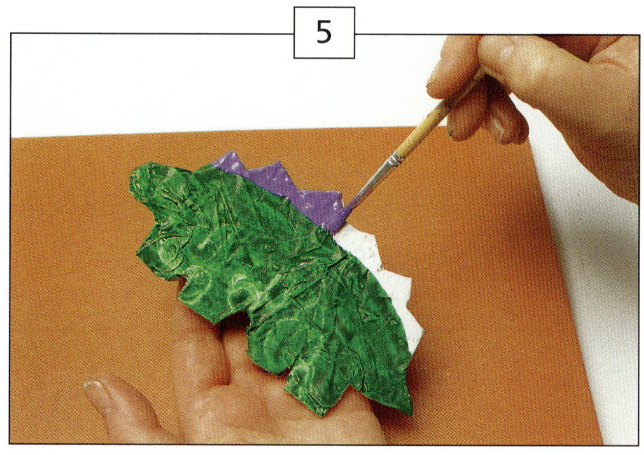

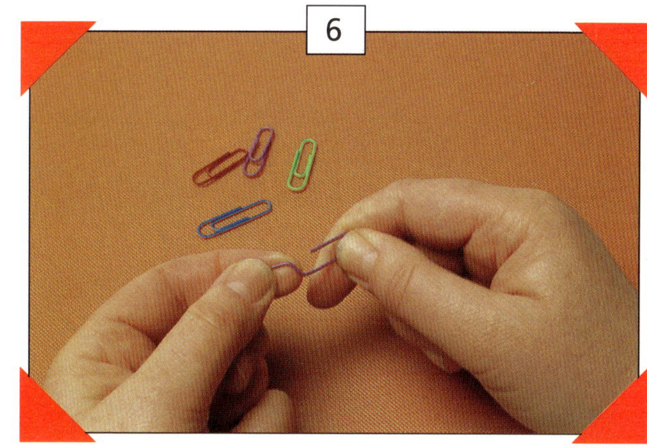

5 When the paint is dry, decorate the dinosaurs in colors of your choice. We used green and purple for the Brontosaurus. Don't forget to cover and paint the main section of the mobile. Use black paint to add eyes to the dinosaurs.

6 **Ask an adult to help you unbend a paper clip. Take care, because the ends can be sharp.**

7 **Make two holes in the top of each dinosaur with a toothpick or something similar.** Thread the paper clip through the holes, holding it firm with a tiny blob of glue.

8 When you have threaded paper clips through the tops of all the dinosaurs, varnish each shape. If you have decorated both sides, allow the varnish to dry on one side before turning it over to varnish the other side.

9 **Attach a paper clip to each of the four corners of the main piece of the mobile. Add one in the center.**

10 Thread lengths of cotton through each of the hooks on the main section of the mobile and attach dinosaurs to each one.

11 Bend under the ends of the legs of the dinosaur to go on top of the mobile. Use strong adhesive to glue it to the center of the top of the main piece. The mobile can be suspended by means of a thread attached to the hook in the top of this brontosaurus, or tied around the dinosaur and threaded through the hook in the center of the leaf.

TIP

☞ Don't tie the thread too tightly at first. Experiment with different lengths of thread until you are satisfied that the mobile is properly balanced, then tie securely in place. The longer the piece of thread, the "heavier" the object suspended from it will seem to be.

Treasure Chest

When you have completed this chest, you could make it extra secure by adding a small padlock to it, so that you can keep your special treasures in it. It is simply made from an ordinary cardboard box – one that contained chocolates or tea bags, for example – but the layers of papier mâché make it sturdy and stable.

YOU WILL NEED

- 1 rounded tablespoon wallpaper paste and 1 cup of water
- Bowl
- Newspaper
- Cardboard box
- Paints: white, red
- Paintbrushes
- Ruler
- Black construction paper
- Scissors
- Craft glue and brush
- Toothpick
- Approximately 43 winged paper clips
- Varnish and brush
- Screw-in eyes (optional)
- Small padlock (optional)

1 Mix the wallpaper paste and water in a large bowl and tear pieces of newspaper to fit the sides of the box. Paste pieces of newspaper to the sides. You can either dip the newspaper in the paste or apply the paste with a brush.

2 Cover the sides, base and top of the box with about six layers of paper.

3 Make sure that you take the newspaper strips over the sides of the box to make a neat edge.

4 Leave the box in a warm, dry room until it is completely dry, then give it a coat of white paint to cover all the newsprint.

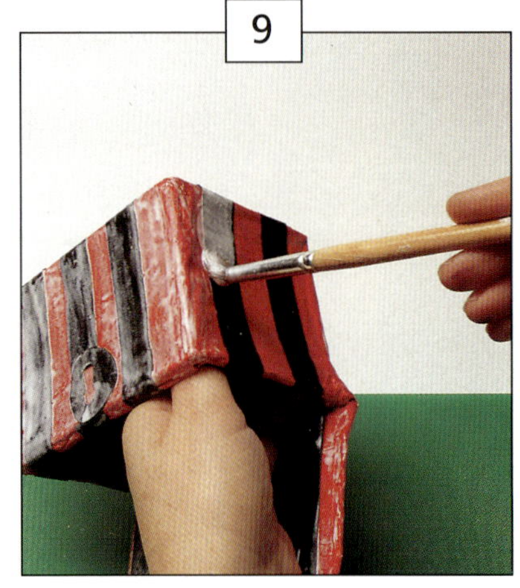

5 When the white undercoat is dry, paint the box red.

6 Use a ruler to measure three strips of black paper. Each strip should be about ¾ inch wide and be long enough to go all the way over the lid and down the back of the box. Measure and cut seven shorter strips, the same width, that are slightly longer than the depth of the box. Trim about 1 inch from one of these strips. **If you use a craft knife to cut the paper, ask an adult to help.**

7 Use craft glue to stick the black strips around the box. Put one at each end and one in the middle. Make sure that the strips are long enough to tuck inside the lid and under the box at the back so that there are no rough edges.

8 Stick the shorter strips to the sides and front of the box, bending the ends neatly under the box and in along the top edge. The shortest strip goes in the center of the front. Cover the ends by sticking a piece of black paper over the inside of the lid. **Cut a circle of black paper, about 1¼ inches across, and cut out**

the shape of a keyhole in the center. Ask an adult to help you cut out the outline. Glue the keyhole to the center front of the box.

9 Apply a coat of watered-down craft glue to the outside of the box.

10 When the glue is dry, **use a toothpick or something similar to pierce a series of holes, about 1¼ inches apart, along the black strips.** Ask an adult to help if the card and paper are now too thick to be easily pierced.

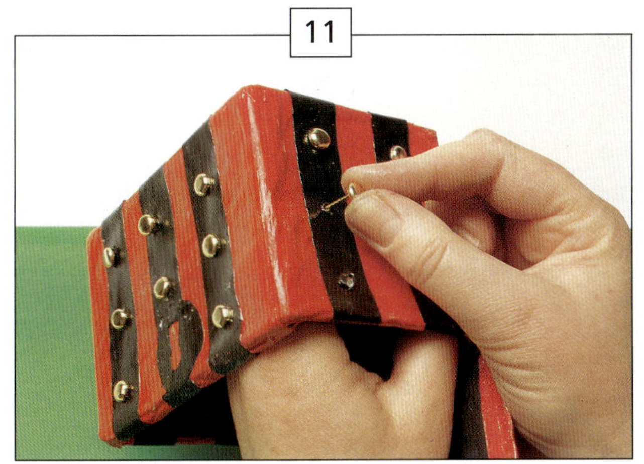

13 If you wish, screw two small round-headed screws into the lid and into the center front of the box. Finish off your box with a small padlock.

11 Insert a paper clip through each of the holes, opening out the wings on the inside.

12 Cut pieces of black paper to cover the inside of the box. Use plenty of glue to make sure that the paper is firmly glued over the opened-out paper clips. Apply a coat of varnish, but take care that you do not varnish the heads of the paper clips.

Dancing Doll

Even though this little doll is wearing clothes, no sewing is necessary. The material is held in place with adhesive and double-sided adhesive tape. The doll is made from bits and pieces that would normally be thrown away. Part of the fun of using these scraps is to make something that looks professionally made, which even has moving legs and arms.

YOU WILL NEED

- 1 rounded tablespoon wallpaper paste and 1 cup water
- Large bowl
- Scissors
- Newspaper
- 2 drinking straws
- Cardboard tube (from inside of toilet paper)
- Masking tape
- Knitting needle
- String
- Paints: white, red, blue, brown
- Paintbrushes
- Black construction paper
- Craft glue
- Double-sided adhesive tape
- Blue and red check fabric, about 6 x 18 inches
- Red rickrack braid
- 3 blue buttons

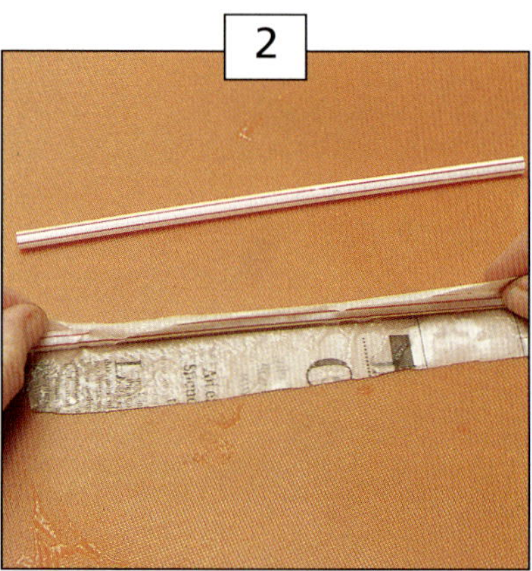

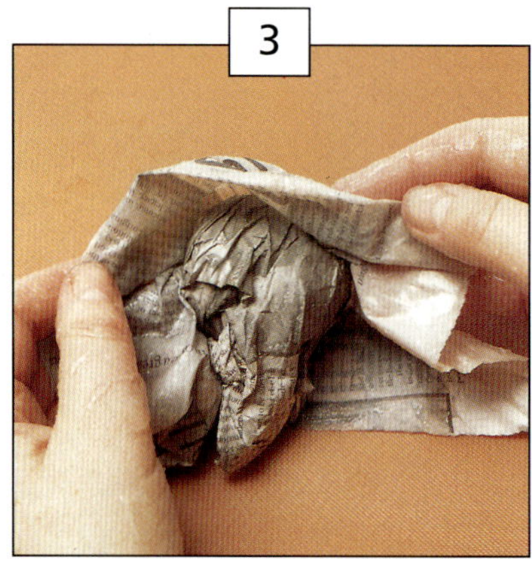

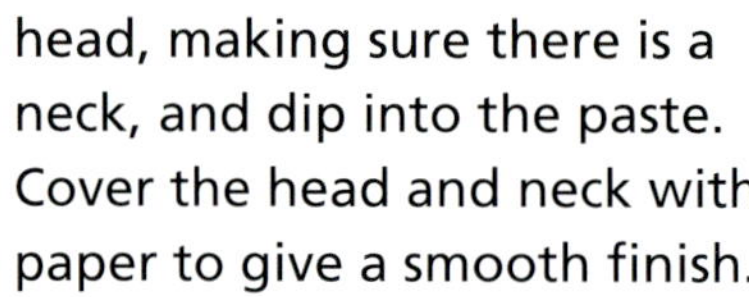

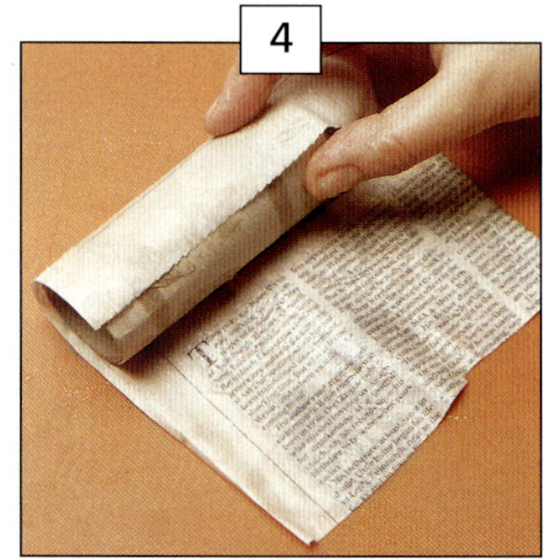

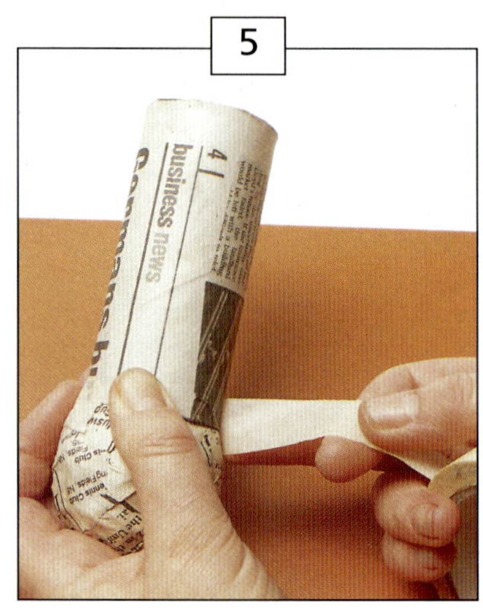

1 Mix the wallpaper paste and water in a bowl and let stand for a while until the paste thickens.

2 Cut two strips of newspaper to fit around the straws. Dip the newspaper in the paste and roll up each straw in a piece of newspaper.

3 Ball up a piece of newspaper to form the doll's head, making sure there is a neck, and dip into the paste. Cover the head and neck with paper to give a smooth finish.

4 Cover the tube with a piece of pasted newspaper and leave it to dry.

5 Use masking tape to hold the head in one end of the tube. When the straws are dry, cut each one in half.

"

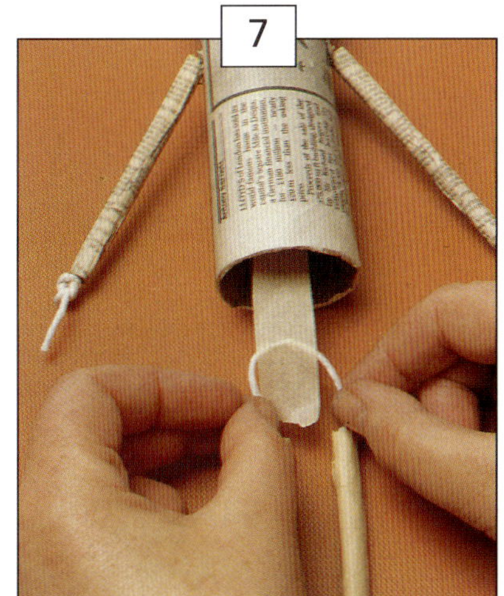

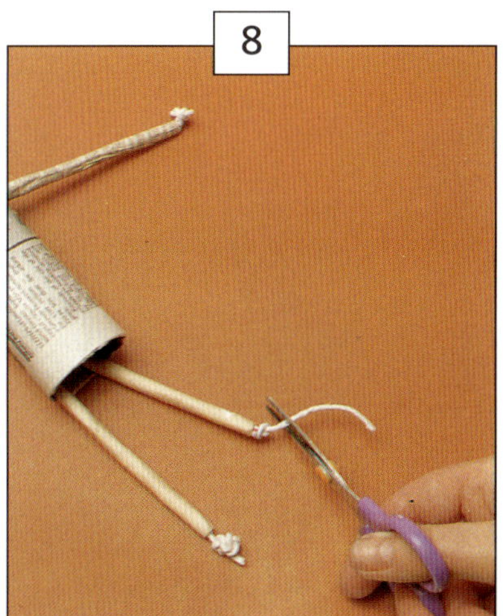

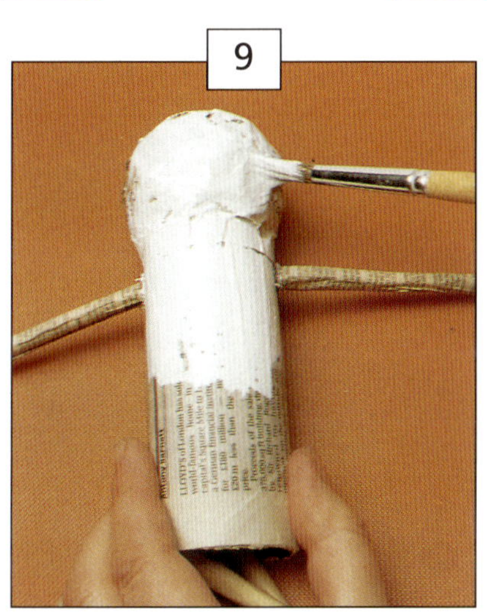

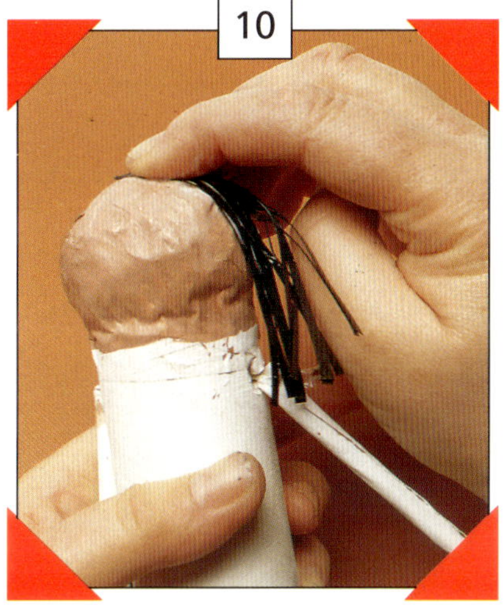

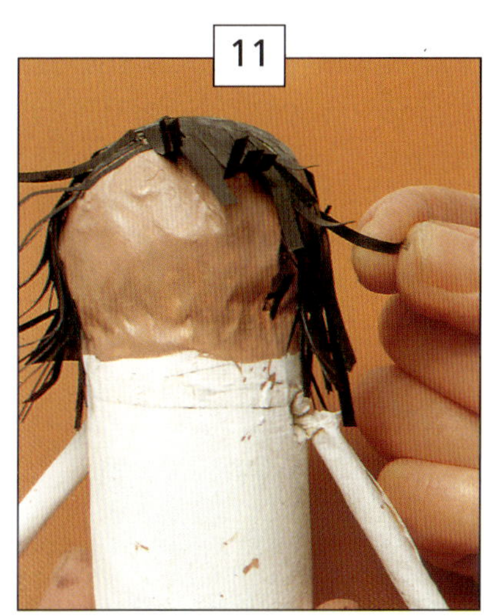

6 **Use a knitting needle to make two holes in the top of the tube, a short distance from the head. Ask an adult to help you thread a length of string through the holes and to thread a piece of straw onto the string to represent arms.** Make sure the string is loose enough for the arms to hang, then tie a knot in each end.

7 Thread a piece of string through the other two pieces of straw. Attach the string inside the tube, holding it in place with a piece of masking tape. Press the masking tape firmly inside the tube.

8 Tie knots in the end of the string to prevent the "legs" from slipping off and then trim the ends.

9 Paint the head and upper body of the doll with white paint to cover all the newsprint. Paint the head a pale brown color.

10 **Cut the black paper into bangs. Ask an adult to help, because this will look better if you can make fine, even bangs.** Use craft glue to glue on the strips of black bangs to look like hair.

11 Trim the black bangs to length. Gently tease out bits of the black bangs to make them resemble curls and waves.

12 Paint the features on the doll's face, including pink cheeks. Paint the upper body and arms of the doll red. Use blue paint to make a pattern of checks and squares on the doll's body, matching the blue of the material you will be using for the skirt as closely as possible. Add a black dot for the pupil in the middle of the doll's eyes.

13 Use double-sided tape to turn under one of the long edges of the skirt fabric to make a hem.

14 Put a piece of double-sided tape around the doll's waist. Gather the unhemmed edge of the skirt fabric and arrange it around the doll, sticking it to the tape.

15 Stick a second piece of double-sided tape around the doll's waist, this time on top of the gathered skirt. Press a piece of rickrack braid around the waist so that it looks like a belt. Stick another piece around the neck. Stick three little buttons down the front of doll's body.

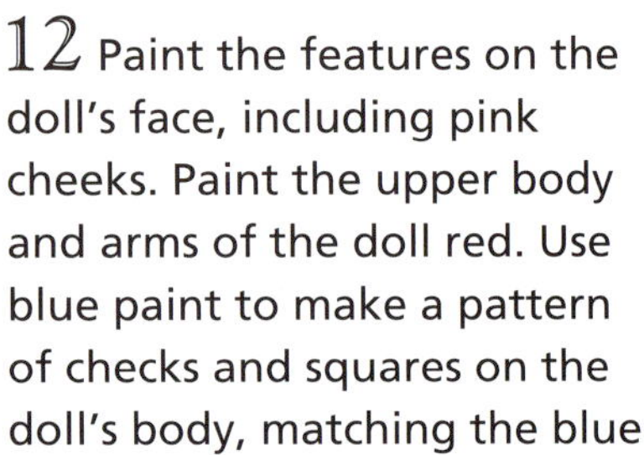

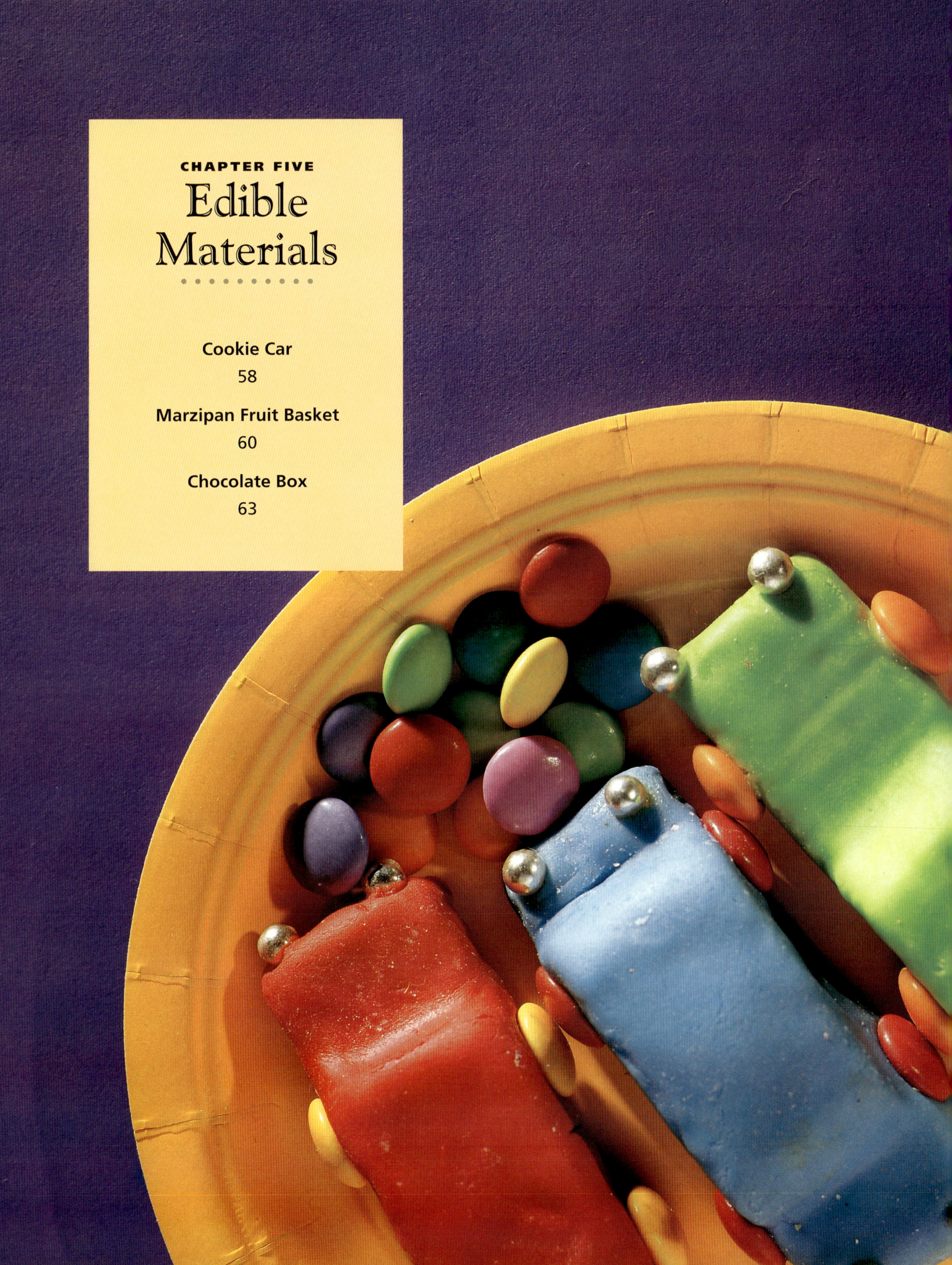

CHAPTER FIVE

Edible Materials

Cookie Car
58

Marzipan Fruit Basket
60

Chocolate Box
63

Cookie Car

It's fun to cook, but sometimes you want to make something quickly, perhaps to give to a special friend or for a party, when there is so much else to do. What could be more enjoyable than to make a car and then to eat it?

YOU WILL NEED

- Plain wafer cookies
- Blunt kitchen knife
- Jam (apricot or something similar)
- Spoon
- Ready-mixed icing sugar
- Food coloring: green
- Rolling pin
- 4 orange M & Ms®
- 4 silver balls (cake decorations)

1 Take two wafer cookies and cut one of them in half. Trim the front and back of the short piece at an angle.

2 Place the cut piece of wafer on the whole piece and cover them both with jam.

3 Take a piece of ready-made icing sugar, about 1½ x 1½ inches, and mix in a little green food color, kneading it with your fingers until the color is evenly distributed through the icing.

4 Scatter a little icing sugar on the worktop and roll out the green icing sugar until it is large enough to cover the wafer biscuits.

5 Carefully lift the icing sugar over the biscuits.

7 Use small pieces of softened icing sugar to attach orange M & Ms® to the bottom of the car to resemble wheels.

8 Place a silver ball in each corner to look like lights.

6 With your fingers, gently press the icing sugar onto the biscuits. Do not press too hard, but make the slopes clear. Trim around the edges with a knife.

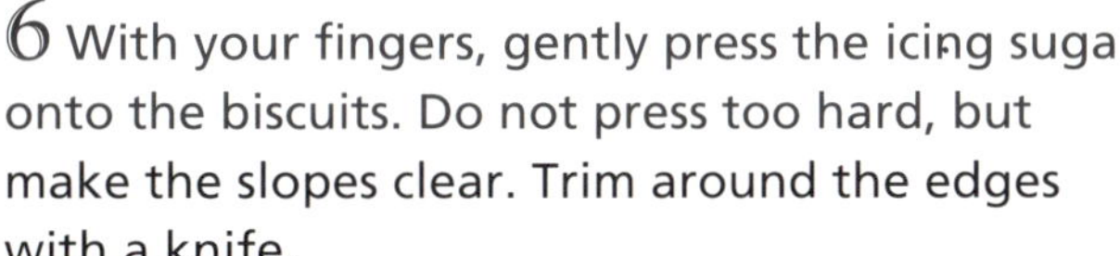

Marzipan Fruit Basket

Working with marzipan is a little like working with modeling clay – except you can eat it. It is easy to use and can be bought ready made. You can color it with food coloring and then use it to make animals and flowers. Decorate it with small candies, nuts, and raisins to make them extra delicious.

- Block of white marzipan
- Kitchen knife
- Food coloring: green, red, orange, yellow, blue
- Teaspoon
- Toothpick
- Kitchen grater (optional)
- Paintbrushes
- Cloves
- Plastic box and netting
- Narrow ribbon

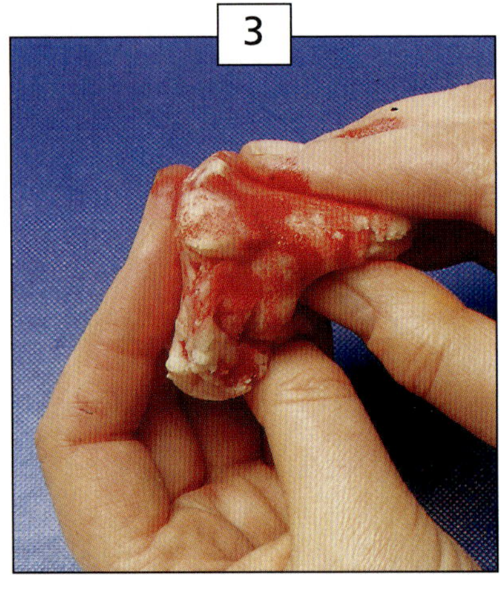

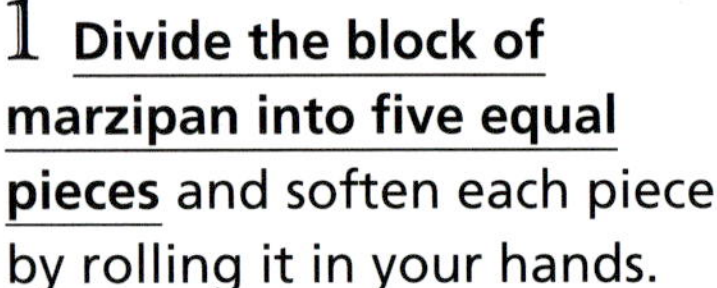

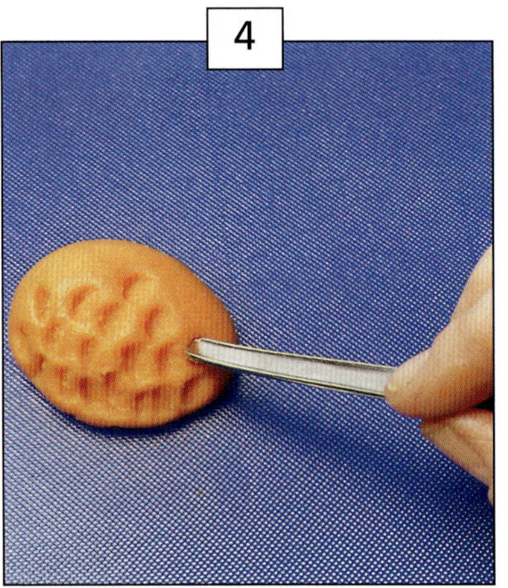

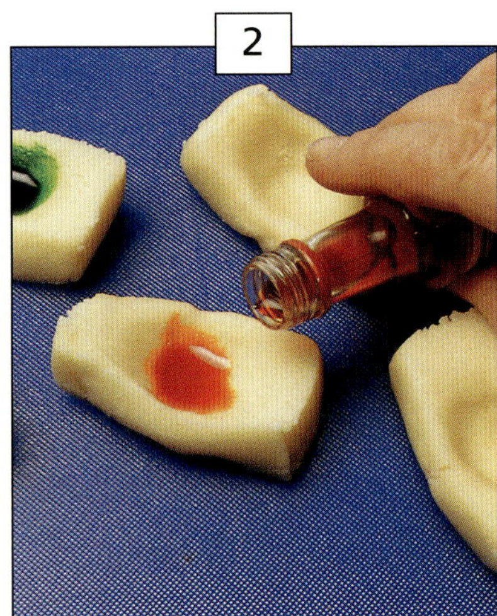

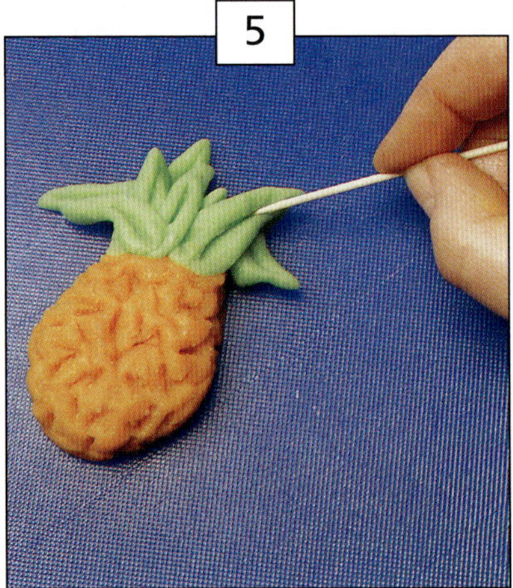

1 **Divide the block of marzipan into five equal pieces** and soften each piece by rolling it in your hands.

2 Flatten each piece and make a slight indentation in the center of each with your finger. Add some yellow coloring to one, some red to another, some green to another and some orange to another. Mix red and blue together to color the final piece purple.

3 Knead each color so that the color is distributed evenly through the marzipan.

4 Begin with orange marzipan and make the pineapple. Mold a piece into an egg shape and use the end of a teaspoon to make a pattern over the surface.

5 Roll some little tubes of green marzipan. Flatten one end and make a point at the other. Press the leaves to the top of the pineapple, arranging them to form a spray.

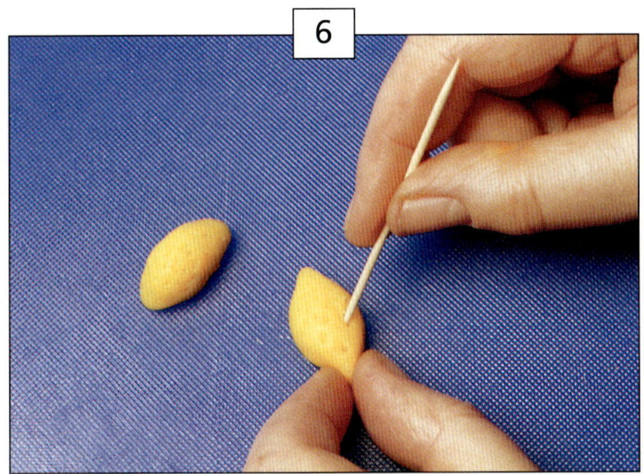

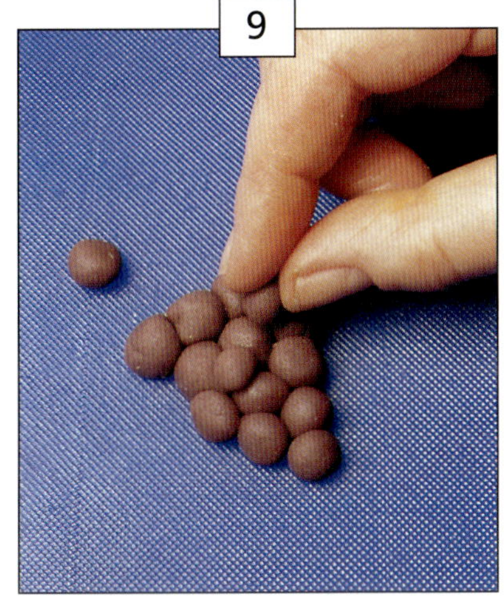

6 Use the yellow marzipan to make four or five bananas and about two lemons. Mold the lemons into little egg shapes with pointed ends, then make a pattern of tiny indentations all over the surface with the point of a toothpick. Or, press each one against the finest side of a kitchen grater.

7 Mold the remaining yellow into the shape of the bananas. Mix a tiny amount of brown coloring from the red, blue, and green, and use a fine brush to draw lines along the sides and to color in the ends.

8 Take small pieces of red and green and roll them together, taking care that the colors do not completely run together, to make apples. Make pears from the green marzipan, molding them with your fingers.

9 Make some balls of different sizes from the purple marzipan. These are going to be arranged into a bunch of grapes. Press the larger balls together to make a triangle. Put smaller balls on top to build up the bunch.

10 Use the red marzipan to make little strawberries. Make a pattern of indentations over the surface with a cocktail stick and attach little green leaves to the top.

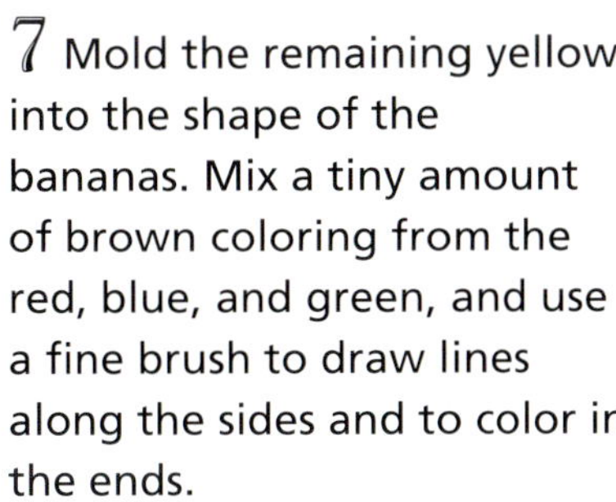

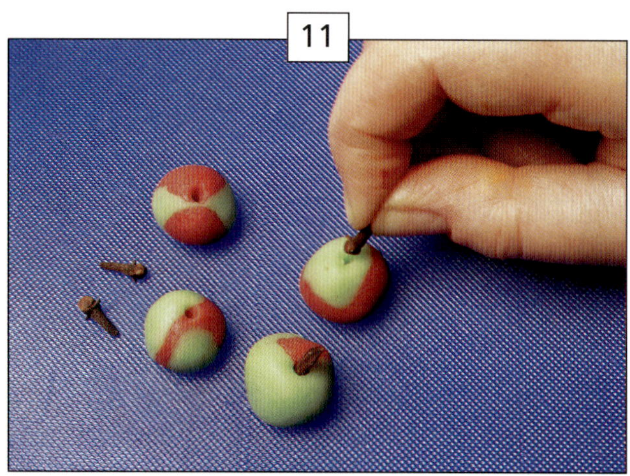

11 Use a toothpick to make an indentation in the top of the apples, grapes, pears, and bananas. Insert cloves in to the tops to represent stalks.

12 Place all the fruit in a small box or basket, arranging them so that the sides of the box are hidden. Tie a piece of netting over the box and hold it in place with a neat bow of narrow ribbon.

TIP

☛ Use any orange marzipan that is left to make oranges. Dimple the surface with a toothpick or grater in the same way as the lemons.

Chocolate Box

This is an ideal project to make for a present for a relative or friend. The chocolates are made in molds, and you can decorate the box in whatever way you want. You could put someone's name on it, or decorate it with shells, ribbons, or flowers. We used silver squares and sequins, which give a sophisticated look to the box, but you could use different colors or a different pattern.

YOU WILL NEED

- Large bar of chocolate (plain, milk, or nut)
- Heatproof bowl
- Saucepan
- Metal spoon
- Selection of chocolate molds
- Silver balls (cake decorations)
- Silver and purple foil
- Ruler
- Pencil
- Purple cardboard
- Cardboard box (empty chocolate box, for example)
- Scissors
- Craft glue and brush
- Silver cardboard
- Silver sequins
- Tissue paper
- Silver ribbon

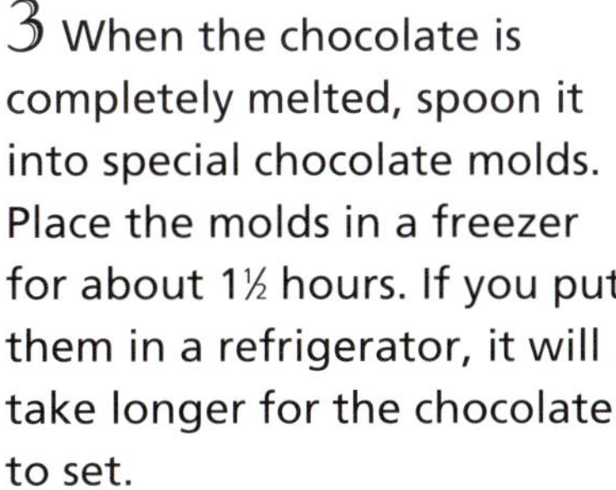

1 Break the chocolate into pieces and place them in a heatproof bowl.

2 **Stand the bowl in a saucepan full of boiling water. Ask an adult to help you with this stage.**

3 When the chocolate is completely melted, spoon it into special chocolate molds. Place the molds in a freezer for about 1½ hours. If you put them in a refrigerator, it will take longer for the chocolate to set.

4 Remove the chocolate from the molds by tapping them sharply on your worktop.

5 Use a little melted chocolate to stick silver balls on the chocolate.

6 Wrap some of the chocolates in silver and purple foil.

7 Use a ruler to mark pieces of purple cardboard that will exactly cover the sides and top of the box.

8 Cut out the pieces of cardboard. Remember to include a piece that will cover the inside of the lid.

9 Glue the purple cardboard over the top and sides of the box.

10 Use a ruler to make a grid of squares, about ¾ x ¾ inch, on the silver cardboard. You will need about 52 squares. Cut out the squares, making sure that the edges are neat and straight.

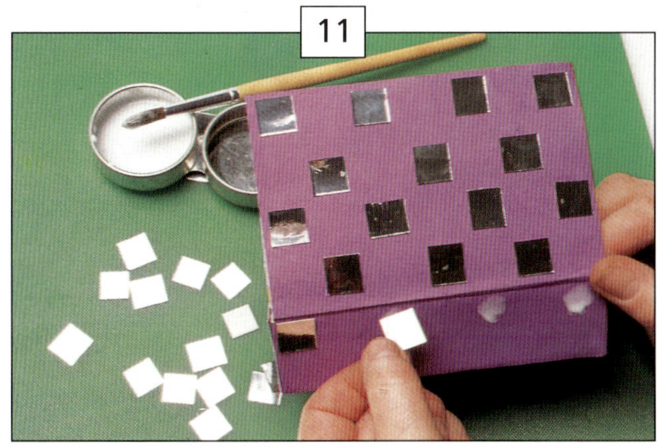

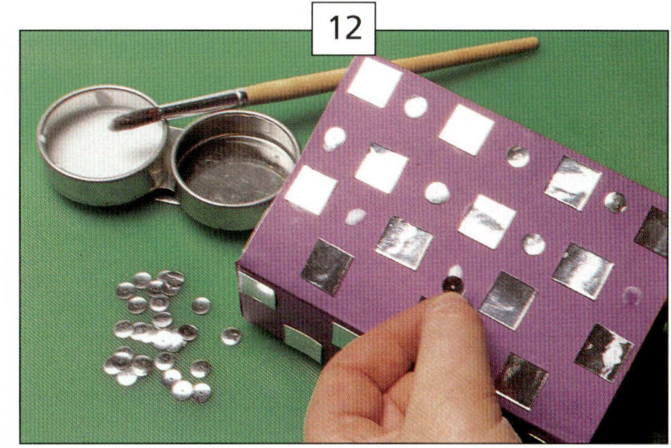

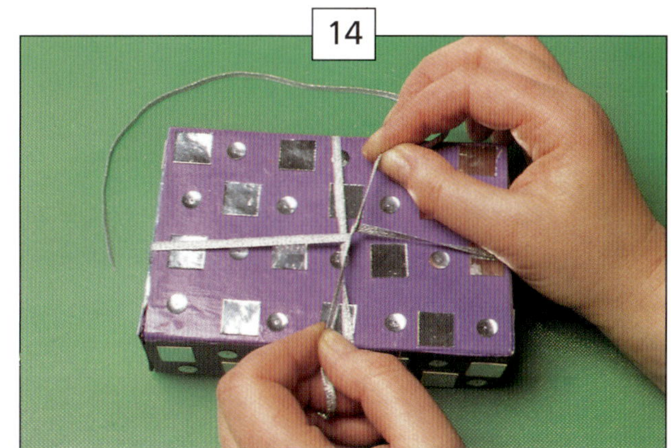

11 Stick the squares in rows on the top and sides of the box.

12 Stick a sequin between each silver square.

13 Put some tissue paper in the bottom of the box and place a layer of chocolates in the box. Cover the chocolates with a piece of silver cardboard and add a second layer of chocolates.

14 Tie a length of silver ribbon around the box and tie a neat bow.

Natural Materials

Rainforest Scene

When you go for a walk in the countryside or along the seashore, you will find all kinds of interesting things – feathers, shells, pebbles, stones, cones, the list is almost endless. You may not have all the items we have used for our rainforest, but our layout will give you ideas for your own version. Let the materials you have suggest ways in which you can develop your own model.

YOU WILL NEED

- Corks
- Craft knife
- Craft glue
- Twigs
- Feathers
- Fine cord
- Black felt-tipped pen
- Pine cones
- Screw-in eyes
- Shallow tray or box
- Blue or green construction paper
- Sand (optional)
- Plasticine
- Grasses, leaves, etc.
- Shells, pebbles, small stones, etc.
- Pieces of bark or driftwood
- Scraps of fabric: red and white
- Scissors

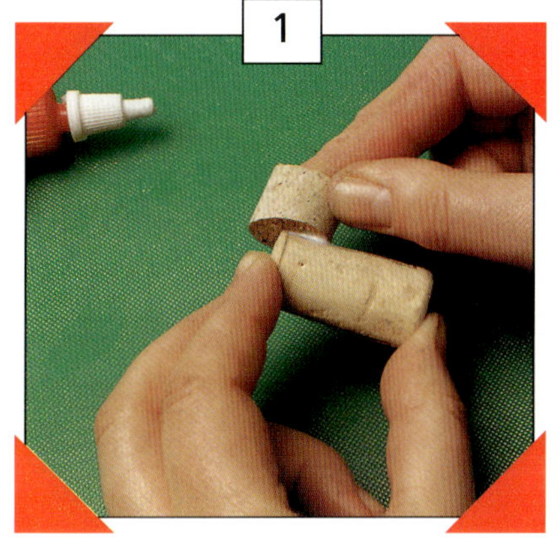

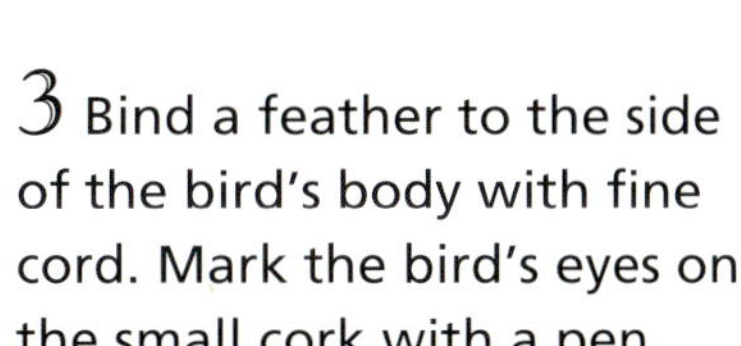

1 **Cut one of the corks in half. If you use a craft knife, ask an adult to help.** Stick the half cork onto a whole cork to form the body and head of a bird.

2 Use a twig to make a hole for the beak in the smaller of the corks. Break the twig until it is about ¾ inch long and glue it in the hole.

3 Bind a feather to the side of the bird's body with fine cord. Mark the bird's eyes on the small cork with a pen.

4 Remove some of the scales from a large pine cone.

5 Stick a scale on each side of another cork. Use a piece of twig to make a beak (see step 3) and stick a feather on top of the cork.

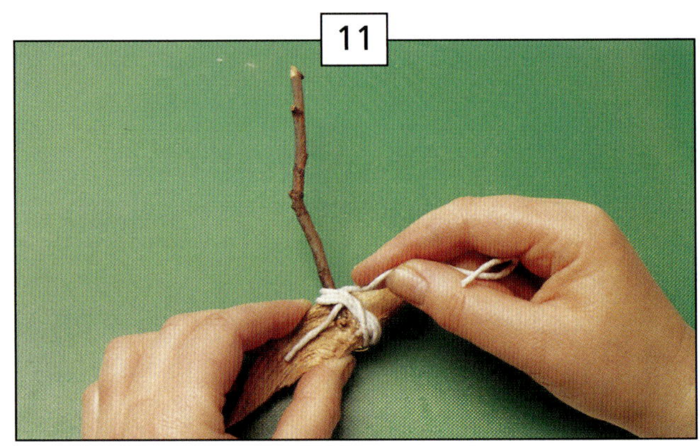

6 Draw in eyes with a felt-tipped pen. Insert a screw eye at the back of the cork so that you can hang the bird up.

7 Make the base of the picture in a shallow tray or box with a rim about ¾ inch deep. Cover the base with blue or green paper, or use a different color at each end and disguise the join by applying a thin layer of glue down the center and shaking sand over it. Shake off any excess sand.

8 Use pieces of Plasticine to make bases for the dried grasses and leaves. Arrange them at the back of the box.

9 Arrange the pebbles, shells, and so on in front of the vegetation. Hang the birds in the trees.

10 Stick a twig in the middle of a piece of bark or small piece of driftwood.

11 Bind cord around the base of the boat and the twig to hold the twig firm.

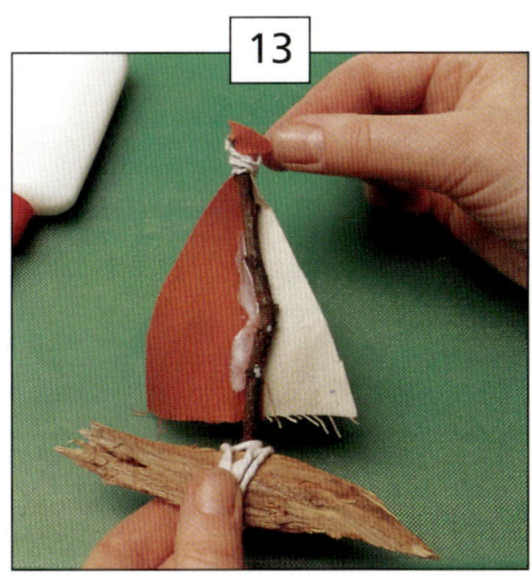

12 Run a line of glue along the twig. Stick the sails in place on the twig.

13 Bind the top of the sails with a piece of fine cord. Cut out and glue in place a tiny flag or pennant for the top of the mast.

14 Place the boat at the front of the arrangement. Try making a raft from twigs and scrap fabric. Add some shells and bits of coral to the ocean end of your model.

Great Greeting Card

Sometimes you want to make something quickly, and this card is ideal. It makes use of the odds and ends you might have collected, such as dried flowers or brightly colored feathers. Choose different colored papers for the base to create a quite different effect.

YOU WILL NEED

- Colored cardboard: yellow and orange
- White cardboard
- Scissors
- Craft glue
- Dried flowers
- Feathers
- Shells

1 Cut a large rectangle of yellow cardboard for the background and fold it carefully in two.

2 Copy the template from page 91 and transfer the outline to stiff cardboard.

3 Cut around the shape in orange cardboard, making sure that the edges are smooth.

4 Stick the orange cardboard to the center of the front of the yellow cardboard.

5 Glue dried flowers to the orange cardboard.

8 Glue on some little shells. Make sure that the glue is dry before moving the cardboard or writing your message inside.

6 Add feathers and shells in a pattern. It is a good idea to try out several arrangements before gluing anything down. Glue on the feathers.

7 Put a dab of glue at each corner.

Cork Necklace

Cork is an excellent material for making jewelry, mainly because it is so easy to make holes in it. It is light and soft, and you do not need complicated tools to work with it. You can leave the cork as it is, or combine it with all kinds of beads and feathers.

YOU WILL NEED

- Craft knife
- 4–5 corks
- Knitting needle
- Paints: white, blue, black, silver, turquoise
- Paintbrushes
- Fine wire (fuse wire)
- Feathers and beads
- Narrow elastic

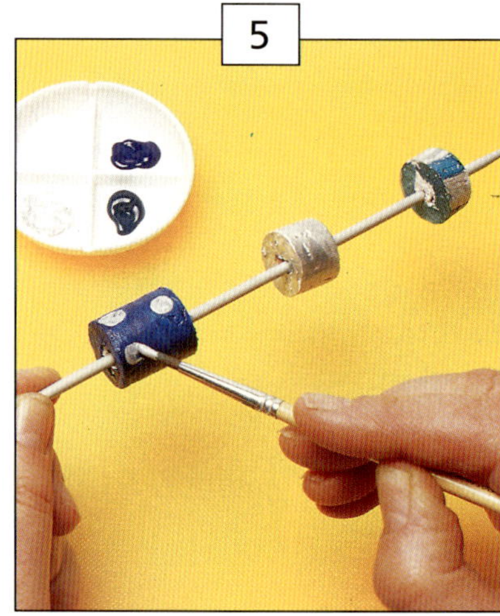

1 **Use a craft knife to cut the corks into various sizes.** The necklace will look more interesting if they are not all the same size. Ask an adult to help you with this.

2 **Thread the corks onto a knitting needle** so that it is easier to paint them. **Take care not to push the point of the knitting needle against your hand.**

3 Give each cork a coat of white paint and leave to dry. This will make the finished color stronger, although you can skip this stage if you want.

4 Paint some of the corks dark blue (blue and black), some silver, and some turquoise. Leave to dry.

5 Decorate the "beads" with spots and stripes of different colors. Try mixing blue paint with silver to create some interesting effects.

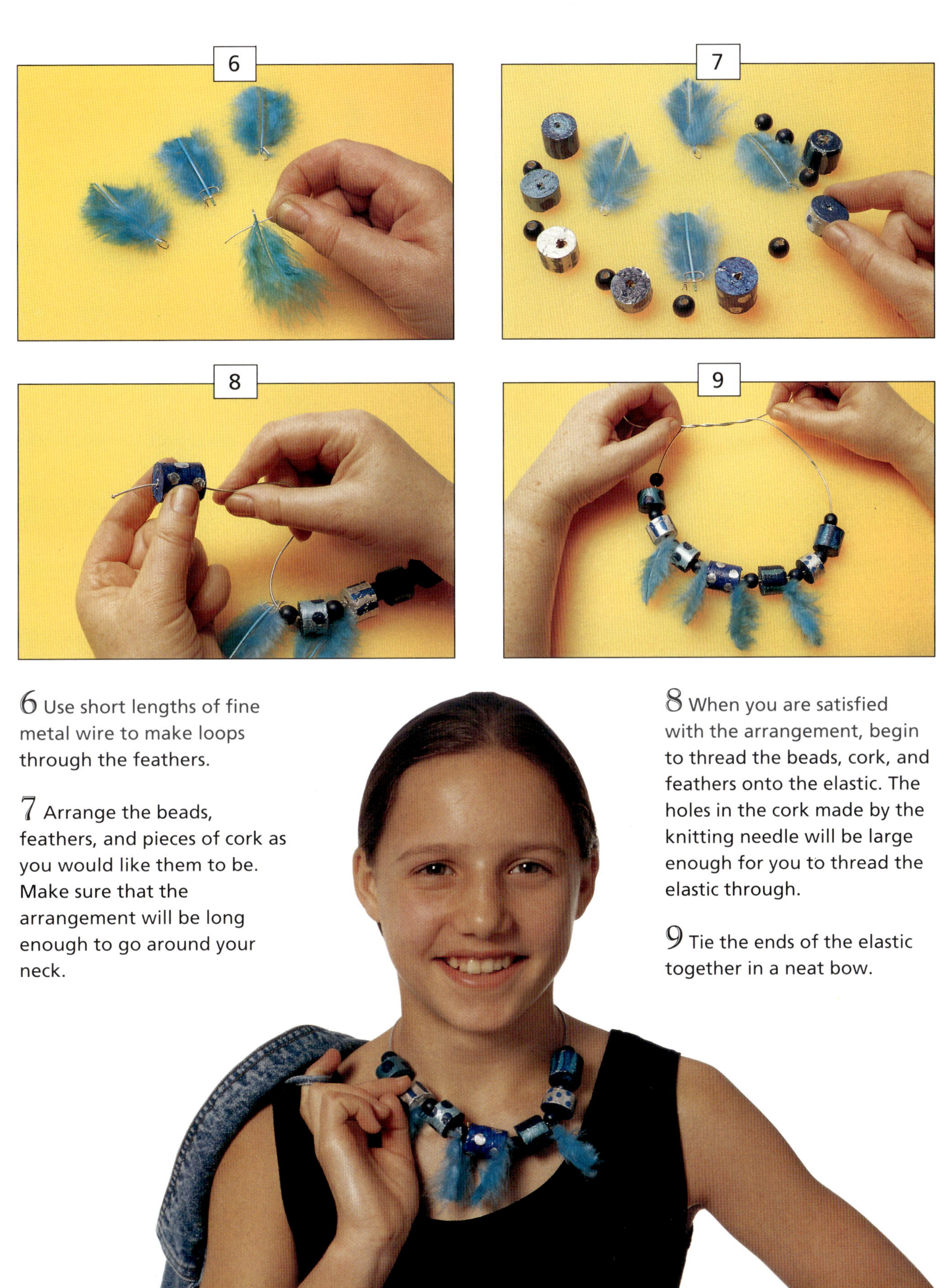

6 Use short lengths of fine metal wire to make loops through the feathers.

7 Arrange the beads, feathers, and pieces of cork as you would like them to be. Make sure that the arrangement will be long enough to go around your neck.

8 When you are satisfied with the arrangement, begin to thread the beads, cork, and feathers onto the elastic. The holes in the cork made by the knitting needle will be large enough for you to thread the elastic through.

9 Tie the ends of the elastic together in a neat bow.

Fly Away!

This glider is a simple project to start off with. It's only got three basic pieces, but it has been designed so that it will fly really well. If you find that you cannot get it to fly smoothly, try adding different weights – paper clips or small pieces of Plasticine, for example – on each side of the nose.

- Pencil
- White cardboard
- Scissors
- Balsa wood: 1 thin sheet (⅛ inch)
- Craft knife
- Sandpaper
- Plasticine
- Paints: white, blue, black
- Paintbrushes
- Adhesive paper, stars, and circles
- Varnish and brush

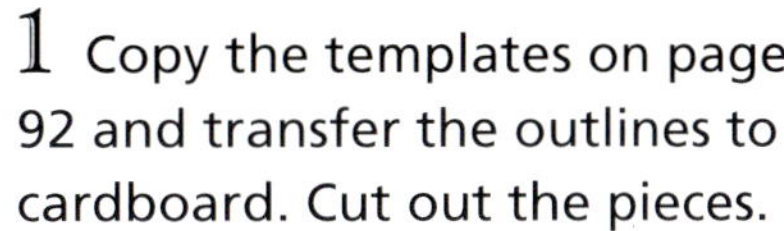

1 Copy the templates on page 92 and transfer the outlines to cardboard. Cut out the pieces.

2 Draw around the cardboard templates to transfer the outlines of the pieces to the balsa wood. Remember to include the slits that have to be cut.

3 **Use a craft knife and ruler to cut out all the pieces.** Use four or five gentle cuts rather than one strong one.

4 **Carefully cut out the slits in the plane's body.**

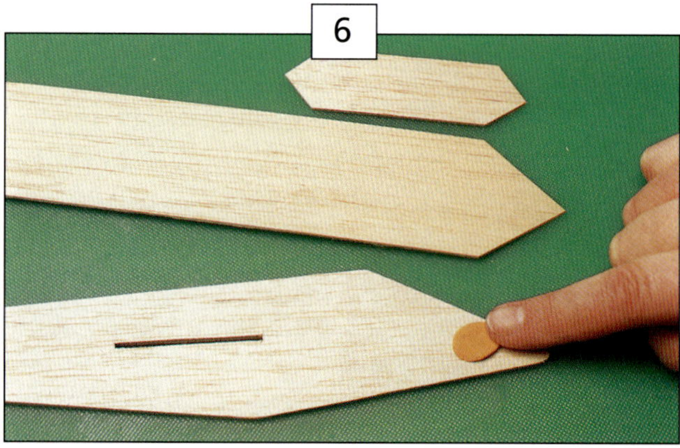

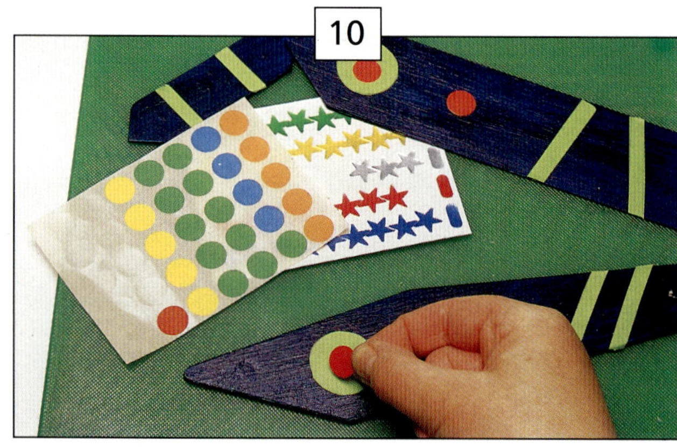

5 Smooth any rough edges with fine sandpaper to give a more aerodynamic shape. Work carefully because the wood is very thin.

6 Place a small piece of Plasticine on each side of the nose as marked on the template. The extra weight will help the glider to fly well.

7 Paint all the pieces with white paint on both sides. Leave to dry.

8 Mix some dark blue paint (blue and black) to paint all three pieces. Leave the paint to dry.

9 Cut some shapes from adhesive paper if you cannot find ready-made ones in the size or color you want.

10 Finish the decoration by adding self-adhesive stars, circles, and so on.

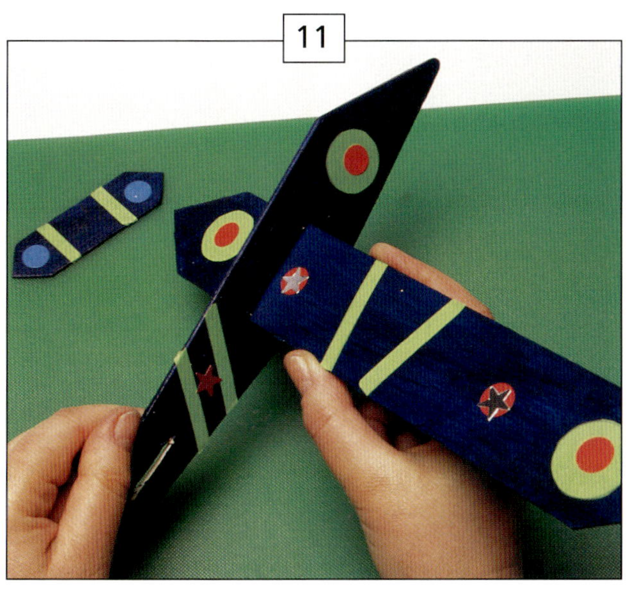

11 Assemble the pieces, sliding the wings through the hole in the fuselage and the tail in the tail piece.

12 Finish by applying at least one coat of varnish to seal the decoration. Remember to allow the first coat of varnish to dry before you apply the next. When the varnish is dry, give your glider a trial flight.

Letter Rack

This is an excellent project for developing your woodworking skills. The simple design is easy to make once you have got used to cutting out the shapes. The paint design was inspired by the design on airmail paper.

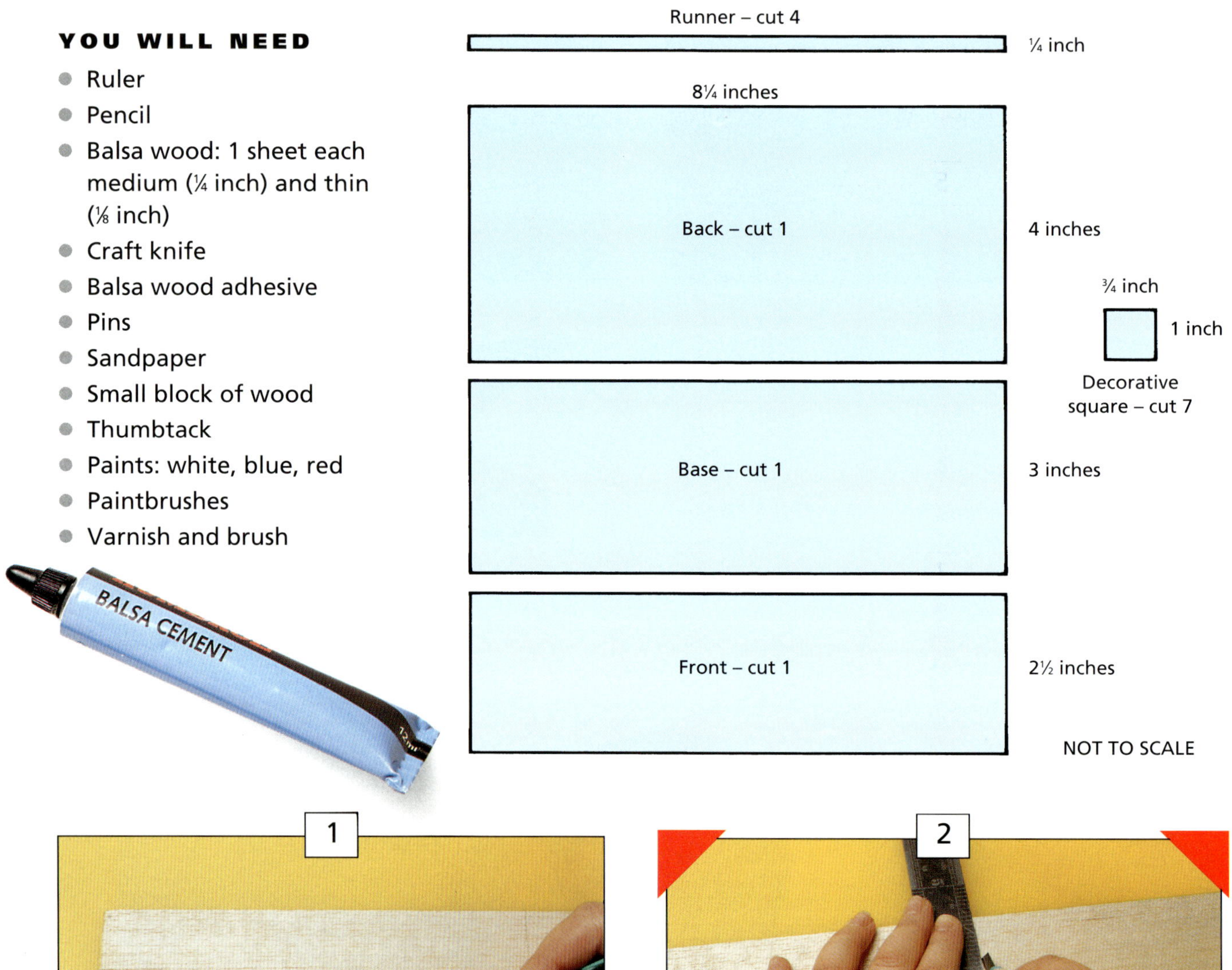

1 Measure out the front, back, and base sections on medium balsa wood, following the cutting diagram, above.

2 Use a craft knife to cut out the pieces. Make several small cuts rather than one strong cut. Press down against the ruler.

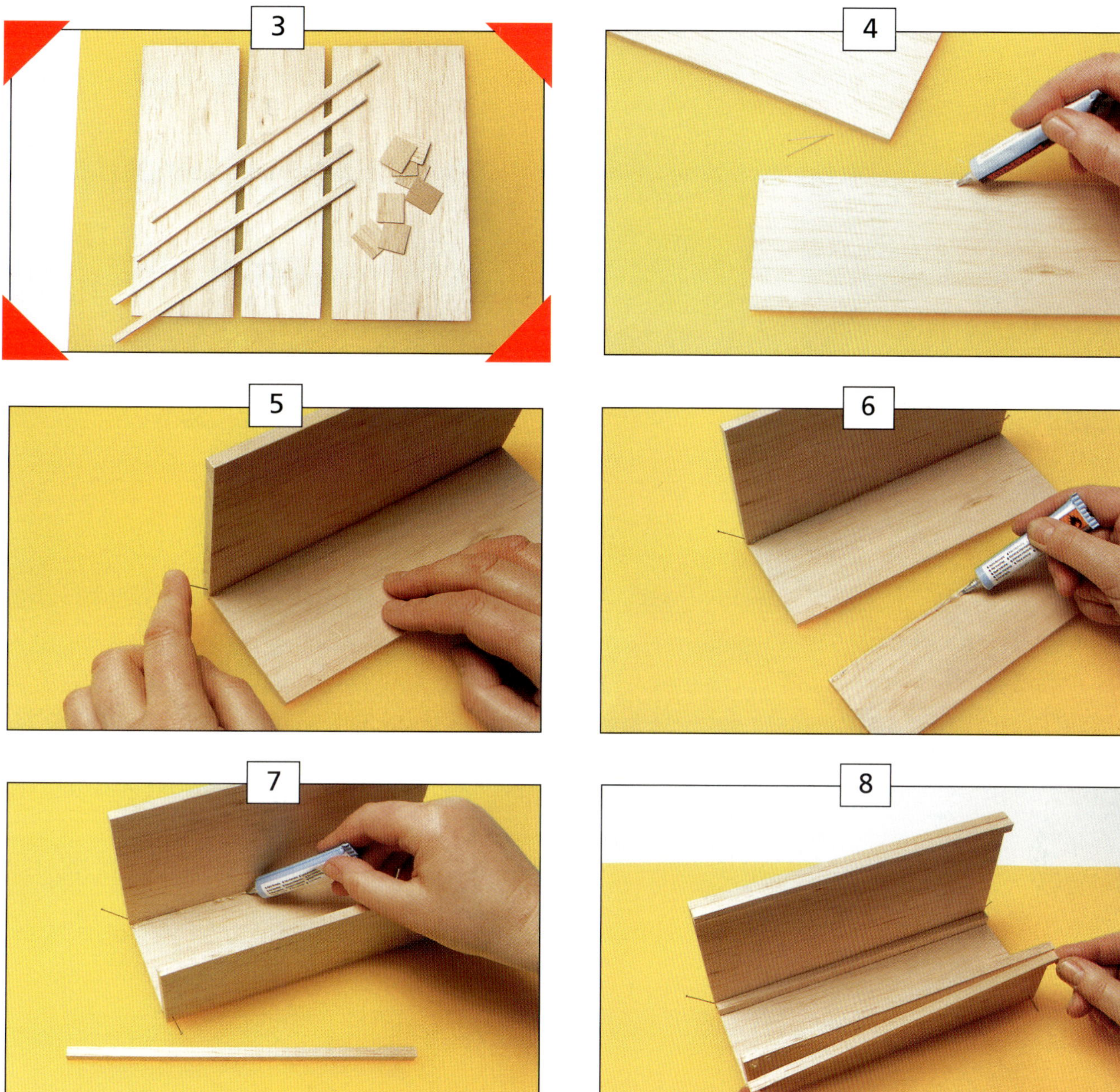

3 **Cut four sticks from the medium wood and seven small squares from the thin wood.** Lay all the pieces out to make sure you have everything you need.

4 Glue the back to the base. Use quite a lot of glue to hold the joints together.

5 Use pins to hold the pieces together. Make sure that the pieces are at right angles.

6 Glue and pin the front to the base in the same way.

7 When the main pieces are dry, which should not take long, glue two of the long, thin pieces along the inside of the joins to strengthen the letter rack.

8 Glue and pin the other two strips along the tops of the front and back. Leave to dry and then remove all the pins.

9 Glue the squares over the front of the letter rack, making sure they are evenly spaced. Do not use too much glue, or it will ooze out when you press them down.

10 Make a sanding block by wrapping a piece of sandpaper around a small block of wood and securing it with a thumbtack.

11 Gently sand all the edges and surfaces to give a smooth finish.

12 Apply a coat of white paint to all surfaces. Paint the background light blue (blue and white).

13 Paint the squares red and add some red stripes along the fronts of the two thin wooden strips.

14 Mix dark blue (blue and black) and paint the top surfaces of the two thin strips and the sides of the letter rack. Add dark blue stripes next to the red stripes.

15 When the paint is dry, varnish all over.

Pooch Pencil Box

If you feel pretty confident making models from balsa wood, then why not have a try at this delightful doggy box? Because you need thicker wood to model the head, you will need a junior hacksaw to cut the wood – take care, as always, with sharp tools.

YOU WILL NEED

- White cardboard
- Scissors
- Pencil
- Balsa wood: 1 sheet each thick (½ inch), medium (¼ inch), and thin (⅛ inch)
- Junior hacksaw
- Ruler
- Craft knife
- Balsa wood adhesive
- Pins
- Sandpaper
- Paints: white, red, black
- Paintbrushes
- Varnish and brush

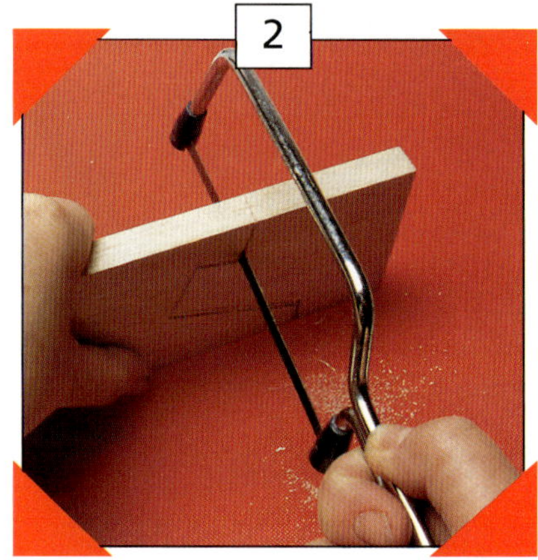

1 Copy the templates of the dog's head and features on page 93 and transfer them to thick cardboard. Cut out all the pieces. Draw around the outline of the template of the dog's head onto the piece of thick balsa wood.

2 **Use a hacksaw to cut around the outline. Ask an adult to help with this because the wood is quite thick.**

3 Measure out the sides, lid, ends, base, and runners on medium balsa wood, using the cutting diagram as a guide. **Cut the pieces out with a craft knife.**

4 **Use the other cardboard templates to cut out all the decorative pieces** – nose, eyes, ears, and collar – from the thin balsa wood. Lay out all the pieces you have cut to check that everything is there.

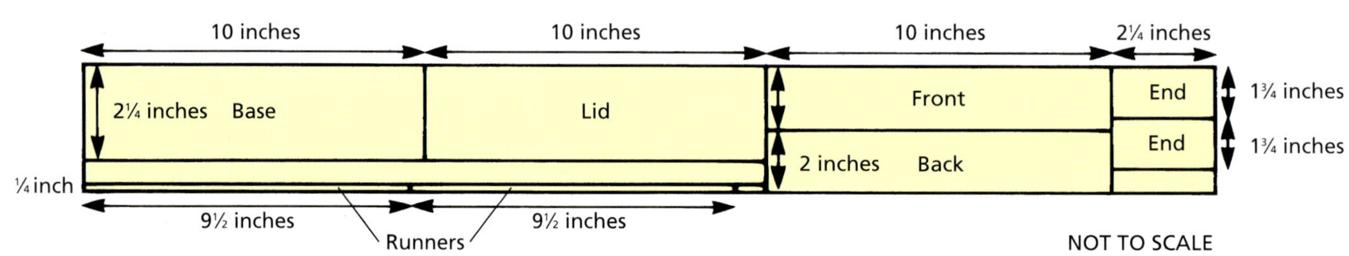

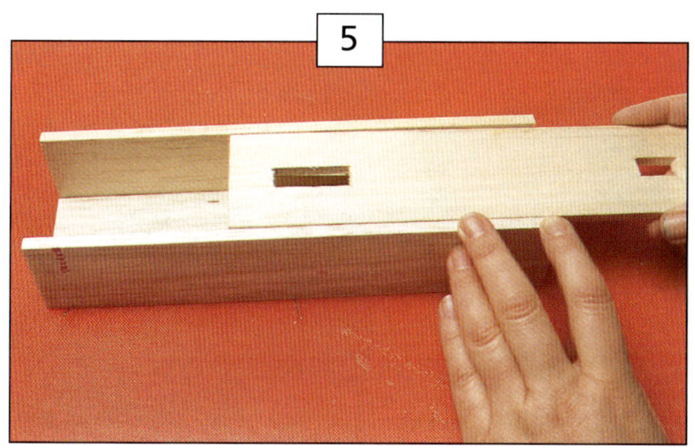

5 Glue then pin the sides to the base. Check that the lid fits between the sides.

6 Measure down about ¼ inch from the top edge of the box. Draw a line at this depth to mark the position of the top of the runners. Glue and pin the runners in place before gluing and pinning the ends on.

7 Glue the dog's tail in position on the box lid. It should be about ¾ inch from one end.

8 Glue the dog's head at the other end, making sure it is the same distance from the end as the tail.

9 Glue the three strips across the top of the box, angling them slightly. Glue them in place. Arrange the other decorative pieces on the dog's head and on the box and then glue them in place.

10 When the glue is dry, carefully sand the surface of the dog and box. It is sometimes easier to smooth the surfaces of the small pieces before they are glued in place.

11 Paint the box white, inside and out.

12 Leaving the triangles white, paint the base of the box black. Paint some red circles inside.

13 Paint the dog's features black and add some dots around the nose to represent whiskers. Paint the collar red, then paint the top of the box black, leaving the three stripes white.

14 When the paint is dry, varnish all over, inside and out.

Penny Pig

This is the most difficult of the balsa wood projects, but it does make a great working piggy bank. We have made it as easy to get your money out as it is to put it in. There is a simple sliding door mechanism at one end, running between two sets of runners, in the same way that a drawer runs in and out.

YOU WILL NEED

- White cardboard
- Scissors
- Pencil
- Balsa wood: 1 sheet each medium (¼ inch) and thin (⅛ inch)
- Craft knife
- Balsa wood adhesive
- Pins
- Paints: white, red, black
- Paintbrushes
- White circular stickers
- Varnish and brush

4¼ inches

Base – cut 1

1¼ inches

4 inches

Top – cut 1

1¼ inches

2½ inches

End – cut 2

Runner – cut 4
1¼ inches

¼ inch   NOT TO SCALE

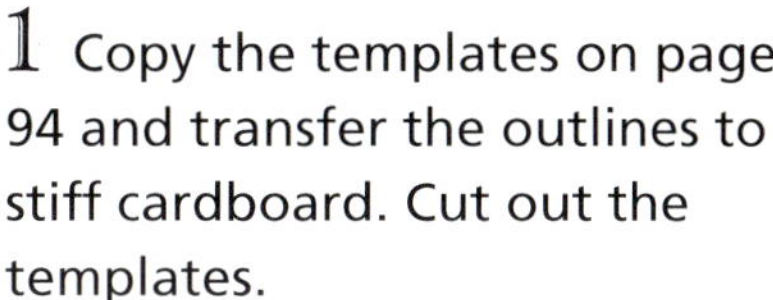

1 Copy the templates on page 94 and transfer the outlines to stiff cardboard. Cut out the templates.

2 Use the templates to draw around the outlines onto the balsa wood. Use the medium wood for the main construction – the pig-shaped sides – and the thin wood for details such as the eyes and ears.

3 **Cut out all the shapes with a craft knife. Go over each cut lightly several times rather than trying to cut through all at once. Cut a slit in the top of the box that is about ¼ inch wide and 1½ inch long.**

4 Finish cutting out all the pieces and lay them out to make sure you have everything, including ears, eyes, and legs.

5 Glue the inner box base and end to one side of the pig. **Cut two small strips from the thin balsa wood** and glue them to the base of the box so that they are about ¼ inch apart. Check that the end piece slides easily between these two pieces.

6 **Cut two more strips, slightly longer**, and position them on the side of the box so that they align exactly with the two shorter strips. Glue and pin the top of the box in position. Glue and pin the runner in place. Check again that the end piece will slide easily between them and slot into the strips on the base.

7 Apply glue all the way round the edge of the box.

8 Place the other side of the pig in place. Glue on the ears and pin everything in position.

9 Glue on the eyes and legs, holding them in place with pins until the glue has dried.

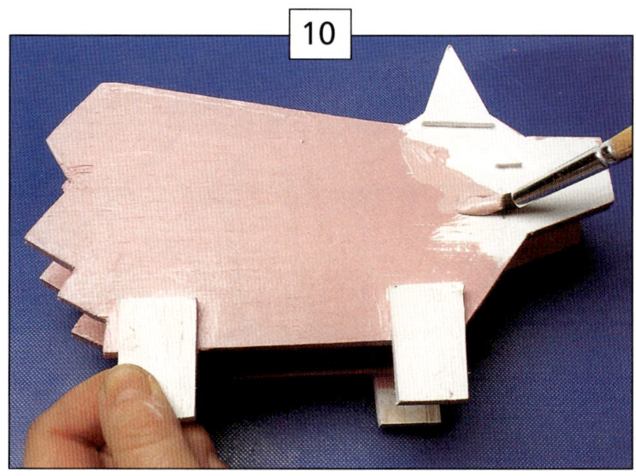

10 Paint the pig white all over. When the undercoat is dry, mix some pink paint (red and white) and paint the pig all over. Leave to dry. Paint the legs grey and the ears and eyes black. Put some white peel-off stickers on the pig's body when the pink paint is completely dry.

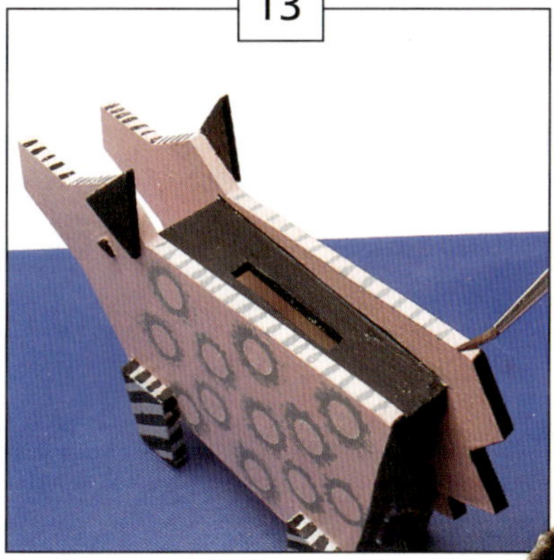

11 Carefully paint around the circles with grey, brushing the paint upwards to make a sort of halo effect. When the grey paint is dry, peel off the stickers.

12 Paint the pig's tail black. Paint fine, black, slanting stripes on the pig's legs.

13 Paint the box black, including the end piece which slides up and down, and decorate the top edge with black stripes.

14 When the paint is dry, varnish the piggy bank all over.

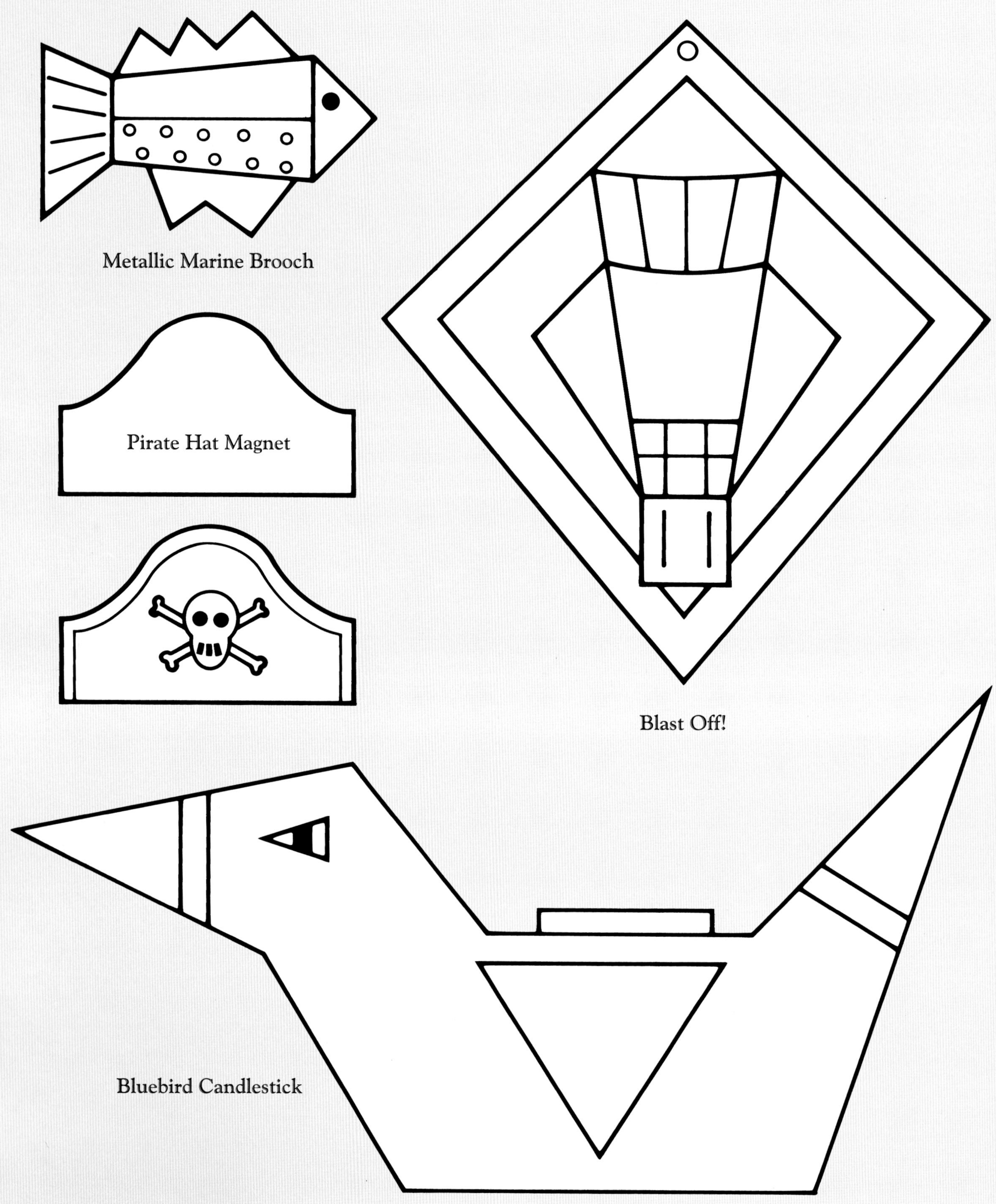

Metallic Marine Brooch
Pirate Hat Magnet
Blast Off!
Bluebird Candlestick

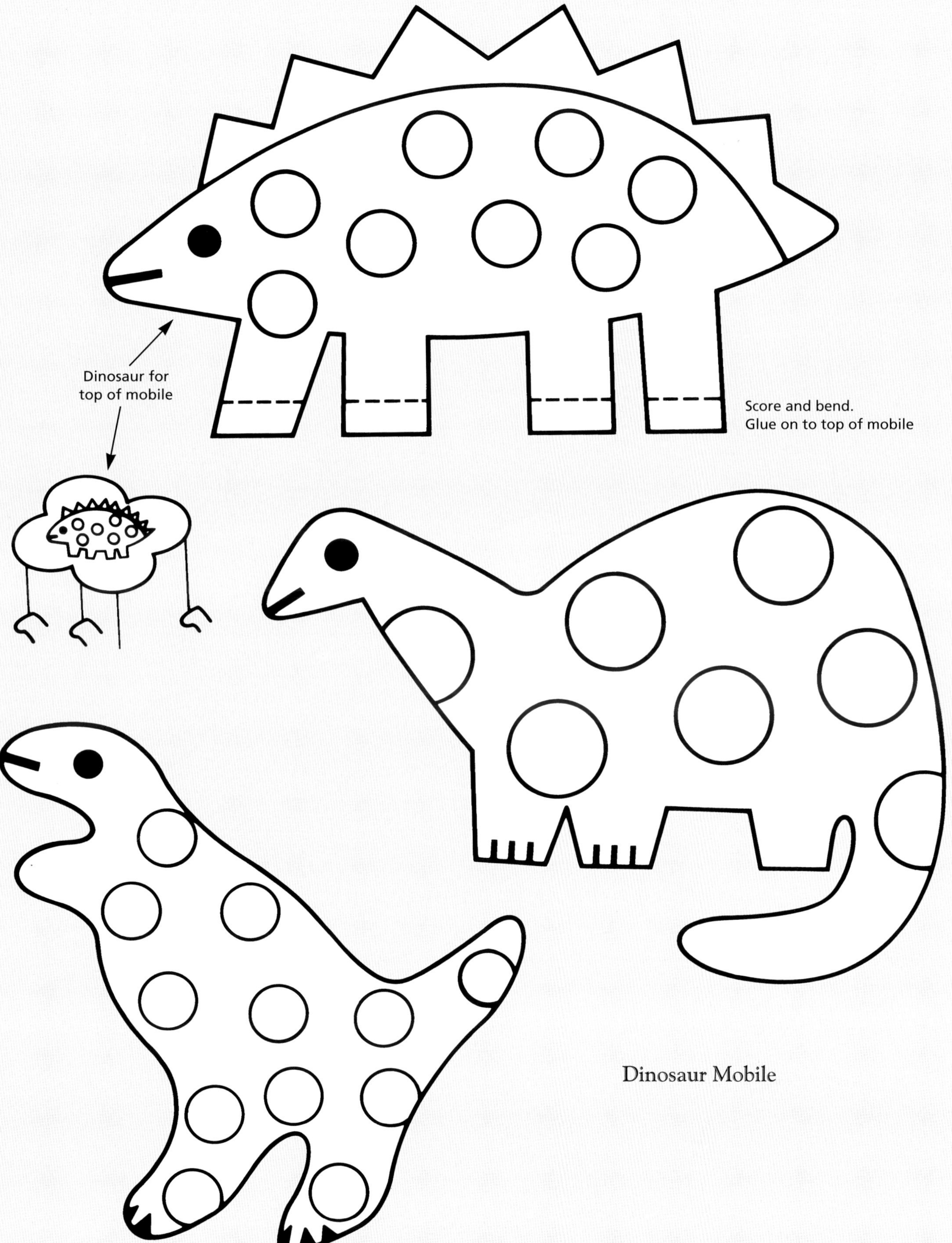

Dinosaur for
top of mobile
Score and bend.
Glue on to top of mobile
Dinosaur Mobile

Dinosaur Mobile

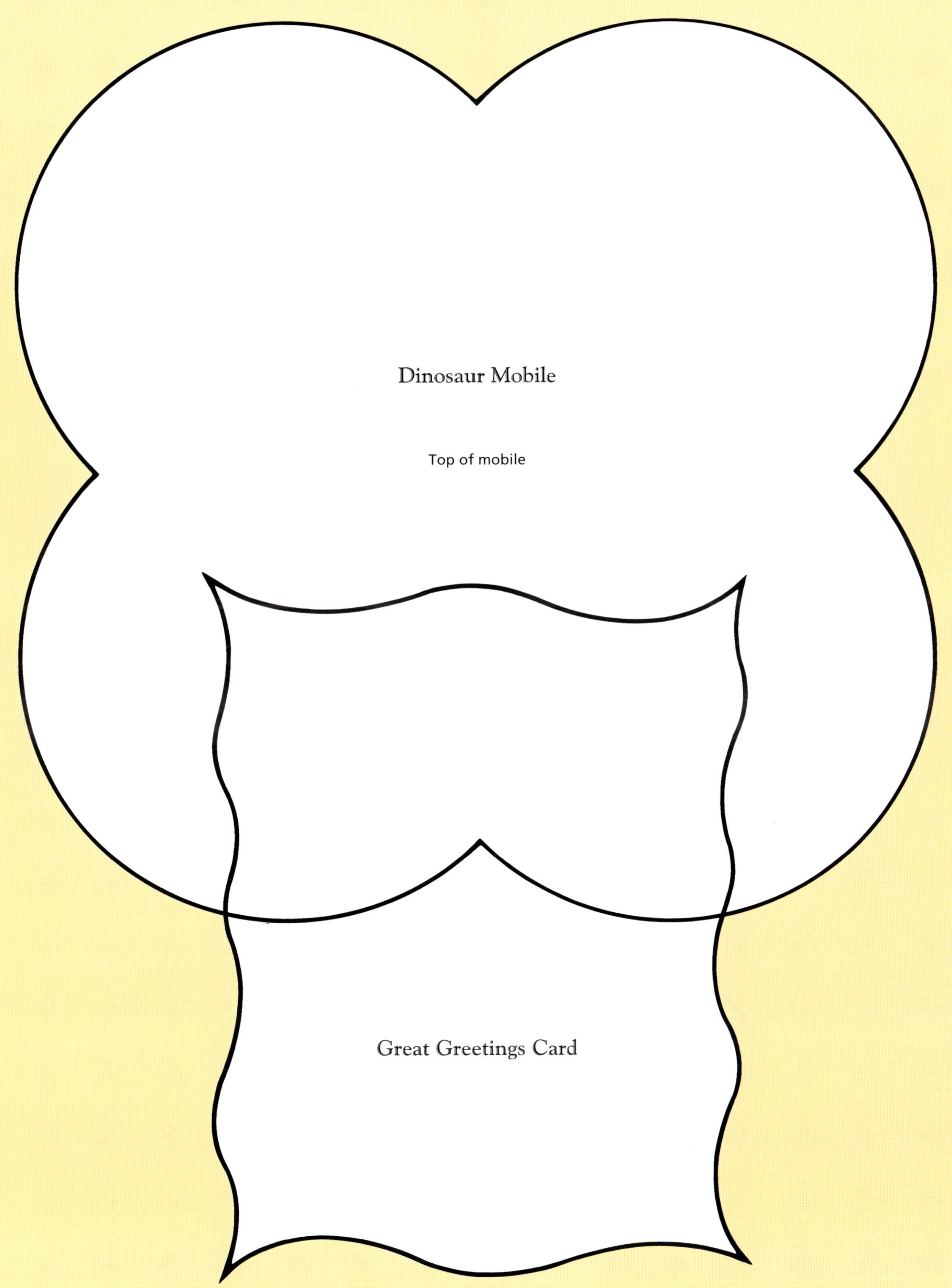
Dinosaur Mobile

Top of mobile

Great Greetings Card

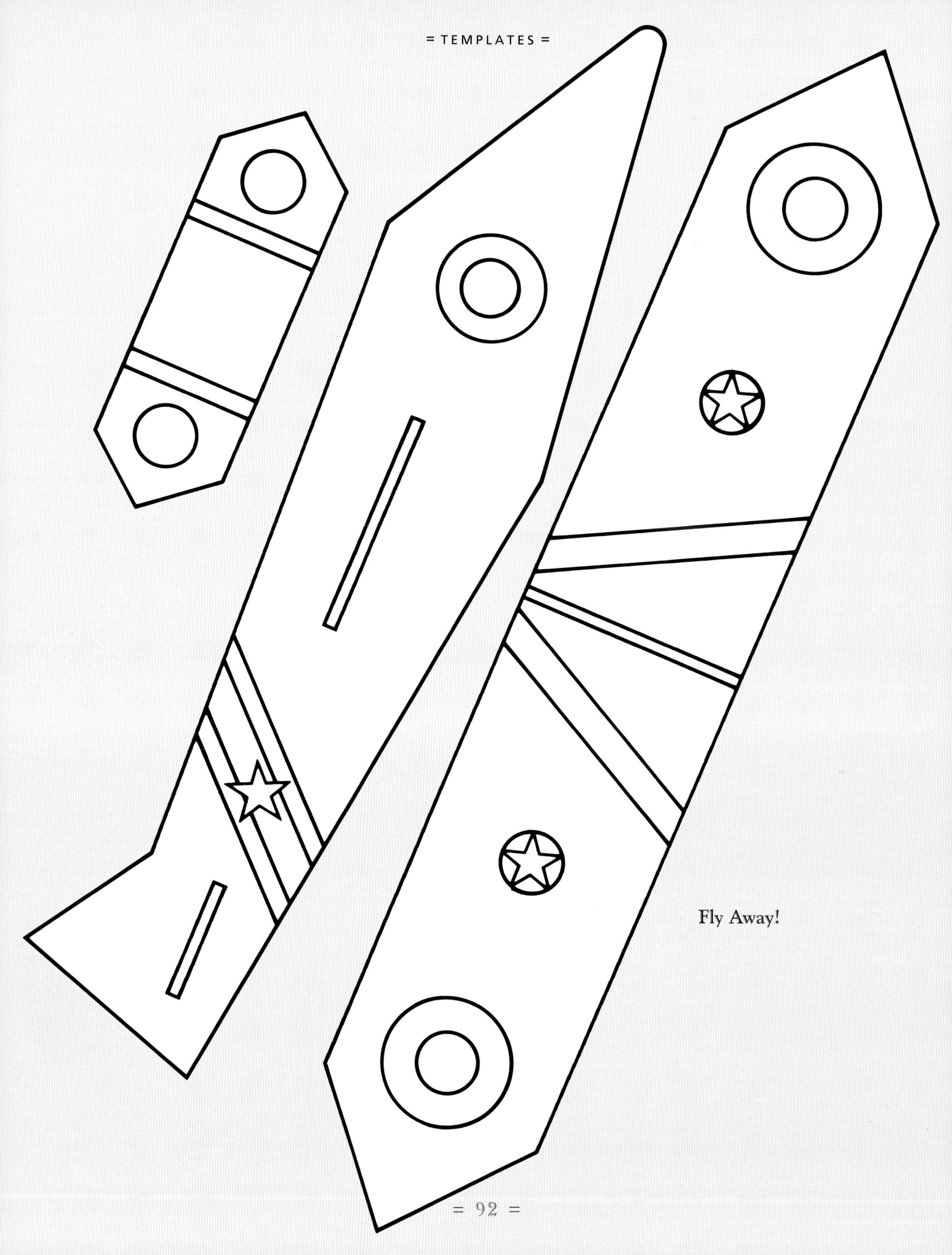
Fly Away!

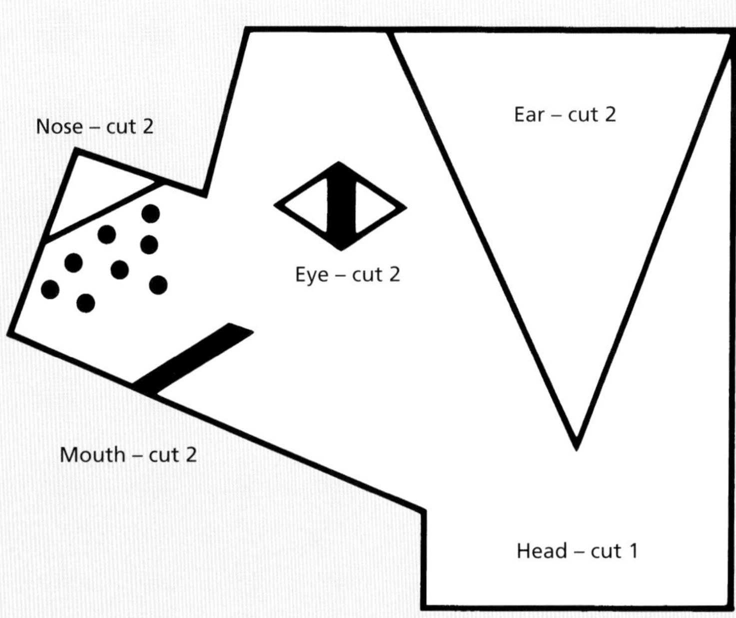

Pooch Pencil Box

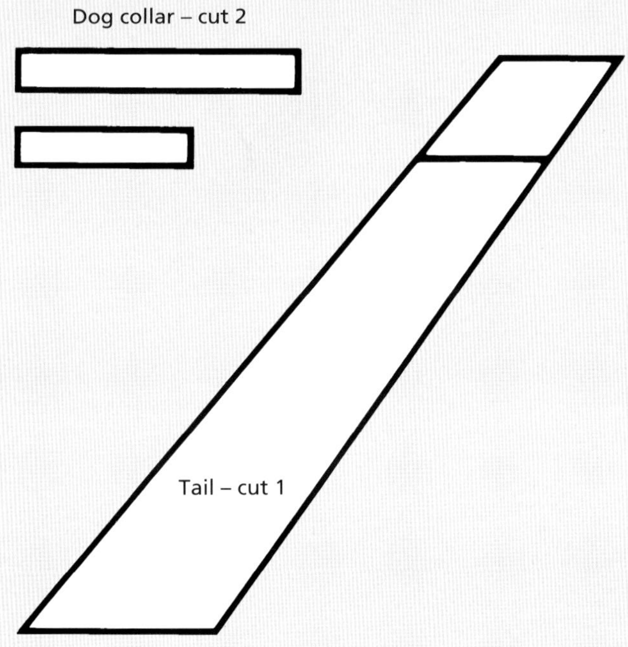

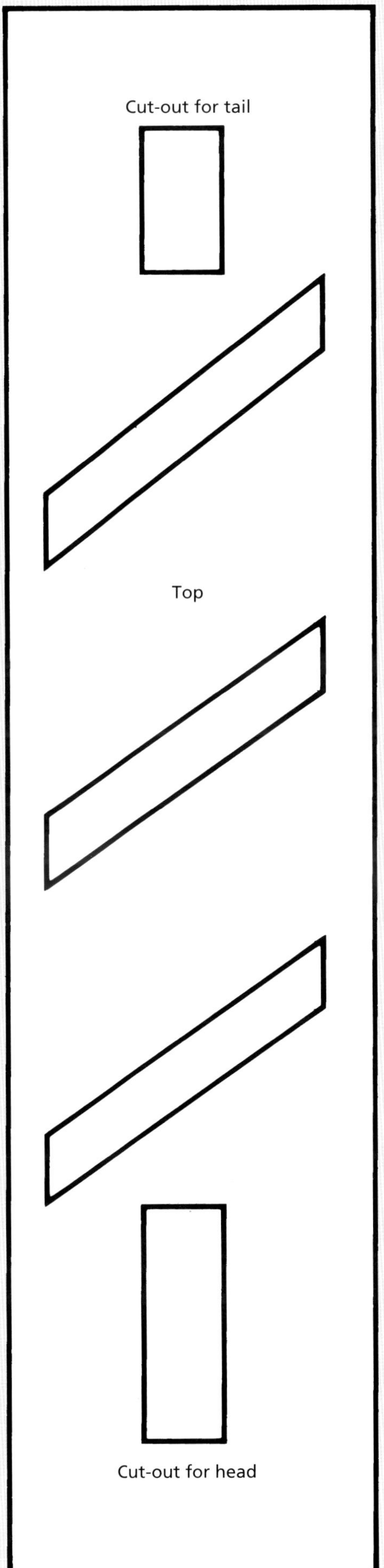

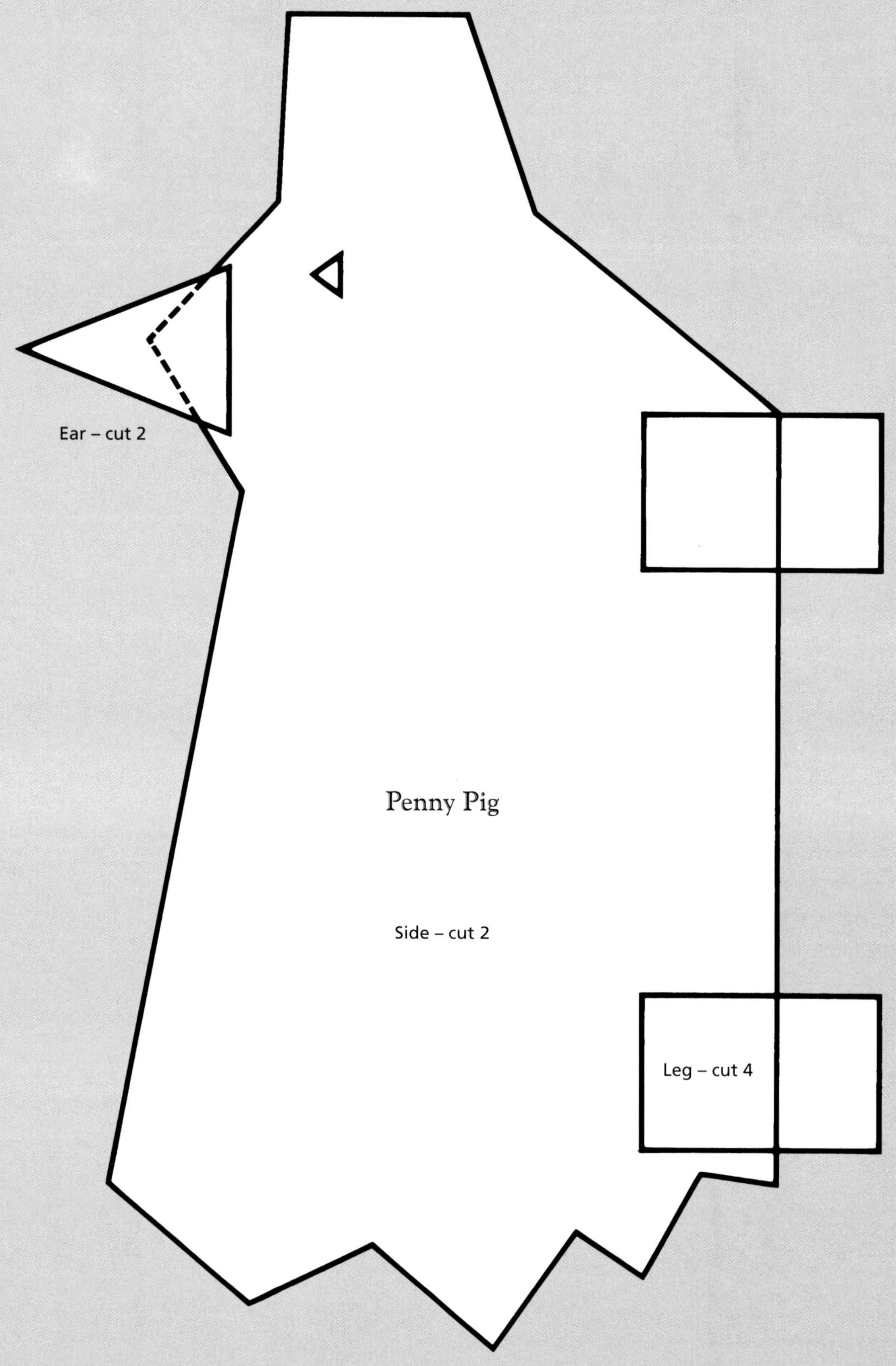
Ear – cut 2
Penny Pig
Side – cut 2
Leg – cut 4

Jewelry

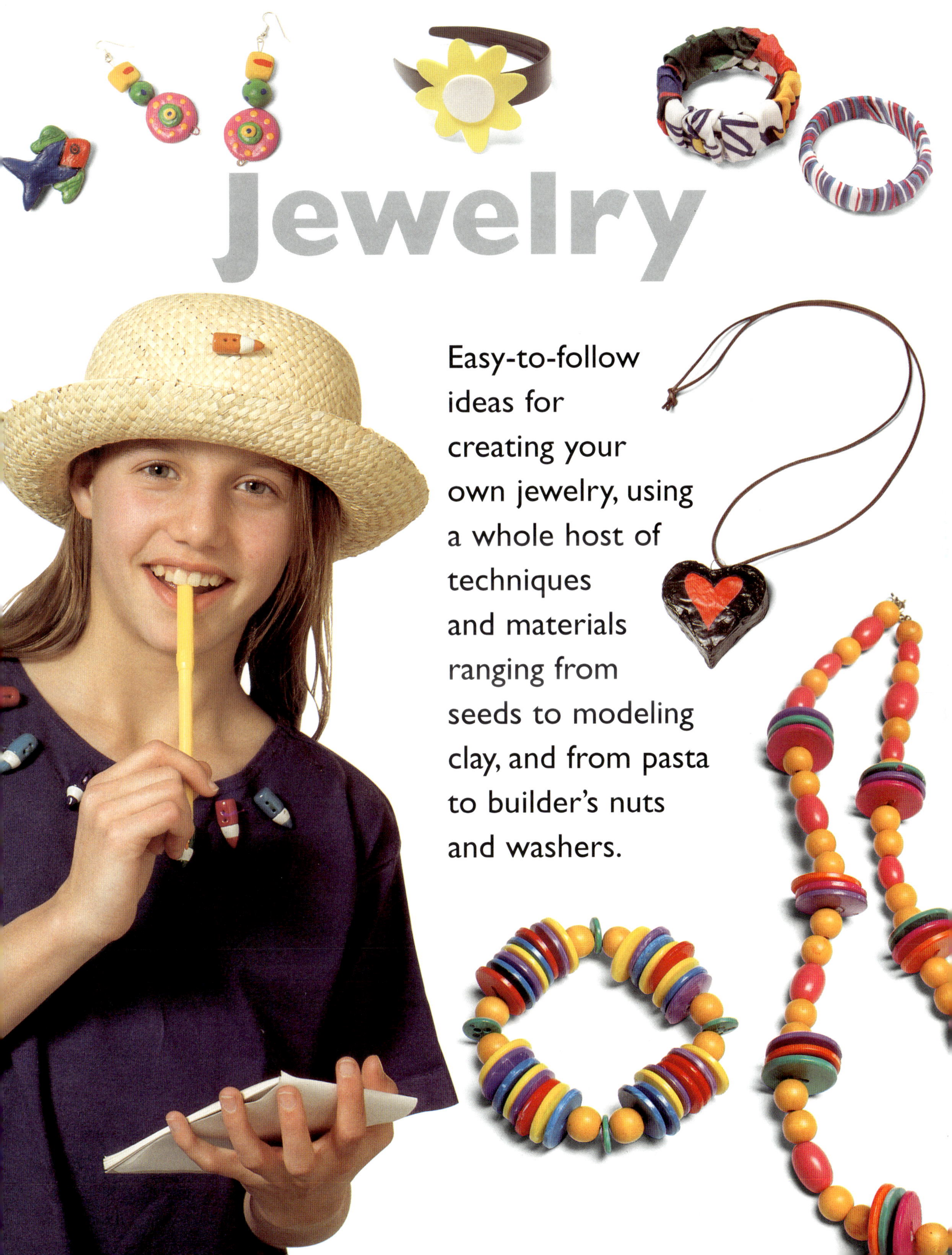

Easy-to-follow ideas for creating your own jewelry, using a whole host of techniques and materials ranging from seeds to modeling clay, and from pasta to builder's nuts and washers.

Getting started

Making your own jewelry is great fun, and not complicated or expensive to do. With just a little imagination, you can make wonderful works of art from almost anything – beads, buttons, scraps of fabric, and even yesterday's newspapers. This book is packed with projects that will suit both the beginner and the more experienced jewelry maker.

It is worth a visit to your local craft or department store, to see what jewelry findings they have in stock. Although findings look fiddly to work with, they are easy to manipulate using pliers, and do give your jewelry a really professional look.

▲ *Totally unique designs can be created from unusual bits and pieces, such as buttons, pasta, unusually shaped beads, nuts, tool box bits, shells, and safety pins.*

Materials

Lots of the projects in this book show you how to make your own beads using materials like salt dough, modeling clay, and even paper. You can also use bead substitutes, such as seeds, nuts, pasta, and shells to make fun jewelry.

The advantage of making beads is that you can decorate them in your own personal style. For this, you'll need poster or acrylic paints, and felt-tipped pens, plus a varnish to give them a shiny, hard-wearing finish.

Nylon or strong cotton line is essential for making your beads up into basic necklaces. Shirring elastic makes bracelets easy to get on and off, while leather thong makes simple pendants look stylish.

To make earrings and brooches you will need to buy small metal "findings" – the bits used to put jewelry together. Simple necklaces and bracelets don't need findings but, for a professional finish, earring and brooch backs, clasp fastenings, jump rings, eye and head pins, calotte crimps, and bails are all essential. They are sold in craft stores or department stores.

The last material you will need is adhesive. PVA is usually suitable, but some projects require an "epoxy" adhesive.

A SHORT HISTORY

Jewelry has been worn since the beginning of time – to highlight a person's social status, to ward off evil spirits, or simply as a means of attracting attention. Prehistoric people wore the teeth or pelts (coats) of their prey. Ancient civilizations wore highly decorative headdresses and collars to display their power and wealth. Archaeologists have found ornate jewelry in the tombs of Egyptian pharaohs, along with wall paintings showing craftsmen working with beads and gold as long ago as 3,000BC.

Designs change constantly, influenced by fashion, the discovery of new materials, and new techniques. The history of jewelry is well worth investigating in your local library.

▲ *This ancient Egyptian necklace is more than 4,000 years old.*

Tools, tips, and techniques

MOST OF THE PROJECTS IN THIS BOOKS ARE easy to make and need very little in the way of specialist tools and equipment. However, there are a few items you might find helpful. You will probably find most of them around the house, but, if not, they are easy to find and should cost very little. Here we show you the basic essentials.

A wooden board is useful for rolling out clay and dough. It is also useful for protecting surfaces when you are cutting, gluing, painting, or varnishing. Use an old chopping board or buy a piece of MDF, or blockboard, from your local DIY store.

For cutting out, you'll need scissors — ideally a pair of small-bladed scissors for intricate shaping, and a long-bladed pair for less fiddly jobs. A craft knife is also useful, but needs to be used under adult supervision.

Needles are used for threading beads together, and for sewing. For decorating your finished design, gluing, and varnishing you will need paintbrushes.

A compass is useful for piercing holes in hard materials, but should only be used under adult supervision. Pliers are also very useful. Here are some other tools you will need for the projects in this book.

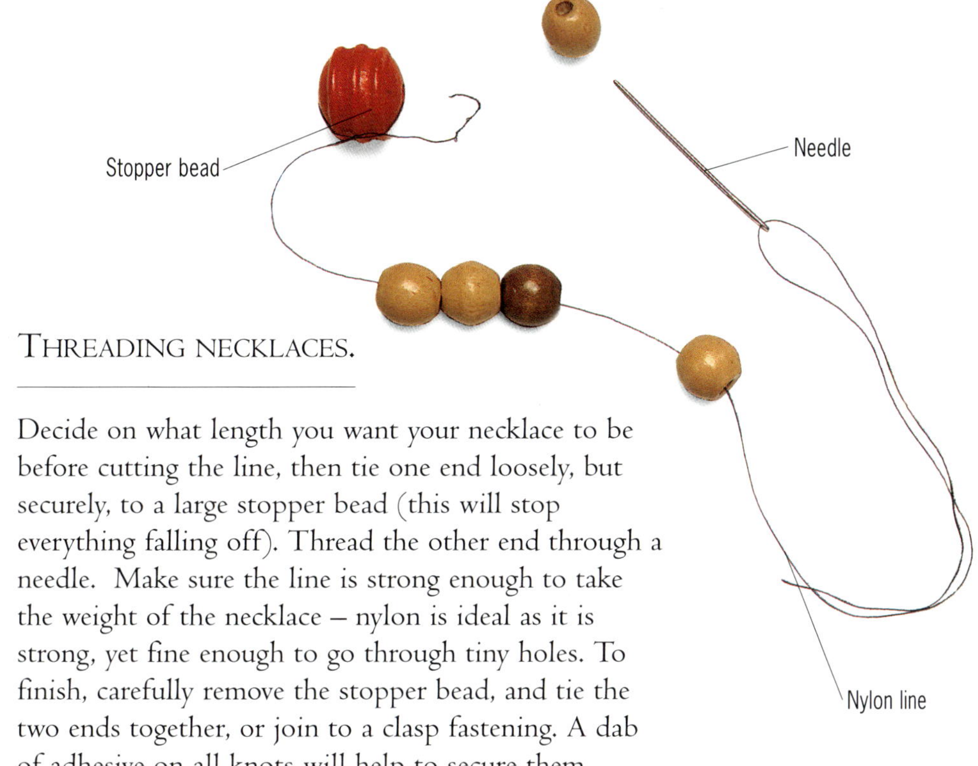

THREADING NECKLACES.

Decide on what length you want your necklace to be before cutting the line, then tie one end loosely, but securely, to a large stopper bead (this will stop everything falling off). Thread the other end through a needle. Make sure the line is strong enough to take the weight of the necklace — nylon is ideal as it is strong, yet fine enough to go through tiny holes. To finish, carefully remove the stopper bead, and tie the two ends together, or join to a clasp fastening. A dab of adhesive on all knots will help to secure them.

DECORATING BEADS

Thread the beads, or bead substitutes, onto a knitting needle or wooden skewer,. Rest each end of the needle/skewer on a ball of Plasticine. This will keep the beads off the surface and make them easier to rotate whilst painting. Alternatively, you can use two pieces of styrofoam packaging to make a frame for the needle/skewer to rest in.

KNOTTING

A simple overhand knot will be secure enough for most necklaces. Don't cut the ends too close to the knot — leave enough line to take each end back through the last few beads on either side. Secure with a dab of adhesive.

Professional techniques

THROUGHOUT THIS BOOK WE HAVE SHOWN you how to make pieces of jewelry from regular materials. Here we show you how to make professional looking necklaces and bracelets from bought beads and "findings." Manipulating the tiny findings may look difficult, but with a little patience you'll soon master the techniques described here.

WHAT YOU NEED

(For Strung Necklace)
Nylon line
2 calotte crimps
2 jump rings
A bolt ring clasp
A selection of colored beads
Small gold beads
Round-nosed pliers
Snipe-nosed pliers

(For Linked Bead Necklace)
Eye pins, head pins, or jeweler's wire
Jump rings
Round-nosed pliers
A second pair of pliers
A selection of beads
Bolt ring clasp

(For Multi-strand Bracelet)
A three-stranded jewelry clasp
6 small looped calottes
Nylon line
A selection of colored beads
Small silver beads
Round-nosed pliers
Snipe-nosed pliers

SIMPLE STRUNG NECKLACE

Decide how long you want your necklace to be, then select a line.

USING CALOTTE CRIMPS

Calotte crimps are useful for concealing knots. Use pliers to open up the two sides of the calotte crimp. Make a large knot in the line, and place in the center on one side of the calotte. Close the other side over it with pliers.

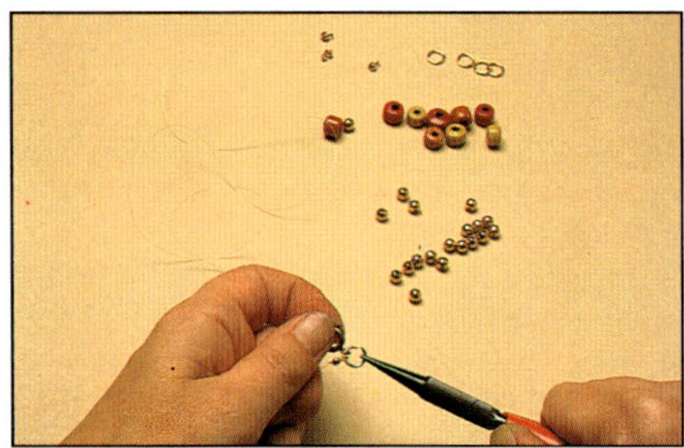

1 Cut the line to the length required, plus a little extra for knotting. Secure with a calotte crimp (see right). Open up a jump ring (see Tip Box, page 102), and slip through the loop on the calotte crimp and the loop on the bolt ring clasp.

2 Close the jump ring by twisting the two ends together until they meet perfectly. Thread the beads until you reach the required length. Knot the line close to the last bead, and conceal with a calotte crimp. Join to a jump ring.

Beads can be linked using wire instead of line. Eye pins are the easiest to use as they have a pre-formed loop, but you can use head pins or jeweler's wire. Headpins are like blunt pins, and you will need to snip off their "head" before making two loops with pliers. Simply loop jeweler's wire.

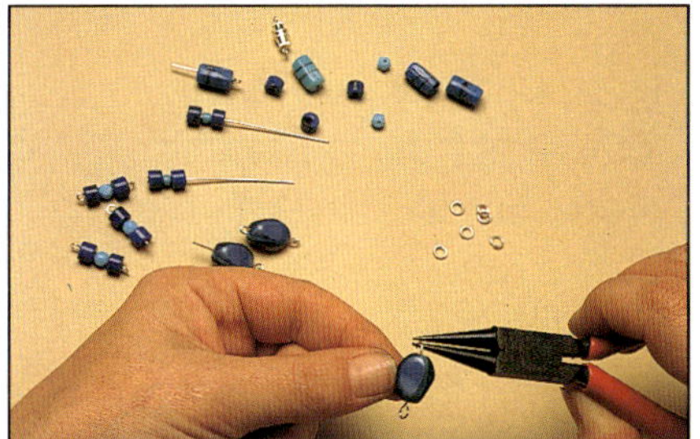

1 Wire the beads singularly, or in groups, by inserting an eye pin, head pin, or jeweler's wire through the hole(s). Trim, and use round-nosed pliers to make a loop in the opposite end.

2 Carefully open up a jump ring, and slip through the loops on each bead, or group of beads. Close the jump ring by twisting the two ends together so that they meet perfectly.

▶ Link the beads until you have the length required. Join a jump ring to one end, and to a bolt ring clasp. Join a jump ring to the other side, and to the second part of the clasp.

Large beads can be wired separately, and smaller ones in groups.

1 Attach each line to a calotte, as described on page 100. Undo each loop, and attach it to a hole in the clasp, using pliers. Thread on as many colored beads as required, placing a silver spacer bead between each one.

MULTI-STRAND BRACELET

As for all projects, work out the length of the finished bracelet before starting. For this multi-strand bracelet, you will need to cut three lengths of line. Looped calottes are useful when working with a multi-strand clasp. They open from the top, whereas regular calotte crimps open from the side. To use, push the nylon line through the hole in the bottom of the looped calotte, and make a large knot. Close the calotte over the knot, and carefully secure using pliers.

◀ Finish the lines by inserting each one through a looped calotte. Knot the line, and close the calotte with pliers. Join the calotte loops to the clasp as before.

Exquisite earrings

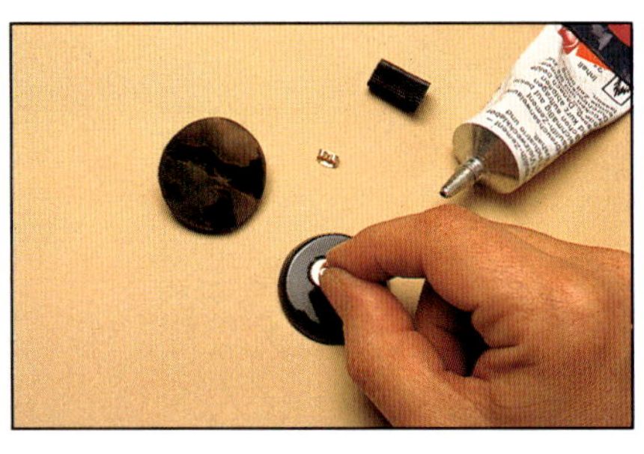

ARRINGS ARE SOME OF THE EASIEST PIECES of jewelry to make, and there are hundreds of styles to choose from. There are lots of other ideas shown throughout the book, but here we show the simplest ways to make professional looking earrings.

It is tempting to just pull jump rings apart to open them, but this distorts the shape, and makes them difficult to close again. The best way to do it is to hold the ring with two pairs of pliers, and twist the ends sideways, away from each other. To close, just twist back together again until the ends meet perfectly.

STUD EARRINGS

These are the simplest earrings to make, and can be put together in minutes. Leave the adhesive to set before wearing them.

1 If working with light bases, the ear stud can be glued to the center of the wrong side. For heavier ornaments, it is important to glue nearer to the top to prevent it falling forward when being worn.

2 Apply adhesive to both the base, and the ear stud, and leave until tacky before sticking together. Leave for 24 hours before wearing.

SIMPLE DROP EARRINGS

Glass beads come in all shapes and
sizes, but these tubes are perfect
for making pretty dangles.

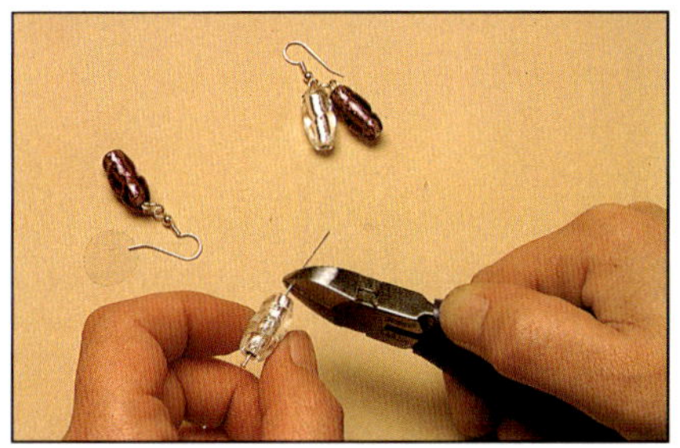

*1 Slip each bead on to a head pin. If the
head begins to slip though the beads,
thread on a small glass rocaille bead first.
Trim the head pin to the correct length,
leaving enough to make loop. Turn a loop
using round-nosed pliers.*

*2 Carefully open up a jump ring, and
slip though the loops at the top of two
beads. Close the jump ring so that its two
ends meet perfectly. Open up the loop at
the bottom of an ear hook, and close over
the jump ring.*

CABOCHAN DROP EARRINGS

These glamorous earrings take no
time at all to make.

Cabochon is the
name for a flat-
backed jewel.

▲ *Make sure that the loop of
the ear clip protrudes just
below the jewel.*

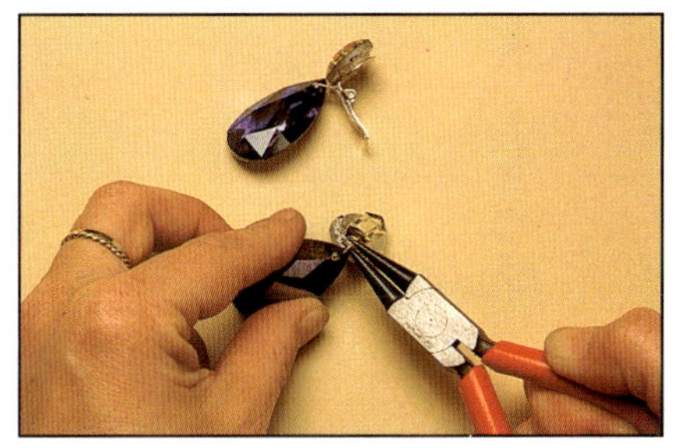

*1 Glue the cabochons to the ear clips.
Leave to dry. Using pliers, open up the
triangle bail, and slip it through the loop of
the ear clip, and then through each side of
the drop bead. Use pliers the squeeze gently
together to secure.*

Rolled paper beads

ROLLED PAPER BEADS ARE VERY EASY TO MAKE. They are simply strips of paper tightly rolled around a knitting needle or wooden skewer. You can have lots of fun experimenting with color, pattern, size, and shape by using different kinds of paper, and by varying the length, width, and shape of the paper strips.

To make your beads last longer, spray them with varnish.

HAND PAINTED PAPER BEADS

You can make interesting beads from almost any kind of paper. Colorful wrapping paper, and pages torn from a glossy catalogue or magazine work well. Even pages torn from an old comic will do. But it's more fun to paint plain paper with your own design.

▼ *Cut out wider triangles from magazine pages to make these long glossy beads. This design is created by cutting two lengths of shirring elastic, and weaving them in and out of the beads.*

1 *Paint your design. On the back, make pencil marks every inch along one edge, starting 1 inch in. Repeat along the opposite edge, but start 0.5 inches in.*

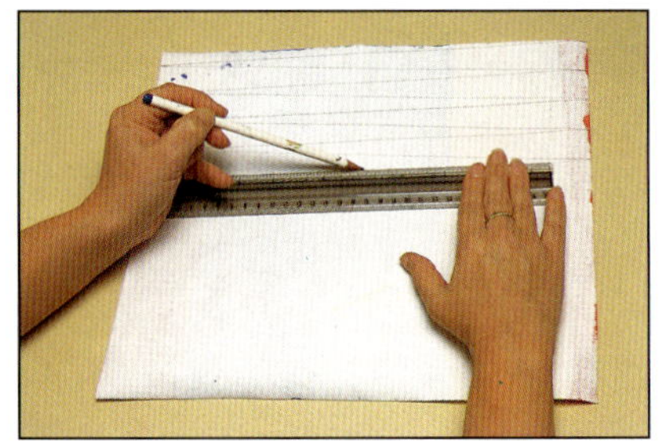

2 *Use a ruler to join the marks on the edges together to create elongated triangles, starting from the 0.5 inches mark. Cut out the triangles.*

3 *Starting at the widest end, roll each triangle around a knitting needle. Just before the end, dab adhesive on the wrong side, then finish rolling. Hold each bead until dry, then slide it off the needle.*

4 *Thread all the beads onto a length of nylon line using the method shown on page 99. Knot the two ends of the line together tightly, and tuck the loose ends in, to complete your necklace.*

To make strong beads, make sure that you roll the paper strips around the knitting needle tightly, with the tapering edges of the triangle in the center.

▶ *These earrings are made from wider strips of paper. To make them dangle, fold a piece of jeweler's wire in half, slip an ear hook onto it, then twist the sides of the wire together. Push the wire into the central hole of the bead with a large blob of clear-drying adhesive.*

▶ *Painting the edges of black paper with gold paint, or a metallic pen, makes the beads look really special.*

◀ *Make a necklace from hand painted paper beads mixed in with beads from an old broken necklace. Use a strong thread such as nylon line, and knot the two ends together. Add a dab of adhesive to strengthen the knot.*

BEAUTIFUL BEADS!

Paper beads look wonderful strung into necklaces, bracelets, and earrings, and make truly special jewelry. Have fun experimenting with different bead shapes, using brightly patterned paper, and paint effects.

Magical Mosaics

CREATE WONDERFULLY INTRICATE MOSAIC designs by decorating cardboard with shiny paper shapes. For the most dramatic results, choose lots of different colors, and mix them all together. A quick look through a kaleidoscope will give you inspiration for shapes, and color combinations. With practice you can use other materials to create similar effects.

Thick cardboard (mount board is ideal)
Pencil
Ruler
Craft knife
Paint
Paintbrush
Gummed shiny paper shapes
PVA adhesive
Varnish
Sharp thick needle or hammer and tack
Large jump ring
Pliers
Leather thong or cord

SQUARE PENDANT

Simple cardboard shapes can be transformed into spectacular pieces of jewelry by decorating them with shiny gummed paper shapes. Any strong cardboard will do, but special mount board, available from art stores, is ideal.

1 Draw a 1.5 inch square on the cardboard, and cut it out carefully, using a craft knife. Paint the square on both sides, and around the edges.

2 Stick the paper shapes all over one side of the square, to cover it. Leave the square to dry, then pierce a hole close to the edge in one corner.

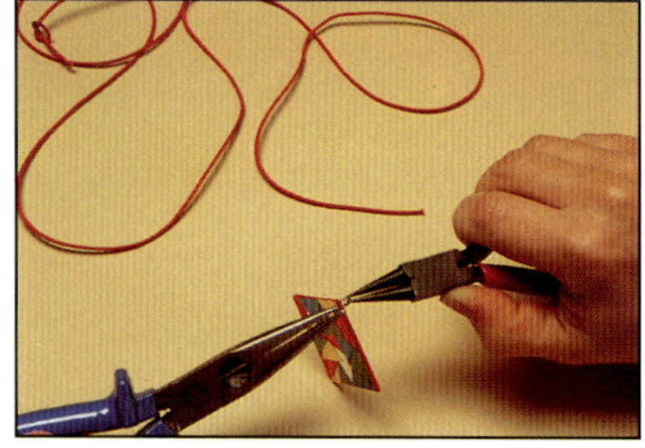

3 Using pliers, open up the jump ring sideways. Thread the jump ring through the hole, and use the pliers to close the ring again.

4 Make sure that both ends of the jump ring meet. Then thread the thong through the jump ring, and knot the ends together.

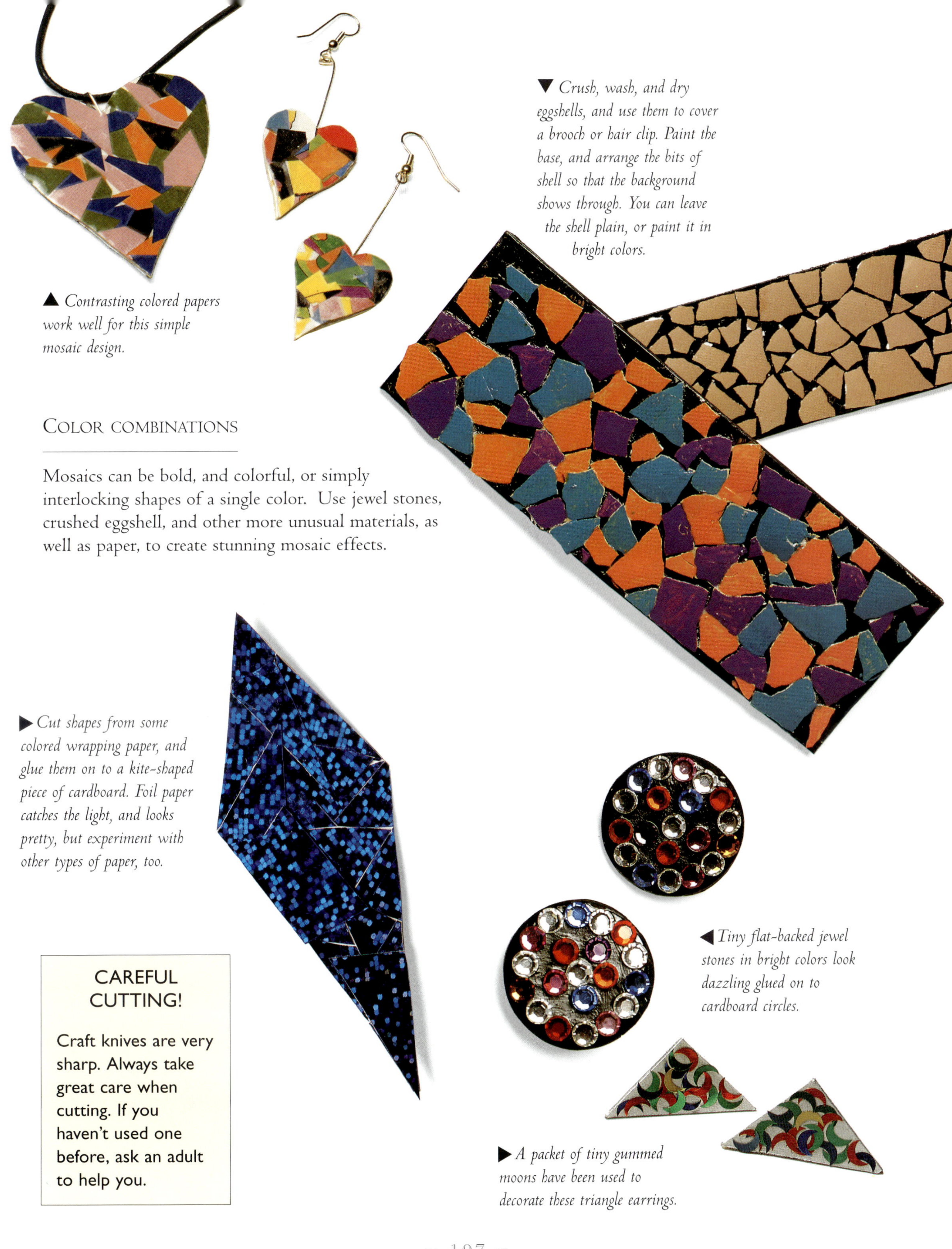

▲ *Contrasting colored papers work well for this simple mosaic design.*

▼ *Crush, wash, and dry eggshells, and use them to cover a brooch or hair clip. Paint the base, and arrange the bits of shell so that the background shows through. You can leave the shell plain, or paint it in bright colors.*

COLOR COMBINATIONS

Mosaics can be bold, and colorful, or simply interlocking shapes of a single color. Use jewel stones, crushed eggshell, and other more unusual materials, as well as paper, to create stunning mosaic effects.

▶ *Cut shapes from some colored wrapping paper, and glue them on to a kite-shaped piece of cardboard. Foil paper catches the light, and looks pretty, but experiment with other types of paper, too.*

◀ *Tiny flat-backed jewel stones in bright colors look dazzling glued on to cardboard circles.*

CAREFUL CUTTING!

Craft knives are very sharp. Always take great care when cutting. If you haven't used one before, ask an adult to help you.

▶ *A packet of tiny gummed moons have been used to decorate these triangle earrings.*

Hero worship

BY DECORATING A PLAIN CARDBOARD SHAPE with a picture of your favorite person, you can make unique jewelry that will be the envy of all your friends. Use a magazine cutting, or an old photograph of someone you love — from a pop star to a pet. Glue the image in place, and make up into a pendant, necklace, earrings, or even a charm bracelet.

Adhesive will help to keep the jump ring in place.

CHARM BRACELET

Cut out photographs of your favorite stars from a comic or magazine, and glue them on to small circles of stiff cardboard to make a fun charm bracelet. Jump rings, clasps, and lengths of chain can be bought from craft stores.

1 Choose your images from old magazines or photographs. Place a coin over each of the chosen images, and draw around it carefully with a pencil. Cut out each of the circles.

2 Place the same coin on the cardboard, draw round it, and cut out a circle for each of your images. Paint one side of each circle a different color. Glue your images in place on the unpainted side of the "charm".

3 Pierce a hole close to the top edge of each charm. Open up the jump rings with the pliers, and insert one ring through the hole in each charm. Do not close up the jump rings at this stage.

4 Lay the charms along the length of the chain, spacing them evenly. Slip each open jump ring through a link on the chain. Close the rings carefully, so that the ends meet, or they will slip off the chain.

5 Join a jump ring to one end of the chain. Join the last jump ring to the other end of the chain, slipping it through the loop on the bolt ring clasp at the same time. Draw a motif on the back of the charm.

▲ Cut out large motifs from colored wrapping paper, and stick on to cardboard. Cut around the shapes carefully, then cover them with self-adhesive plastic. Make into brooches by sticking a brooch finding, or a safety pin, to the wrong side.

Instead of using self-adhesive plastic, you can protect your images by spraying them with varnish. If you take them to a local print shop, and laminate them, this will give them a very hard-wearing finish.

OUT OF THIS WORLD!

Here are some other ideas for "hero jewelry." If you use your imagination, the sky is the limit!

◄ A stickpin is a fun idea, and can look great on a hat, coat, or jumper. These pins have rubber caps, and can be bought at specialist craft stores. If you can't buy a pin, use a safety pin instead, and keep it in place with a sticky label.

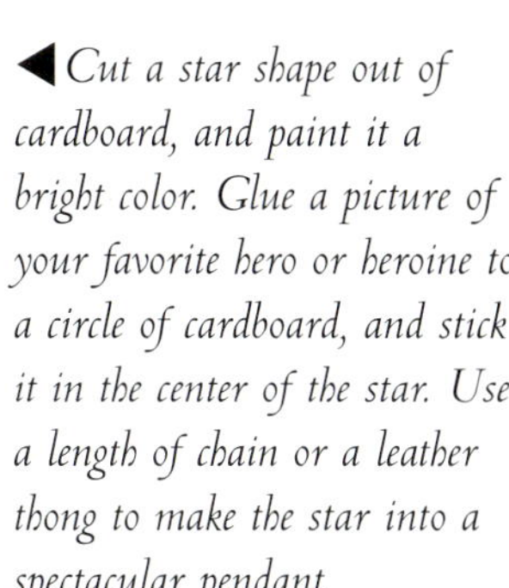

◄ Cut a star shape out of cardboard, and paint it a bright color. Glue a picture of your favorite hero or heroine to a circle of cardboard, and stick it in the center of the star. Use a length of chain or a leather thong to make the star into a spectacular pendant.

Oriental influences

THE TRADITIONAL JAPANESE ART OF PAPER FOLDING is known as origami, and has been practiced for centuries. You can use this ancient craft to create exotic and stylish jewelry. We show the simplest techniques here, but you can get even more inspiration by borrowing a book on origami from your local library.

LINKED BRACELET AND EARRINGS

This linked bracelet and earrings set is much easier to make than it looks. You can buy special origami paper from good art and craft stores, which comes in packs of assorted brightly colored sheets.

1 Fold the squares in half and open out. Fold one side edge in to meet the center crease. Repeat with the opposite side edge. Cut the square into four strips along the creases.

2 Fold each strip along the length, then the side edges in to the center crease. Refold along the center to form a thin strip. Fold this strip across the width, and fold each end to the middle.

3 Take two folded strips and push the end of one through one of the folds of the other. Repeat with more folded strips.

4 When it is long enough to fit your hand, secure the folded ends with a dab of adhesive to complete the circle.

▼ *To make these earrings, link together 5 strips for each side, and glue the open ends to secure them. Pierce the top of one link with a needle, and insert a jump ring through the hole, and the loop of an ear hook at the same time. Close the jump ring.*

This bracelet is m
using origami pape
wrapping paper
marbled paper, an
work just as we

◀ *Make kite shapes from bigger paper squares, and stitch them to a narrow braid to create a necklace.*

◀ *These pretty shell shapes are made by pleating a half circle. Glue the edges together at the base, and insert a wire loop. When dry, thread on to a necklace, with beads.*

▶ *Choose interesting handmade papers to make earrings to match the necklace.*

▶ *To make these "fan" earrings, fold the corner points of two 5.5 inch squares to the center. With one point at the top, fold the side points across, to meet the middle line. Fold the paper in half along the middle line, to enclose all the other folds. Make a loop from jeweler's wire and glue it inside the last fold of one square, at the top. Place the two shapes with the pointed edges facing, and them tuck together, overlapping the edges. Add an earring wire to the top metal loop.*

Papier-mache beads

THE ART OF PAPIER-MACHE HAS BEEN USED FOR centuries all over the world. Its name is French, and means "mashed paper," although it is thought the Chinese invented the craft. The simple technique used here to make beads is known as "layering." The beads can be decorated in brilliant colors and used to make exciting jewelry.

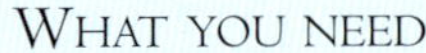

By varying the shape of the newsprint base bead, you can create differently shaped beads.

BASIC BEAD NECKLACE

Papier-mache is an easy way to make you own beads. It can be a little messy, but the results are well worth the sticky fingers. Paint the finished beads in bright colors, and string them into necklaces, and bracelets.

▲ *This necklace has been made using multi-colored beads, but jewelry made using single color beads can look equally effective.*

1 *Scrunch squares of newsprint into rough balls, applying a little adhesive to help set. Tear paper into strips, paint with adhesive, and wrap over a base ball, until covered. Smooth the ball into shape as you wrap. Give the ball two more layers, but leave to dry between each one.*

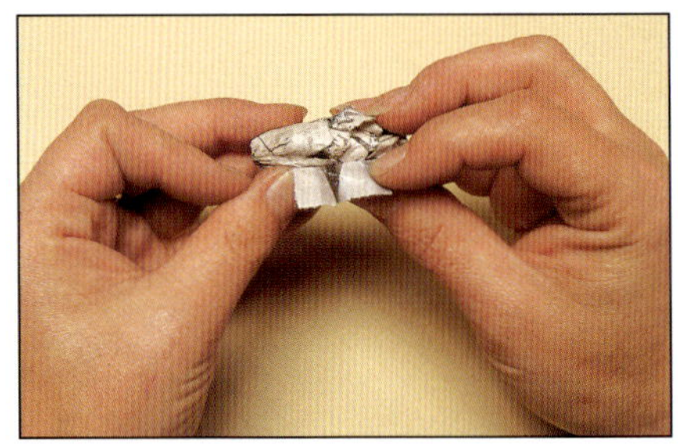

2 *Pierce the balls with the needle, and push on to a knitting needle. Rest on two lumps of Plasticine — so you can turn the beads as you paint. Give each bead an undercoat of white poster paint and leave to dry. Paint the beads in bright colors. Allowing to dry before adding any detail.*

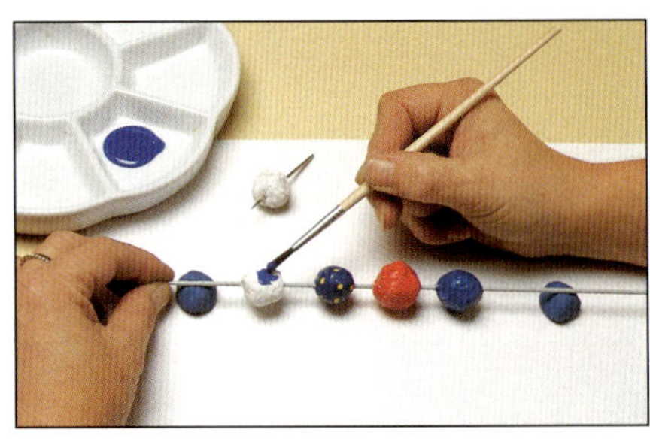

3 *Thread the beads onto a length of nylon line, using the method shown on page 99. Try to mix the colors evenly. Knot the two ends of the line together tightly and tuck the loose ends back through the beads on either side of the knot, to hide them.*

Papier-Mache Magic!

Once you feel confident making basic papier-mache beads, you can start to experiment with shape and size. With a bit of practice, you will soon be able to create all sorts of original bead shapes.

Arrange the beads in a pattern with the largest at the center. Add decoration with colored permanent markers, or metallic pens.

▼ *Experiment with different shapes, such as papier-mache "hearts". To make these fun earrings, fold a length of jeweler's wire in half. Slip one end through an earring hook loop, then twist the edges of the wire tightly together. Push it into the papier-mache bead, and thread on a few bought beads. Glue the end of the wire.*

▶ *Make a bracelet by threading a colorful mixture of beads onto shirring elastic.*

More papier-mache ideas

H ERE ARE MORE WAYS TO USE THE LAYERED
papier-mache technique. Pieces of card,
with the ends joined together to
make a circle, can be covered with
strips of newsprint to create
unusual bangles. Oblongs or
squares of card, layered in the
same way, can be made into
hair slides and brooches.

*▲ This bracelet looks dramatic
in black and gold. Use a
metallic pen to draw your
design on to four squares.
Pierce holes in all the corners
of each square, and thread
with black shirring elastic.*

Pencil

A piece of corrugated cardboard

Marker pen

Scissors

Newsprint, torn into strips

PVA adhesive

Hair slide base (from craft stores)

Paint

Paintbrush

Varnish

HAIR SLIDE

Make a jazzy hair slide by layering
strips of old newsprint over a
cardboard template. Ensure that
the crown shape is completely
covered — try to keep the points of
the crown well defined.

MAKING A HAIR SLIDE

1 *Draw a crown shape on to
corrugated cardboard. Draw over
the outline in marker pen, and cut out
carefully with scissors.*

2 *Paint the newsprint strips with
adhesive, and cover the card shape
with an even layer. Repeat once or
twice, leaving to dry between each layer.*

3 *Open the hair slide, and place on
the crown. Layer adhesive-covered
newsprint over the hair slide base.
Leave to dry. Repeat to secure.*

4 *Decorate with bright paints, then
leave to dry. Finish with a coat of
varnish, and leave to dry for 24 hours
before using.*

▶ *Scrunch up a length of paper, and bring the ends together, to make a circle. Use sticky tape to hold the ends together. Layer with pasted paper until rigid, then decorate with a bold design.*

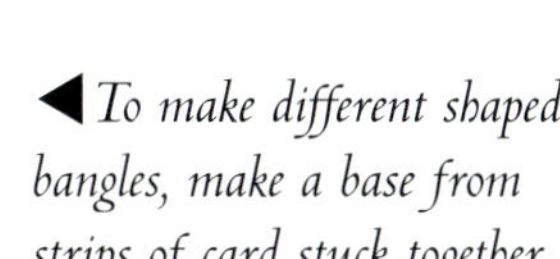

◀ *To make different shaped bangles, make a base from strips of card stuck together with sticky tape.*

PILES OF PAPER

Use the layered paper technique to make all kinds of interesting jewelry. Cut out different shaped templates, or join cardboard together with sticky tape to make circles for a bangle.

▼ *Paint your hair slide in bold colors. This design is easy to copy, but you can have lots of fun designing your own.*

▲ *Use strips of wrapping paper to give a new look to a hair band, and bangle. You only need one layer of paper, just to cover the surface, and a couple of coats of varnish to protect it.*

Pressed paper pulp

This papier-mache technique uses paper pulp made from tissue paper or newsprint. The paper is soaked in water until soft, then mashed with a fork, or – if allowed – with an electric blender. The pulp is then squeezed until almost dry, and shaped into beads, pressed into cookie cutters, or molded on to card templates, which when decorated can be used for earrings, brooches, or pendants.

▲ *Cut out the bird shape from cardboard, and add a little pulp to give texture. Paint in bright colors, then add the detail in black, or another contrasting paint.*

CHUNKY NECKLACE

Paper pulp is a lot of fun to work with. This chunky necklace is an easy design to start with, but once you get going you will soon want to move on to more complicated pulping ideas.

1 *Cut the tissue paper, or newsprint, into tiny pieces, place in a bowl, and cover with warm water. Leave to soak for several hours until soft, then mash.*

2 *Strain the mixture through a sieve, lightly squeezing out the water. Return to the bowl, and mix with a tablespoon of wallpaper paste. Strain again.*

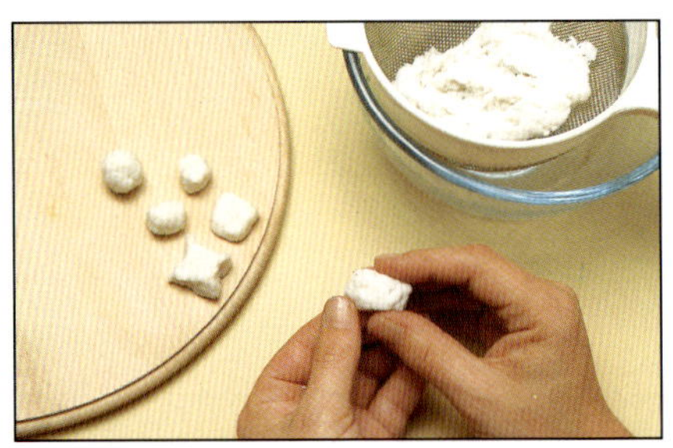

3 *Mold the pulp into beads shapes, and leave to dry somewhere warm. Putting them on a cake rack will speed up the drying time. When almost dry, pierce with a cocktail stick.*

4 *Paint the beads with white poster paint first, then, when, dry in the colors of your choice. Finish with a coat of varnish if required. When completely dry thread onto nylon line.*

PULP SCULPTURES

Cut out cardboard templates to use as a base for novelty designs, then sculpt layers of pulp into the shape.

PULP FICTION?

Newsprint will take longer to soften than tissue paper. Don't squeeze out too much water, or the pulp will become an unworkable mass. Excess pulp can be stored in a plastic bag and kept in the refigerator.

Fascinating foil

With a little creativity, regular aluminium foil can be transformed into stylish pieces of jewelry for next to nothing. Scrunch it up, and roll into beads to make dazzling necklaces, or mold into all sorts of different shapes to use as earrings or brooches. Use the foil as it is, or decorate with jewel stones for a more spectacular finish.

Look out for jewel stones at thrift stores, and yard sales.

FOIL BROOCH

Roll aluminium foil into tight balls to create an exquisite brooch, and finish it off with a jewel stone at its center.

1 Tear the foil into squares, scrunch up, and roll into balls in the palm of your hands. (Make a couple of practice balls first to see how big the foil square needs to be.) Make seven evenly sized balls, each about 0.5 inch in diameter.

2 To make the center, roll a slightly larger, looser ball, about 0.75 inch in diameter. Flatten one side, and press your thumb into the middle of the other side. Press the jewel stone into the indentation to ensure a perfect fit.

3 Glue the foil balls around the outer edge of the center ball, and leave to dry. Glue the jewel stone in place.

4 Glue a brooch finding the wrong side of the brooch, and leave to dry for 24 hours before wearing.

▶ *Try molding other shapes
from foil, and decorate with
jewel stones to give a
glamorous touch. Stick on to
eye pins, with co-ordinating
beads, and join to an earring
hook to make pretty earrings.*

FOIL FUN!

Pierce balls of rolled
up foil with a
needle, and thread
on nylon line to
make a necklace. To
make pretty foil
wrappers go further,
use them just to
cover a bead rolled
from aluminium foil.

FANCY FOIL

Colorful foil candy wrappers,
especially the more decorative ones
covering Easter eggs, or Christmas
treats, can be recycled, and look
really impressive wrapped over
basic bead shapes, or twisted, and
glued to hair combs or slides.

▶ *Twist candy wrappers at
the center, and stick to a hair
comb to make an unusual
hair ornament.*

Clay beads

W ITH TODAY'S SYNTHETIC MODELING CLAYS, IT IS easy to make beautiful beads in unusual shapes, and different sizes. The big advantage poly clays have over air-drying clays is that they set hard at low temperatures in an oven, and won't shatter if dropped. They also come in an amazing range of colors.

WHAT YOU NEED

Modeling clay in two or
three different colors
Round-bladed kitchen knife
Knitting needle
Varnish
Leather thong

MARBLE BEAD NECKLACE

Make beautiful marbled beads to create a stunning necklace. Varnish the beads to bring out the depth of the colors, then thread onto leather thong.

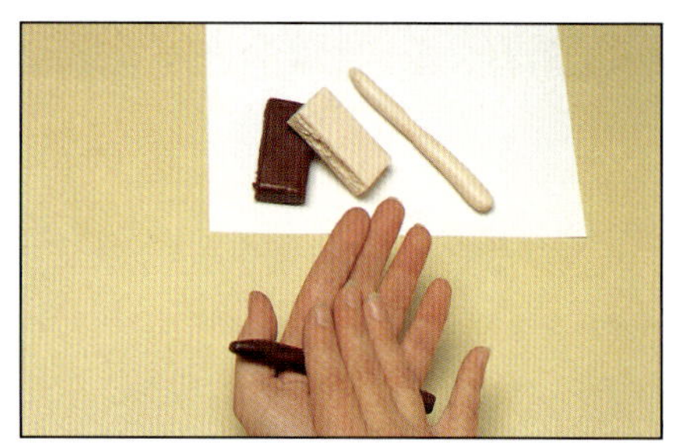

1 Break off a piece of modeling clay, and knead until it becomes soft, and pliable. Then roll into a sausage in the palms of your hands. Do the same with each of the colors — wash your hands carefully when changing between colors.

2 Wrap the colored sausages around each other, as shown. Then twist them, and start to knead the different colors together, rolling the sausages carefully in the palms of your hands until they combine to form another sausage.

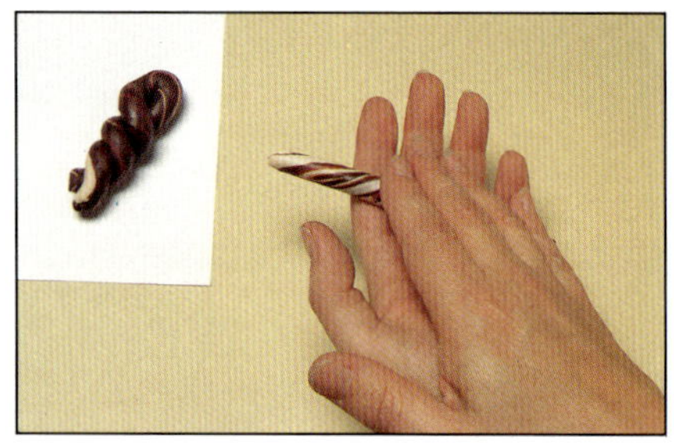

3 Fold the sausage in half, twist the two halves together, and knead again. Roll into another sausage, and repeat the process until all the air bubbles have gone, and you have a marbled effect. Don't knead too much, or the colors will merge completely.

4 Place the sausage on the work surface, and cut off small pieces. Roll these in the palms of you hands to make ball or tube shaped beads. Make as many beads as you need to make a necklace, rolling out more pieces of clay if required.

5 Make a central hole in each bead using a knitting needle. Smooth any rough edges, and reshape by rolling in the palms of your hands. Bake in a low temperature oven, following the instructions on page 122. When ready, thread onto a thong.

Tie a knot either
side of each bead.

BEAUTIFUL BEADS

Have fun molding clay into a variety
of shapes to make unusual beads.

▶ *This necklace and earring set
is made from lots of different
bead shapes, decorated with tiny
blobs of other colors.*

Insert the
metal wire
before baking.

◀ *Roll modeling clay into thin
sausages, and link both ends to
make a small circle. When
baked, varnish, and use to
space out larger beads.*

◀ *Roll out long worms of
clay, and wrap them around a
knitting needle to make
unusual beads. Dust them
with modeling clay bronze
powder before baking, to
make them sparkle.*

◀ *Make chunky beads, and
transform into a stylish
bracelet to go with the
spiral earrings.*

Sculptured clay jewelry

Y OU CAN HAVE GREAT FUN SCULPTING CLAY
into different shapes. Building up a design on a
flat base – like these sheep, ladybugs, bees, and
flowers – is the easiest way to start. Include
loops, or holes, so the finished
design can be hung as a pendant,
or drop earrings. Leave an area
flat for brooches, badges, hair
slides, and stud earrings.

Pigs make great
earrings.

SHEEP PIECES

These fun sheep earrings, and
stickpin are much easier to make
than they look. Once you've
mastered the basics, try making
other animals, too.

BAKING CLAY!

Set your oven to
110°C/200°F/Gas Mark
3, and place the clay on
a cookie sheet. Bake
until completely dry.
This may take between
five and eight hours,
depending on the size
and thickness of the clay.
Ask an adult to help, as
even low temperatures
can burn if you don't
take care.

1 *Break off a piece of white clay, and
knead with your fingers until it
becomes soft, and pliable. Then roll into a
sausage, approximately 0.5 inch in
diameter. Slice off the uneven end, then cut
two slices, each measuring 0.25 inch wide.*

2 *Break off a small amount of black
modeling clay, and mold two tiny
balls for each earring. Press firmly to one
edge of each white circle to make the feet.*

3 *From black clay, mold four ears, and
two triangle faces. Soften the points of
the triangle with the tip of you finger, and
press into place. Press the ears in position.
Make three tiny white balls for each
earring, and use for eyes and nose.*

▲ *Glue earring findings onto the back of sculpted ladybugs to make cute earrings.*

CLAY CAPERS

Almost any shape can be recreated in modeling clay. Once you get used to using it you could try making cars, buses, fruit, and even miniature people.

▲ *Mold features from tiny bits of modeling clay. Don't forget to wash your hands when changing between colors.*

Position one point of the triangle between the two feet.

A jewel stone glued to the center after baking gives the perfect finishing touch.

▲ *A caterpillar creeping across a leaf shape makes an amusing brooch.*

▼ *Knead the clay until it is really soft, break off small balls, and mold into petal shapes using your thumb. Pinch the ends and press together to make a fun flower brooch.*

◀ *Make the stickpin in the same way as the earrings, but use a slightly larger base.*

▲ *Loop long sausages into flower shapes, add a center made from a flattened ball, and brush with gold modeling clay powder, before baking, for a dazzling earring and pendant set.*

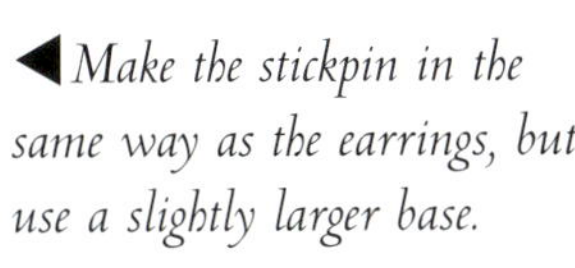

◀ *Bake in a low temperature oven, following the instructions on the left. When the sheep are cool to the touch, glue the earring findings (or stick pin) in place, and leave to set.*

Quick and easy clay shapes

MODELING CLAY CAN BE ROLLED OUT JUST LIKE pastry, cut into all kinds of shapes – using templates or cookie cutters – and then made into stunning jewelry. The shapes can be left as they are or, before baking, press a small jewel stone into the clay to make an indentation where you the stone to go. Remove the jewel, bake, and then replace.

▲ *The shapes were put onto eye pins, and painted with glitter powder before baking. The sections were joined, and the jewel stones added afterward.*

FLOWERY HAIR SLIDE

Roll out the clay, and add a flower in a contrasting color for a pretty hair slide. Rolling the clay on a foil-covered board helps stop the clay sticking.

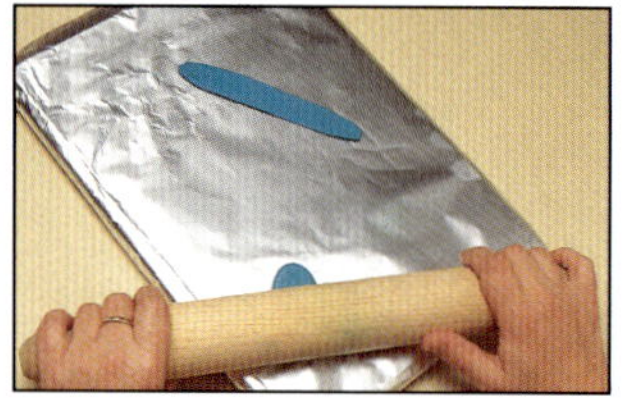

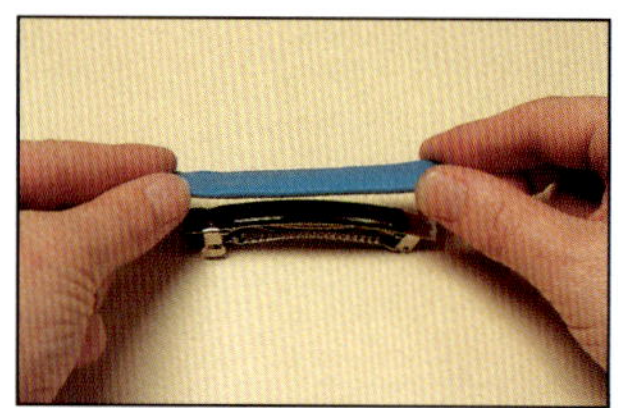

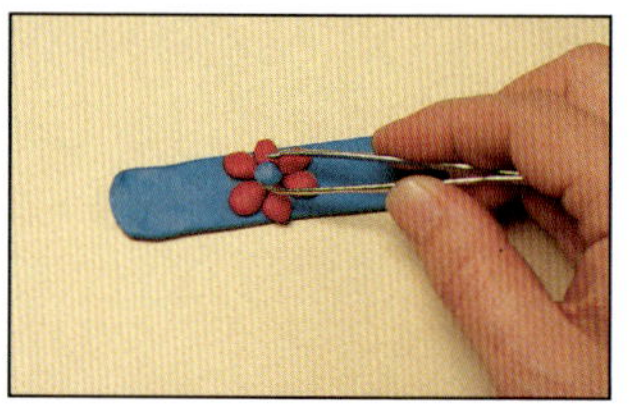

1 *Break off some modeling clay, and knead until it becomes soft and pliable. Roll out a strip approximately 0.25 inch thick, and a little larger than the hair slide base.*

2 *Smooth out any indentations, caused by wrinkles in the foil, with your fingers. Check that the strips is the right size, and curve the ends to neaten.*

3 *Roll balls in the contrast color. Mold into petal shapes, and pinch the ends between your thumb and forefinger. Press the petals in a flower shape on the base.*

4 *Flatten a ball of the base color, and press over the center point. Press the completed design over the hair slide, and bake, following the instructions on page 122.*

▶ *Baking the design over the clip will make it curve. It is unlikely to stay in place, and will need gluing to secure.*

◀ *Cut shapes out of brightly colored clays, and place them on top of each other for fun geometric jewelry.*

▲ *A metal wire was inserted before baking the sections of these earrings. They were eased out after cooking, and a bead was placed in the center, then the wire was reinserted through the bead, and looped over an ear hook at the top, and a wired bead at the bottom.*

SPECIAL SHAPES

Use different colored clays together to make striking designs, or decorate plain colors with special glittery powders, and ceramic paints.

▶ *Modeling clay glitter powder, mixed with varnish, has been painted over these cookie cutter earrings after baking to give them a special finish.*

▼ *Brush a blob of clay with glitter powder, and bake on a ring finding.*

Glue the ring finding, and jewel stone in place after baking.

▼ *Cookie cutters were used to shape these stars. The stars were then covered with yellow ceramic paint to make them look like china. The earring findings were glued in place before painting to help hold the shape.*

Decorative effects

PRESSED COTTON BALLS ARE CHEAP TO BUY, AND make A great base for experimenting with different paint techniques. You will soon discover that different sorts of paints can give very different finishes, and that different materials can be mixed to create stunning effects. The ideas discussed on these pages can also be used to decorate plain wooden beads, and polystyrene balls.

Wooden beads have been decorated with acrylic paints, and varnished.

COTTON BALL NECKLACE

Pressed cotton balls are usually used in simple toy making, but they make great beads, too. Decorate with paint, and add detail with marker pens for a really original necklace.

1 Use a knitting needle to pierce holes through the center of the cotton balls. (Cotton balls are frequently used as heads in toy making, and usually have a hole that goes part way through.)

2 Thread the beads onto the knitting needle, and rest on two lumps of Plasticine — to make it easy to turn the beads as you paint. Paint the beads in different colors, and leave to dry.

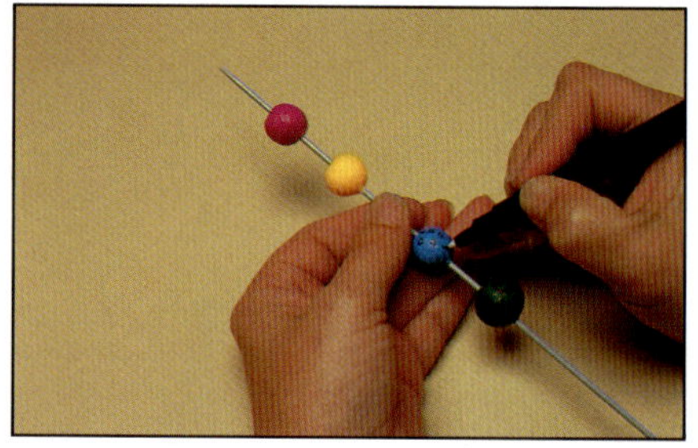

3 Draw patterns on the beads with a marker pen. Varnish the beads, to give them a harder wearing finish. Leave to dry for 24 hours before threading onto nylon line to make into a necklace.

BEAUTIFUL BEADS

Interesting paint effects give a new look to ordinary wooden beads. It's a good idea to experiment on paper first, before decorating the actual beads.

◀ *Graduate the size of the beads as you thread them on.*

▲ *Cut decorated cotton balls in half, using a craft knife (ask an adult to do this), and glue to a hair slide base.*

◀ *Plain beads have been given a striking design with a fine marker pen, then mixed with bought black beads to make stylish earrings.*

◀ *Link together different sized beads with jeweler's wire. Use pliers to make a loop at the bottom to stop the beads falling off, and one at the top to insert an earring hook through.*

▶ *Nail varnish has been used to paint these beads, and gold felt pen to draw the spots.*

Dough craft

OUGH SCULPTURE IS A traditional craft that is inexpensive and easily mastered. The dough is made from ingredients found in most kitchen cupboards — flour, salt, and water. When mixed together, they make a wonderfully versatile modeling medium that can be sculpted, rolled, or cut out, like pastry, into different shapes. Once the design is completed, the shapes are baked in an oven to harden like biscuits — but are not to be eaten! Once painted and varnished, the dough shapes make bright, fun jewelry pieces that cost next to nothing.

▲ *Bright coloured brooches make great gifts for friends or family.*

BAKING DOUGH

Set your oven to 110°C (200°F) and place the design on a baking tray. Bake until completely dry. This may take between five and eight hours, depending on the size and thickness of the dough.

FUN FISH BROOCH

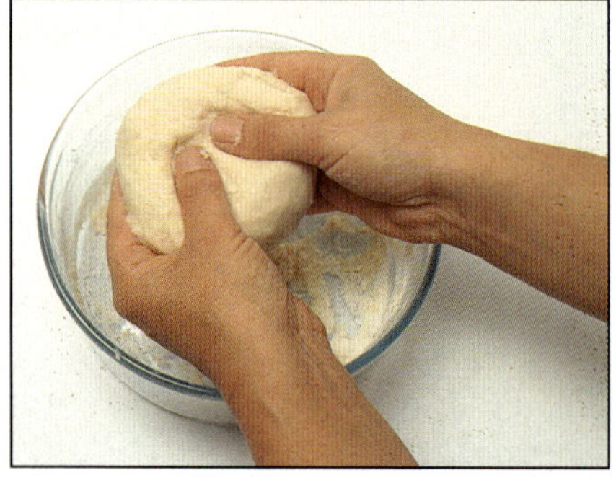

1 *Put the flour in a mixing bowl and stir in the salt. Mix in the water and oil slowly, first using a fork and then with your hand until the dough is stiff but not too sticky.*

2 *Turn the dough out onto a board and knead it for about ten minutes, until it becomes smooth. Roll out a small piece and cut out your shape, using a cardboard template if needed. Here, it is a fish shape.*

3 *Place the dough in a plastic bag or container for about an hour. Lightly moisten any add-on pieces with water and press together carefully. Bake the shape following the instructions shown above.*

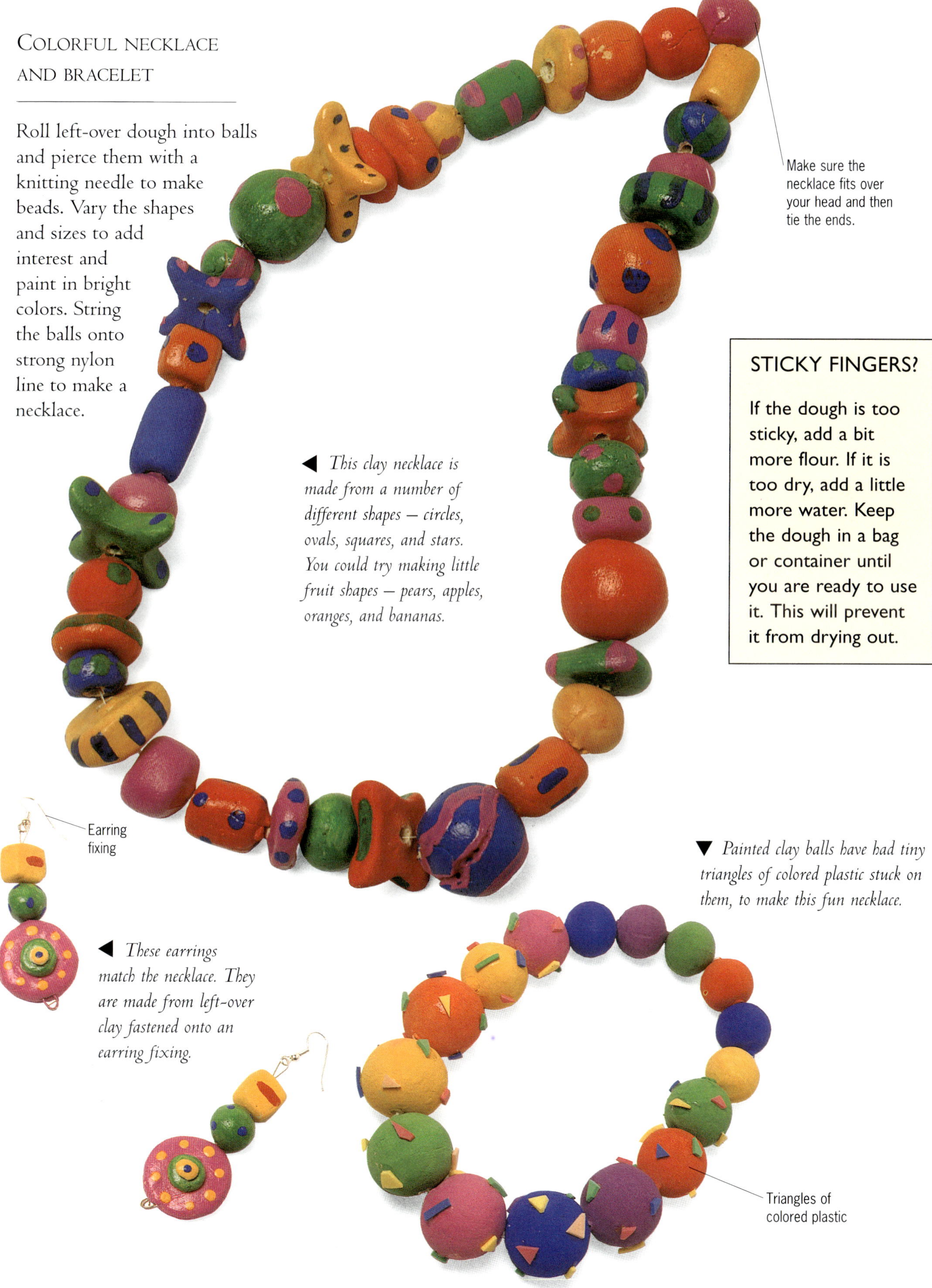

COLORFUL NECKLACE AND BRACELET

Roll left-over dough into balls and pierce them with a knitting needle to make beads. Vary the shapes and sizes to add interest and paint in bright colors. String the balls onto strong nylon line to make a necklace.

Make sure the necklace fits over your head and then tie the ends.

◀ This clay necklace is made from a number of different shapes — circles, ovals, squares, and stars. You could try making little fruit shapes — pears, apples, oranges, and bananas.

STICKY FINGERS?

If the dough is too sticky, add a bit more flour. If it is too dry, add a little more water. Keep the dough in a bag or container until you are ready to use it. This will prevent it from drying out.

Earring fixing

◀ These earrings match the necklace. They are made from left-over clay fastened onto an earring fixing.

▼ Painted clay balls have had tiny triangles of colored plastic stuck on them, to make this fun necklace.

Triangles of colored plastic

= 129 =

Magnificent millefiori

Gᴌass Millefiori, or "a thousand flower" beads, were made by people living in Venice, Italy, several hundred years ago, and were much sought after all over the world. Today, a similar effect can be achieved with simple modeling clay. Different colors are rolled, and wrapped around each other to make the "millefiori cane," which is cut into slices, and used to cover a base bead. The cane can also be used on its own to make eye-catching jewelry.

Millefiori beads

Create beautiful millefiori-style beads from different colored modeling clay. Spraying with paint or varnish will bring out the lovely colors, but leave for 24 hours before making into jewelry.

Getting started

Knead the modeling clay with your thumbs and fingers, until really soft and pliable. Wash your hand when changing colors – to prevent one rubbing off on the other, and spoiling the finished effect.

MAKING BEADS

1 Roll out two sheets of colored clay to a depth of about 0.1 inch. Place one on top of the other, and press gently together, smoothing out any air pockets. Roll together like a Swiss roll, smooth the edge, gently compress, and roll between the palms of your hands.

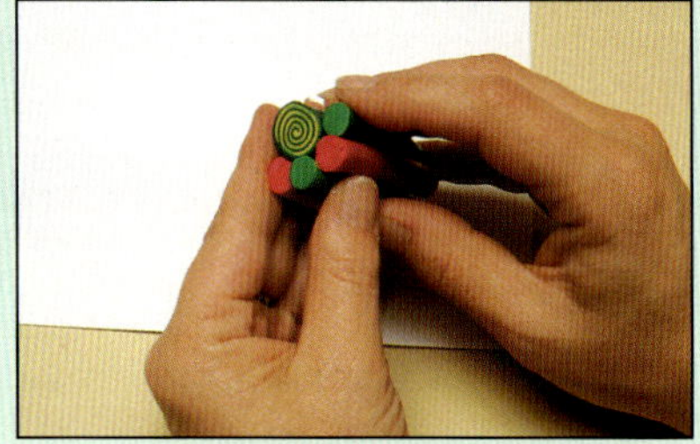

2 Roll out four sausages of equal lengths from each of the remaining colors, to a diameter of 0.5 inches. Build the cane by alternating these sausages around the two color spiral, as shown. Gently compress together, and roll between the palms of your hands.

3 Roll out another sheet of modeling clay, choosing one of the colors used for the spiral, and use to wrap around the outside of cane. Smooth the joining edge, gently compress together, so that there are no air pockets, and roll between the palms of your hand.

SIMPLE SLICES

Slices from a thick millefiori cane can be used on their own to make colorful jewelry. Follow the basic instructions, but don't roll out the cane as thinly.

▶ Cut slices that graduate in size, and use a cocktail stick to pierce holes, from side to side, instead of through the center. After baking, string together on nylon line to make a colorful necklace.

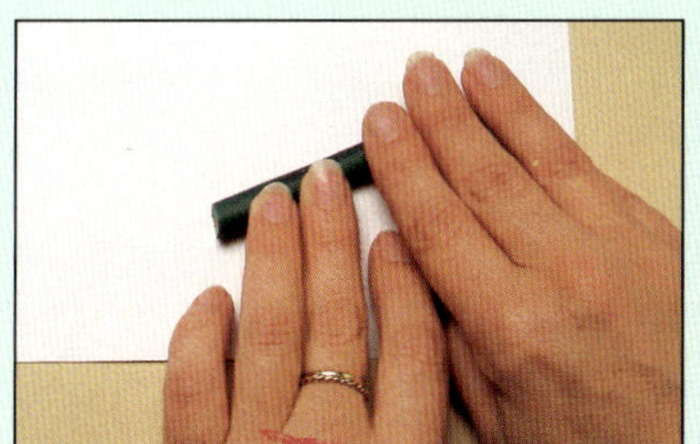

4 *Roll the cane carefully, and evenly on a flat surface with the tips of your fingers, until the diameter is about 0.25 inch. The diameter of the cane should be roughly the same throughout its width. Try to ensure that no air pockets build up.*

5 *Cut off the end of the cane. Discard this first bit, as it will be misshapen, then cut the rest of the cane into thin slices. Put these aside, and gently roll the clay into balls, or tubes between the palms of your hands, to make the base beads.*

6 *Cover each bead with the millefiori slices, and roll gently to merge them together. Leave for several hours before piercing a hole in each with a knitting needle. Bake in a low temperature oven, following the instructions on page 122. (Ask an adult to supervise this stage.)*

Fabric jewelry

Y OU WOULDN'T NORMALLY THINK OF USING FABRIC to make jewelry, but if you can use a needle and thread, you can easily transform any odd scraps into stylish earrings, necklaces, and bracelets. Look out for interesting off-cuts, remnants, and even old clothes from thrift stores and yard sales. Collect sequins, and beads to use as decoration and to give a special finish.

STRAWBERRY EARRINGS

Scraps of felt and a few beads can be turned into pretty strawberry earrings to wear throughout the summer months.

1 *Trace the strawberry shape from the template, and transfer on to card. Place on the felt, and cut out 3 shapes for each earring. Sew a few black rocailles at random to each section.*

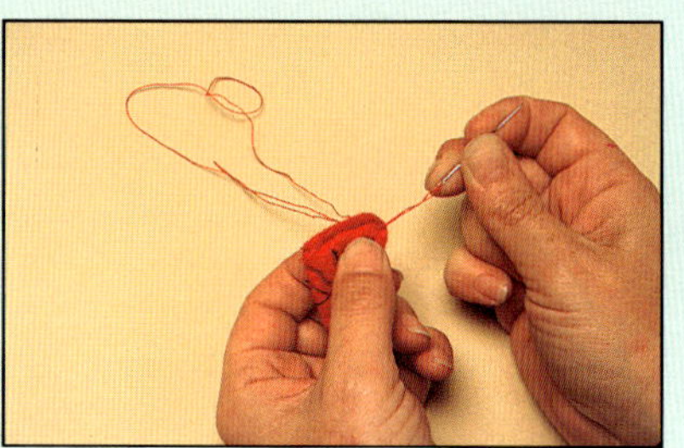

2 *With wrong sides facing, backstitch the section together, leaving an opening at the top edge.*

3 *Pad each earring out with a little piece of wadding. Gather the top edge and secure with several stitches.*

4 *Cut strips of green felt. Make one edge jagged. Gather the straight edge, and stitch to the top of each strawberry. Oversew a jump ring to the top of each one. Use pliers to join the ear hook.*

More unusual necklaces and bracelets are easy to make from tubes of bright silks, filled with wadding and twisted together. Dramatic earrings and pendants can be made from simple shapes cut from felt and decorated with sequins and embroidery.

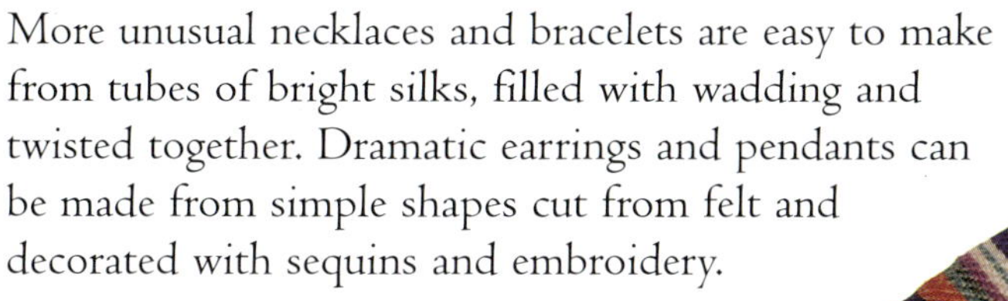

▲ *If you make the tube much longer than you need and cut the wadding to the right length, the fabric will form natural gathers to give a ruched effect.*

Knot tubes together at their centre point then stitch jump rings and a clasp to the ends to make a fun bracelet.

▼ *Sequins have been sewn to one side of the fish to look like scales. Decorate first before joining together, and padding out with wadding. Make into a brooch by stitching a pierced brooch finding to the undecorated side.*

Leaving the tail unstitched gives the fish a three dimensional look.

More fabric jewelry

Glamorous fabrics, such as velvets, net, satins, and lamés can be soaked in PVA adhesive and used to create interesting effects. Ribbons come in wonderful colors, and look great woven together and mounted on cardboard, or gathered up and turned into mini rosettes for pretty earrings. Once you start playing with fabric, you'll soon come up with your own ideas.

ROSETTE EARRINGS

Colorful strips of ribbon gathered into rosettes make pretty earrings.

1 *Join the ribbon strips to make two circles. Work either French seams or flat seams to enclose raw edges.*

2 *Work a row of gathering stitch close to one edge and draw up tightly to form a rosette. Oversew the ends to secure.*

3 *Carefully stitch the wrong side of each rosette securely to a pierced disc.*

4 *Position the disc over a matching ear clip and bend over the clips with pliers.*

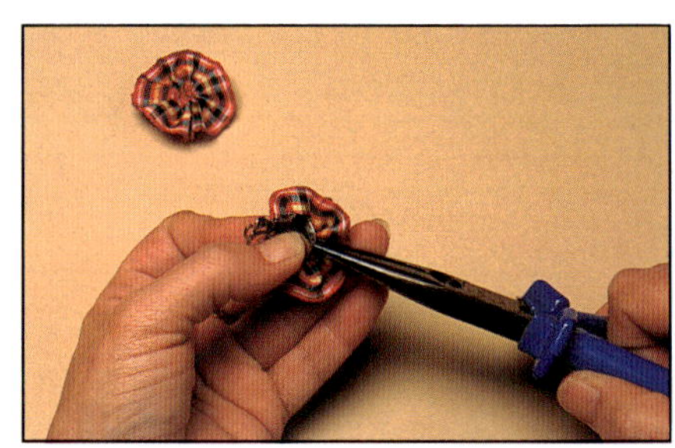

FUN FABRIC FANCIES

Different types of fabric can be used in all sorts of
ways to make unusual jewelry.

Beautiful buttons

Buttons can be used to make brilliant pieces of jewelry and there are lots of different ways they can be linked and threaded together for necklaces, earrings, and bracelets which can look stylish or fun. You can also stick buttons onto hair slides, hair bands, and bracelets to give plain basics a different look. To build up a collection of buttons, take them off any old clothes you've grown out of before they get thrown away.

BLACK-AND-WHITE BRACELET

With their ready-made holes, buttons make a great substitute for beads and are easy to string together. Plain white buttons can be painted in different colors using acrylic enamel-finish paints. Alternating black and white buttons strung together on shirring elastic make a striking looking bracelet

1 Thread the needle with a double length of shirring elastic long enough to slip over your hand and sit on your wrist comfortably. Tie one end loosely to a large bead to prevent the buttons from falling off.

2 Take the needle and double thread through one hole in each button until you have threaded on enough buttons to go around your wrist. Then secure the thread with a firm knot.

BUTTON HUNT

Look out for unusual buttons at yard sales and thrift stores and ask friends and adults if they have any they don t need — many people have a button box filled with an interesting assortment.

BUTTON BONANZA

Buttons can be used to make brilliant pieces of
jewelry and there are lots of different ways they
can be linked and threaded together for necklaces,
earrings, and bracelets.

Making your own buttons

Now you've seen what can be done with buttons, you can have fun making your own to create unique jewelry. Use brightly colored poly clays, add decorative paint finishes to air-drying clay, or leave natural. Like beads, you can make all kinds of different shapes, and sizes, other than the traditional styles. Try making them look like candies, animals, flowers, or anything else you fancy. Then turn them into fun earrings, bracelets, or necklaces.

A pack of terracotta air-drying clay
Rolling pin
Small cookie cutters
Knitting needle
Permanent marker pens
Nylon line
Selection of beads

FUNKY NECKLACE

Using air-drying clay, it is easy to make your own buttons shapes. Thread your buttons with beads to make a fun necklace.

1 Roll out clay until it's about 0.25 inch thick. Use cookie cutters to make some shapes. Mold others with your hands.

2 Use a knitting needle to pierce holes in each shape to make them look like buttons. Leave to harden.

3 Decorate the edges of the hardened buttons with markers. Thread your buttons, along with beads, on to line.

Buttons Galore

Have fun making your own buttons, and transform them into unique pieces of jewelry. Brightly colored poly clays, or air-dry clays can be molded into all sorts of different shapes and sizes, as well as into the traditional button styles.

▶ *These buttons have been threaded with beads to make them go further.*

Thread beads, and buttons on to nylon line, following the instructions on page 99.

◀ *Use cookie cutters, and icing tubes to cut out different shaped buttons from terracotta clay.*

▼ *Paint white buttons bright colors, then add stick on eyes, and fun features in permanent marker pens. Glue the button faces to a hair clip, or brooch back.*

Brightening up basic bangles

BASIC PLASTIC OR WOODEN BANGLES CAN BE GIVEN A new lease of life with a little creative thought. One of the easiest ways is to cover them with decorative cord, raffia, fabric, or even colored ribbon. Glittering, flat-backed jewel stones can be used to add a touch of glitz, and glamor, or you can simply paint them with brilliantly colored acrylic paints.

Cord is easy to wrap over bangles.

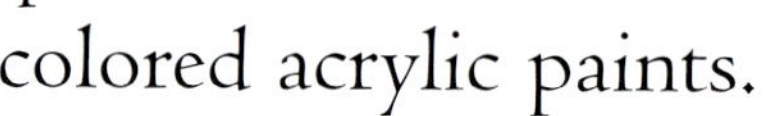

BRILLIANT BANGLES

Wrapping a plain plastic or wooden bangle with jazzy cord, or decorating with brilliant jewel stones, turns something ordinary into something really special.

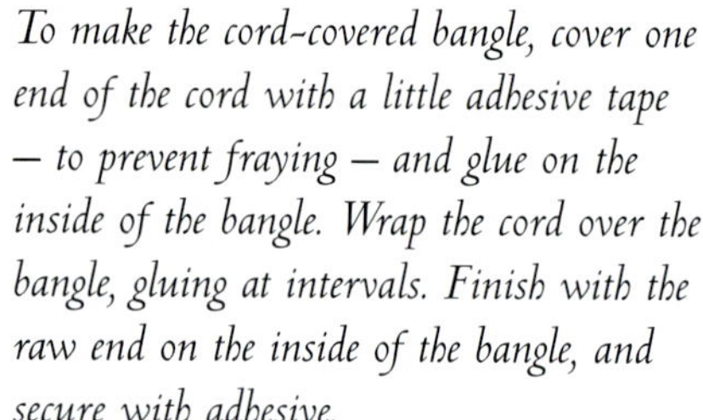

To make the cord-covered bangle, cover one end of the cord with a little adhesive tape — to prevent fraying — and glue on the inside of the bangle. Wrap the cord over the bangle, gluing at intervals. Finish with the raw end on the inside of the bangle, and secure with adhesive.

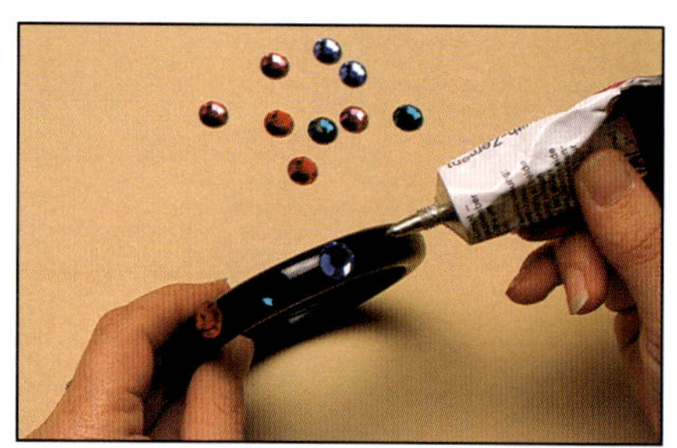

1 *To make the jewel-encrusted bangle, measure the circumference of the bangle, and decide how many stones you want to use. (It's also a good idea to plan how you're going to mix the colors.) Put a small blob of adhesive on the side of the bangle, and leave until slightly tacky.*

2 *Place the first flat-backed jewel stone on the glue, and hold in position until firmly set. Repeat with the remaining jewel stones, until the whole circumference of the bangle is covered — you can place the jewel stones side-by-side, or leave a regular gap between each one.*

Fabric soaked in PVA adhesive can be used to achieve interesting effects. When it dries, it becomes hard and rigid, and can be scrunched, pleated, or molded into many different shapes.

▲ *Braid colored raffia, or even string, and use to cover old bangles. Paint with varnish to give them a glossy hard-wearing finish.*

▶ *Mold PVA-soaked fabric onto a bangle for a different look.*

Terrific tassels

A TASSEL CAN BE USED TO ADD THE PERFECT finishing touch to a necklace, worn as a stylish pendant on it's own, or made into pretty earrings. You can make them from beads, or thread, in designs as simple, or as elaborate as you choose. Thread tassels are the simplest, and are made by wrapping long lengths over a piece of cardboard.

▲ *Wrap lengths of embroidery thread over a piece of cardboard, the length you want the finished tassel to be. Thread a tapestry needle, and slip under one looped end of the threads on the cardboard, and tie tightly. Slip the threads off the cardboard, and wrap a contrasting thread tightly near the top. Snip the other end with scissors, and fluff out the tassel. Join an earring wire to the top thread.*

BEADED TASSEL NECKLACE

Beaded tassels add an elegant finishing touch to a necklace.

MAKING A BEADED TASSEL NECKLACE

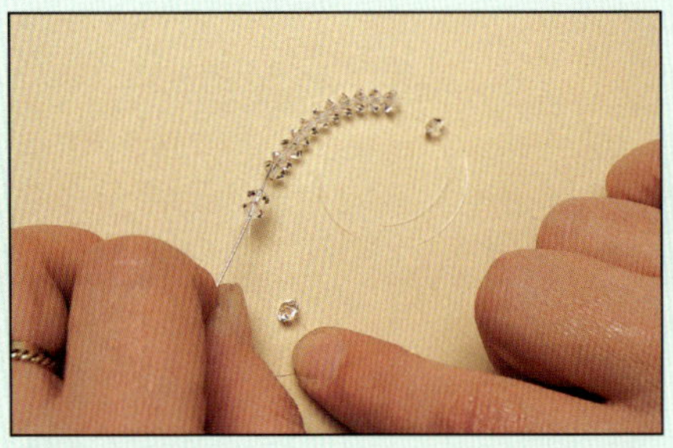 

1 *Decide on the number and length of strands you want to make the tassel. Thread the beading needle with line, and string on the beads. Take the needle back through all the beads, except the last one — this prevents the others falling off.*

2 *Take both tails of each beaded strand through the large bead. When all the strands are through the bead, knot them securely close to the bead — make a loose knot, insert a needle in its center, and use it to push it up close to the bead.*

TASSELING TIPS

You can make a tassel from one color, or from lots of
different colors. The more thread you use the fatter
the tassel will be.

3 Open up a calotte crimp with pliers,
and close it securely over the knot by
squeezing it firmly with pliers. Trim the
ends of line close to the calotte. String more
beads on to line, to make a necklace the
length required.

4 Knot the necklace ends securely.
Thread 1 to 1.5 inches of line back
through the beads on either side of the knot,
and trim. Open up the loop on the calotte
crimp with pliers, and close over the
necklace at its front center point.

Colorful threads

Y OU CAN MAKE BRILLIANTLY COLORED
FRIENDSHIP bracelets, hair ties, and unusual
necklaces by knotting, braiding, and weaving
cotton embroidery threads together. Mix
different colors together to get striking
combinations, and add your own personal
touch by stitching co-ordinating or
contrasting beads to the finished design.

Experiment with different
numbers of threads and
a mix of colors

GETTING STARTED

Cut two 30-inch-long strands from each skein of cotton
and knot them together 5 inches in from one end. Stick
the safety pin through the knot and secure to the
pincushion. Hold the pincushion between your knees as
you work. Separate the strands, so that the two on the
outside are the same color, the next colors in toward the
center are the same, and the two middle ones are the
same.

FRIENDSHIP BRACELET

Make your own friendship
bracelets from brilliantly colored
cotton embroidery threads.

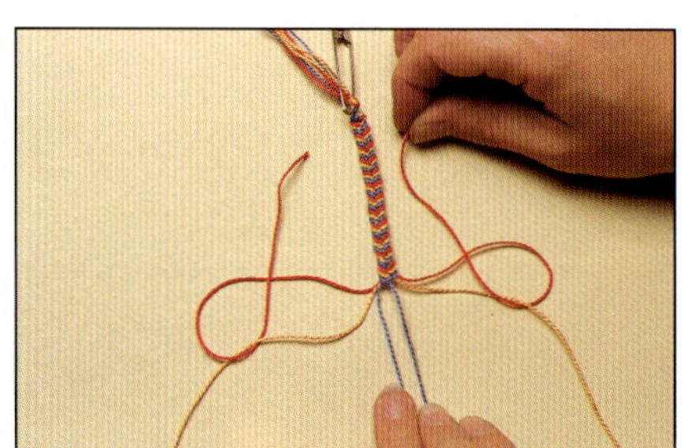

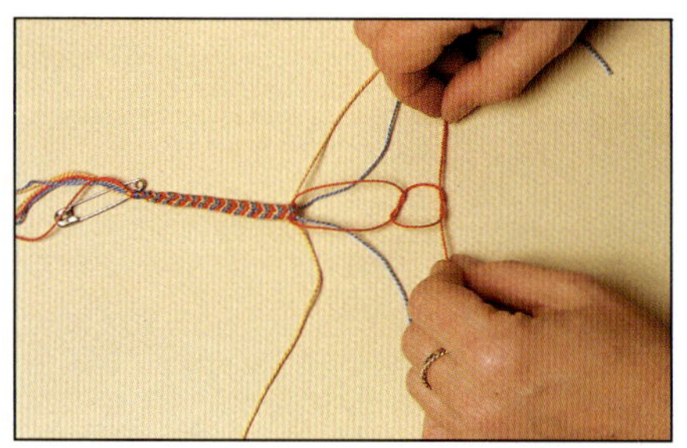

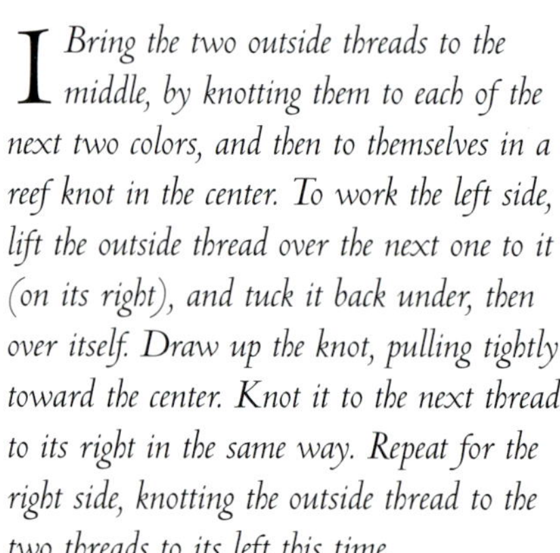

*1 Bring the two outside threads to the
middle, by knotting them to each of the
next two colors, and then to themselves in a
reef knot in the center. To work the left side,
lift the outside thread over the next one to it
(on its right), and tuck it back under, then
over itself. Draw up the knot, pulling tightly
toward the center. Knot it to the next thread
to its right in the same way. Repeat for the
right side, knotting the outside thread to the
two threads to its left this time.*

*2 When the two outside threads have
reached the middle, knot them to
themselves by taking the left over the right,
and under, then the right over the left, and
under. This completes one row. Continue to
work as many rows as you need to make a
strip long enough to fit comfortably around
your wrist, taking the outside threads to the
center each time in the same way, and
always working with the same color thread
on both sides.*

Braid, knot, and weave bright threads together to make
bracelets, hair ties, and unusual necklaces.

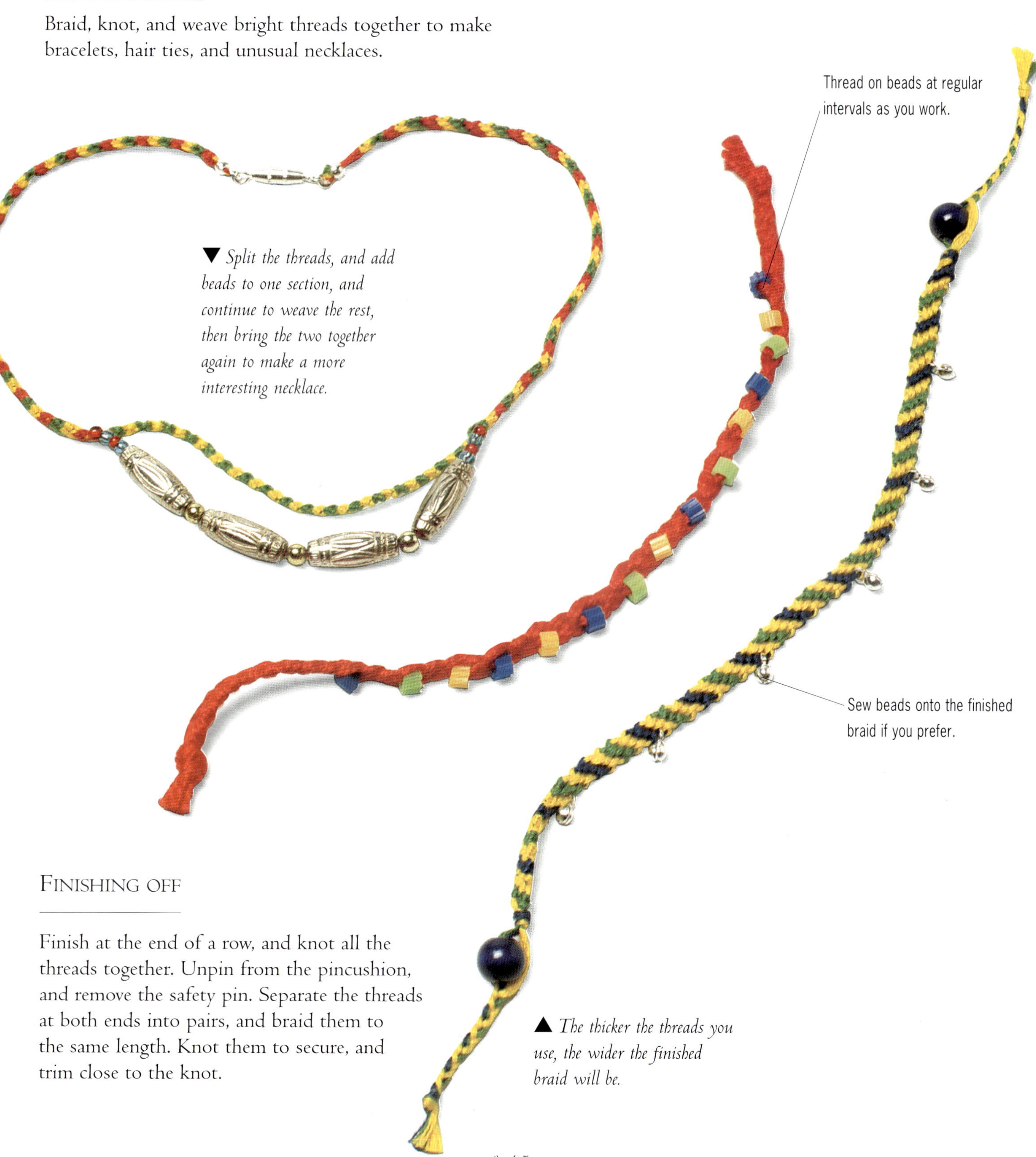

Thread on beads at regular
intervals as you work.

▼ *Split the threads, and add
beads to one section, and
continue to weave the rest,
then bring the two together
again to make a more
interesting necklace.*

Sew beads onto the finished
braid if you prefer.

FINISHING OFF

Finish at the end of a row, and knot all the
threads together. Unpin from the pincushion,
and remove the safety pin. Separate the threads
at both ends into pairs, and braid them to
the same length. Knot them to secure, and
trim close to the knot.

▲ *The thicker the threads you
use, the wider the finished
braid will be.*

Loom weaving

METAL OR WOODEN LOOMS ARE EASY TO FIND IN craft stores and can be used to create all kind of wonderful jewelry designs. Look for inspiration from colorful native American and African beadwork. Looms are simple to thread and can be used to make elaborate designs not only with beads, but cotton line too. Weaving with thread is very rewarding but takes a lot of time and concentration and you won't be able to use the loom for anything else until you've completed the piece.

Roughly work out a design on a piece of graph paper first; here, we are making a colorful pendant. Once the loom is threaded, it is much easier to work the designs than it looks.

1 Thread the loom with one more "warp" (lengthways) line than you need for the pattern. Add 5 inches to the finished length of your project or the loom (whichever is bigger). Cut the lines and knot together at one end.

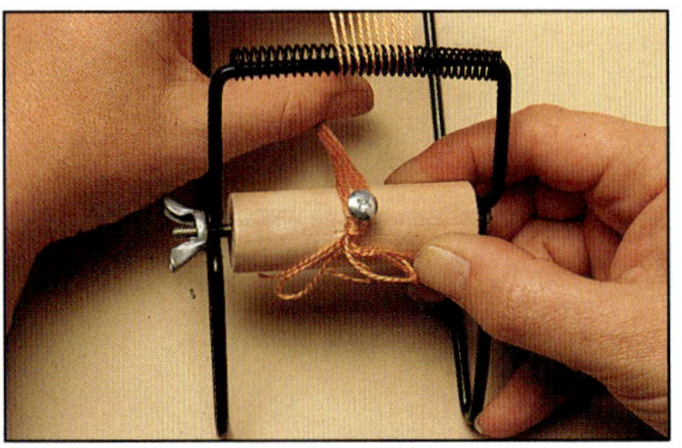

2 Separate into two halves and loop over the screw in one roller. Turn the roller until you can knot and place the lines over the screw in the other roller. Turn this until the lines are taut and separate each line into its own slot on the separator bar.

WHAT YOU NEED

A small beading loom

Colored silk embroidery line

Fine polyester or silk beading line

A fine beading needle

Selection of beads

Screw clasp

Pliers

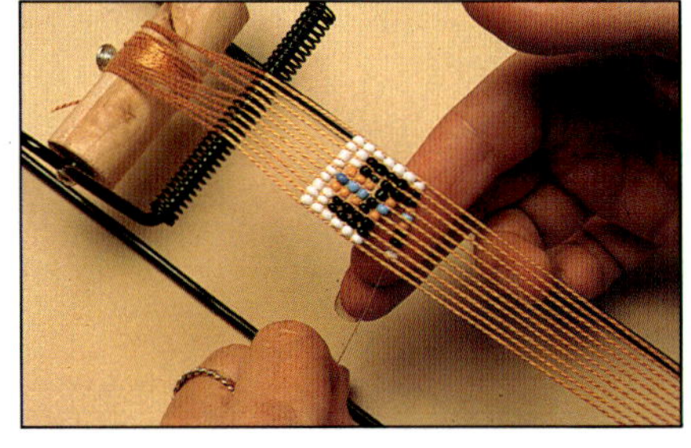

3 Work out how much beading line you need by multiplying the number of rows in the design by its width, then adding an extra 12 inches. Knot the thread neatly to an outside warp thread leaving a 3-inch tail.

4 Thread the needle and pick up a row of beads, bring them up under the warp threads and push them up between each warp thread. Take the needle back through the beads making sure it is above the warp threads. Add beads in rows.

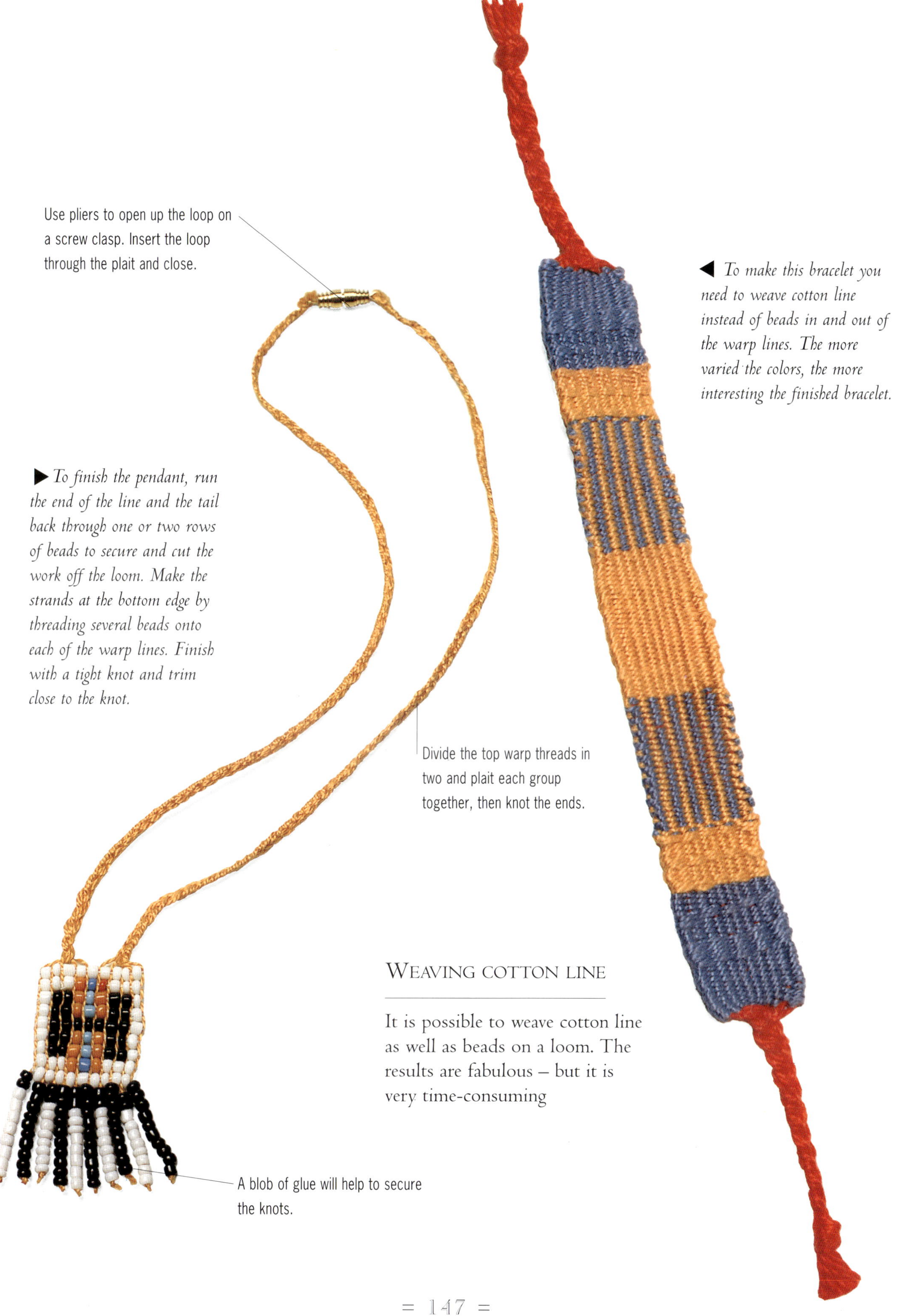

Use pliers to open up the loop on a screw clasp. Insert the loop through the plait and close.

▶ To finish the pendant, run the end of the line and the tail back through one or two rows of beads to secure and cut the work off the loom. Make the strands at the bottom edge by threading several beads onto each of the warp lines. Finish with a tight knot and trim close to the knot.

Divide the top warp threads in two and plait each group together, then knot the ends.

◀ To make this bracelet you need to weave cotton line instead of beads in and out of the warp lines. The more varied the colors, the more interesting the finished bracelet.

WEAVING COTTON LINE

It is possible to weave cotton line as well as beads on a loom. The results are fabulous – but it is very time-consuming

A blob of glue will help to secure the knots.

Fun with feathers

You can buy feathers in fantastic colors from department stores, and use them to make jewelry that's glamorous and fun to wear. With findings, you can turn them into earrings, necklaces, and brooches or, alternatively, simply glue them to hair bands or slides for a really glamorous finish. Always use clean feathers, and if you find any when out walking, check with an adult before working with them.

▲ *Glue a large feather to a brooch back or stickpin to make a pretty brooch.*

FEATHER EARRINGS

A brightly colored feather duster was used for these easy to make earrings. Choose co-ordinating beads to really set the feather off.

1 *Trim feathers from the duster. Lay two to three on top of each others and insert the ends through beads. Wrap wire tightly around the ends of the feathers, and make a loop to attach to the ear hook.*

2 *Use the pliers to open up the loop on the ear hook, and slip it through the loop you've made with wire on the feathers. Close the loop again securely. Neaten the feathers if necessary.*

◄ *Dramatic black feathers look glamorous decorated with a jewel stone and glued to a clip-on earring back.*

FEATHERY FUN

American Indians are experts at making fabulous necklaces from feathers. Look at pictures of their designs to get different ideas.

▼ *Use larger feathers to make a pendant. Follow step 1 for making earrings, then hang the pendant from a thong or brightly colored ribbon.*

▲ *Glue different colored feathers to a hair clip base to make a fun hair slide.*

◄ *Wrapping a length of wire tightly around the ends of the feathers sticking out through the beads helps to secure them, and can be folded into a loop to attach to an ear hook.*

Be creative with cork

A COLLECTION OF CORKS CAN BE TRANSFORMED INTO really unique jewelry. Cork is easy to work with, but you might need an adult's help with cutting, slicing, and piercing holes. Corks look great left their natural color, and simply varnished, or you can give them a bright painted finish. Thread them together on their own, or mix with home-made clay, or bought beads for different effects.

CORK NECKLACE

Slices from an ordinary wine bottle cork look great painted bright colors, and strung into necklaces alongside other beads.

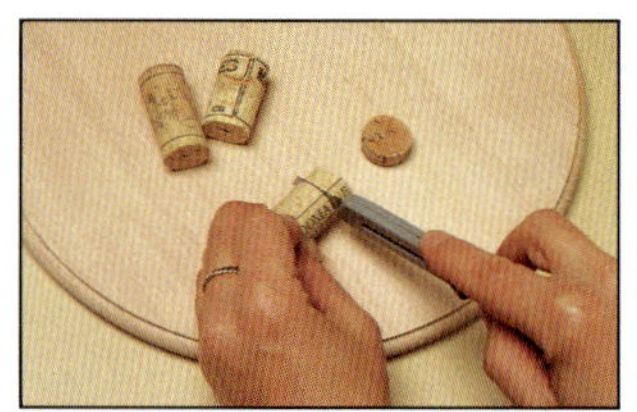

1 Ask an adult to help you cut the cork into slices about 0.25 inch wide.

2 Pierce a hole through the center of each cork slice using a sharp thick needle.

3 Slip the cork discs on to a knitting needle. Rest this on two lumps of plasticine — this will make it easy to turn the discs as you paint. Paint the discs in different colors, and leave to dry. Varnish, if desired, and leave to dry for 24 hours before making up into jewelry.

4 Knot one end of a length of nylon line securely to a bolt ring clasp. Thread on a selection of beads, then start adding the cork slices, placing a bead between each disc. Finish with the same number of beads as you started with, and knot the line securely to a jump ring.

▶ The selection of identical beads allows the necklace to hang evenly on your neck.

Varnish will give the cork beads a shiny finish.

CORKING IDEAS

Use different sorts of cork to create truly
stunning jewelry.

Stylish seashells

Next time you are down at the beach, look out for shells to turn into exquisite necklaces, earrings, and bracelets. Some shells are soft enough for holes to be made with a big needle, but for others you will need an adult to use a bradawl or drill. Large shells can simply be threaded on to cord to make a pendant. Smaller ones can be linked together to make bracelets and earrings.

▲ *Attach jump rings to shells to make attractive drop earrings.*

SHELL HAIR BAND

Keep any small shells you collect on holiday, and use to decorate a plain hair band.

1 Lay the shells out in front of you, and work out a design before your start to stick them in place. Put the adhesive on the edges of the shell that will actually touch the hair band.

2 Wait until slightly tacky, then stick in position. Stick two or three shells on at a time, then leave to dry, resting the hair band somewhere that will keep it upright.

For a more glamorous finish,
paint the shells gold or silver.

◀ A collection of the same shells, in graduating sizes, look pretty glued to a plain hair band.

▼ Hair slides with wide tops look lovely decorated with tiny shells.

Seashore styles

Once you get the feel for making shell jewelry, you could try bringing in other elements of the seashore by incorporating bits of driftwood, or even pebbles the sea has worn holes in.

▲ Some shell are just the right size and shape to glue earrings backs to.

▶ A large single shell makes a spectacular pendant. Ask an adult to drill a hole in the top, then paint it gold, and thread a piece of leather thong or ribbon through the hole.

Seeds and nuts

SEEDS AND NUTS ARE OTHER MATERIALS FROM nature that you can use successfully in jewelry making. Nuts, stung on to nylon, make unusual necklaces. Melon seeds, washed and dried, or sunflower seeds look wonderful strung together for necklaces, bracelets, and even earrings, but can also be used to decorate other plain bases.

A bag of monkey nuts

A thick sharp needle

Gold paint

Paintbrush

Nylon line

Pearl beads

PEANUT NECKLACE

It's easy to make holes in the shells of monkey nuts with a large tapestry needle. Paint them gold, and string together with pearl beads to make a pretty necklace.

▲ Make earrings to match a necklace to create a pretty set.

PEANUT NECKLACE

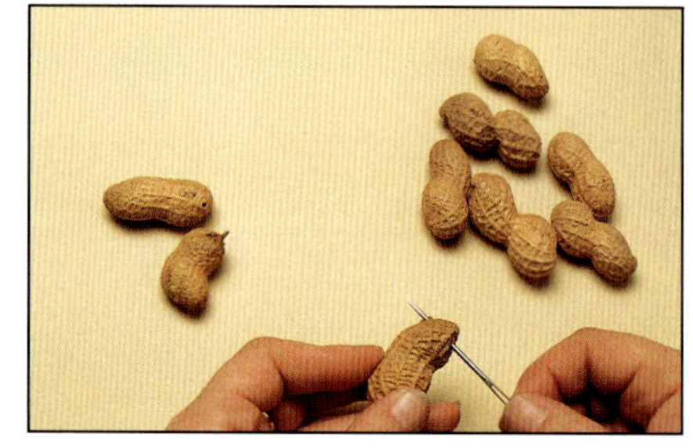

1 Pierce a hole through the top of each nut with a sharp thick needle.

2 Paint the nuts gold. Inserting a cocktail stick through the hole will make it easier to hold and rotate the nuts while painting.

3 Loosely tie the nylon line to a pearl bead to stop all the others falling off. Thread several pearl beads on, then add the peanuts, putting a pearl bead between each one. Finish the necklace with the same number of pearl beads as at the beginning. Untie the end bead, and knot the two ends together. Trim any excess nylon.

Tie on a stopper bead before threading the seeds.

▶ *Next time you eat a melon, keep the seeds, and make them into a delicate necklace. Wash, and dry them first, then use a needle to thread them on to nylon line*

Seeds and pulses look really good painted and used to decorate basic cardboard bases.

▲ *Decorate a circle of card with sunflower seeds to make an unusual brooch.*

▲ *Stick pumpkin seeds to a cardboard base to make a flower shape, then add earring backs.*

Pasta and pulses

R AIDING THE PANTRY CAN PROVIDE YOU WITH ALL
sorts of materials to use in jewelry making. Dried
pasta tubes can be painted in brilliant colors, and
transformed into fun necklaces. Lentils and other pulses
can be stuck to all kinds
of bases — cardboard
shapes, bangles, plastic
hair bands, and slides.
Paint with metallic paint for
a glamorous finish.

▲ *A cardboard tube was cut in
half lengthways, covered in lentils,
and painted a dramatic black.*

▶*Pasta shapes can also
make pretty earrings.*

PASTA NECKLACE

Dried pasta comes in a whole range of fun
shapes, which look wonderful painted, and threaded
into necklaces. Don't squeeze the pasta shapes too
hard, or they will shatter, but don't worry if just a few
bits break off .

1 *Push the needle gently through the
pasta shapes to make a hole for the line
to go through. Try not to use too much
pressure.*

2 *Put the shape on top of a wooden
skewer, and paint with a fine brush.
Stick the skewer into a foam pad, or ball
of plasticine, and leave to dry.*

3 *When dry, outline the edges in a
contrasting color. Leave to dry, then
varnish, if desired. Leave for 24 hours
before threading into a necklace.*

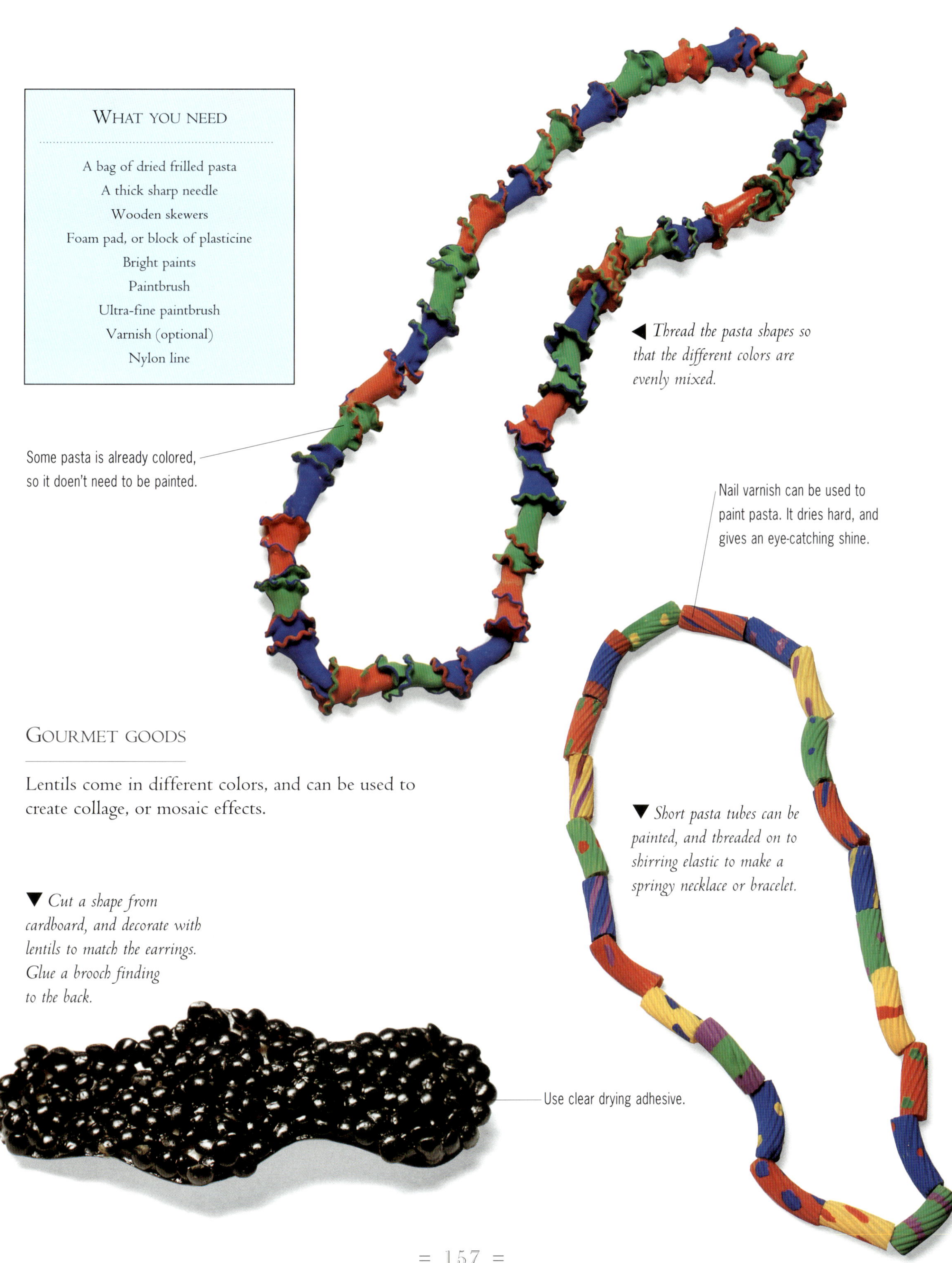

Some pasta is already colored,
so it doesn't need to be painted.

◀ *Thread the pasta shapes so that the different colors are evenly mixed.*

Nail varnish can be used to paint pasta. It dries hard, and gives an eye-catching shine.

GOURMET GOODS

Lentils come in different colors, and can be used to create collage, or mosaic effects.

▼ *Short pasta tubes can be painted, and threaded on to shirring elastic to make a springy necklace or bracelet.*

▼ *Cut a shape from cardboard, and decorate with lentils to match the earrings. Glue a brooch finding to the back.*

Use clear drying adhesive.

Fun foam

THE FINE FOAM USED FOR this jewelry can be bought from craft specialists. It comes in sheet form and is available in lots of different colors to add a new dimension to jewelry making. You can treat it like card and cut out simple shapes. These can be used to decorate plain bases, such as hairbands, hairslides, brooches, and bracelets. It is also flexible enough to be rolled and twisted into interesting three dimensional shapes. If this inspires you, but you cannot find the foam, try out the ideas using thin washing-up sponges.

▲ *This hairslide and these daisy earrings look striking because the colors and shapes used are simple and "unfussy."*

◄ *Fine foam makes cutting out shapes an easy job. This daisy is one example — choose shapes that you like.*

Foam sheets
Tracing paper
Pencil
Card
Scissors
Glue
Plain hairbands
Slides and bracelets to decorate
Earring backs

DAISY HAIRBAND, EARRINGS, AND BRACELET

1 *To make templates, trace daisy shapes and centers and transfer this to card to cut out. The small templates are for earrings and the bracelet and the larger one is for the hairband. You will need one large flower and center for the hairband, and two small flowers and centers for the earrings and the bracelet.*

2 *Put the templates on the foam and draw around them in pencil. Carefully cut this out with scissors, following the lines. For traditional daisies, choose yellow for the flower and white for the center. But for fun variations, choose brilliant clashing colors, such as pink and orange.*

3 *Glue a center to the middle of each flower and leave to dry. To make the hairband, try it on first and mark where you want the flower to go. Glue the flower in place and leave to dry. To make the earring, glue an earring to two small daisies. To make the bracelet, space the daisies out evenly and glue in place.*

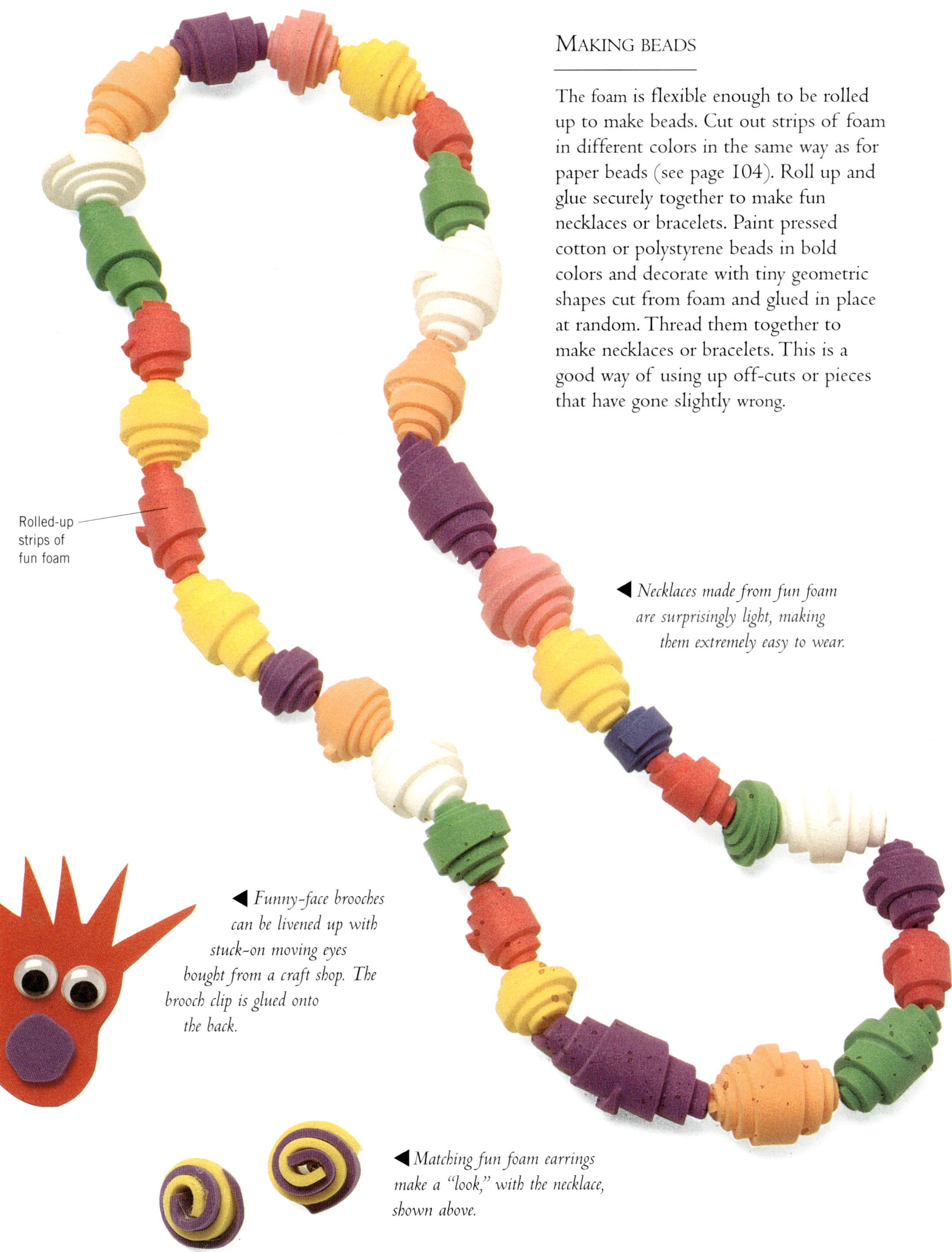

MAKING BEADS

The foam is flexible enough to be rolled up to make beads. Cut out strips of foam in different colors in the same way as for paper beads (see page 104). Roll up and glue securely together to make fun necklaces or bracelets. Paint pressed cotton or polystyrene beads in bold colors and decorate with tiny geometric shapes cut from foam and glued in place at random. Thread them together to make necklaces or bracelets. This is a good way of using up off-cuts or pieces that have gone slightly wrong.

*◀ Necklaces made from fun foam
are surprisingly light, making
them extremely easy to wear.*

*◀ Funny-face brooches
can be livened up with
stuck-on moving eyes
bought from a craft shop. The
brooch clip is glued onto
the back.*

*◀ Matching fun foam earrings
make a "look," with the necklace,
shown above.*

Tool box treasures

ONCE YOU GET THE JEWELRY MAKING BUG, YOU'LL start to look for all sorts of different materials to use. You'll be amazed at what you can find to use in a basic household tool box. Silvery nuts and washers can be linked together, and mixed with beads to look really glamorous. Washers can be painted with enamel paints to give them a bright fun look. Even plastic covered wire can be twisted or braided together into truly original bangles.

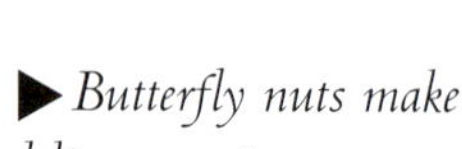

▲ *Stick three nuts together, and add earring backs.*

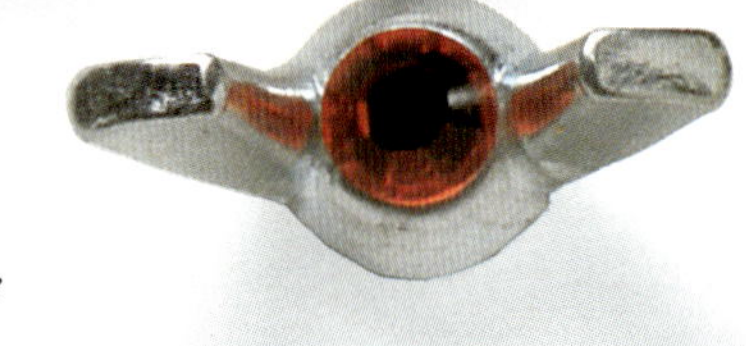

▶ *Butterfly nuts make delicate earrings.*

WHAT YOU NEED

....

A packet of small metal washers

Jump rings

A screw clasp

Pliers

WASHER BRACELET

Metal washers can be linked together to make a fashionable chain bracelet.

1 *Use pliers to carefully open a jump ring sideways. Slip the loop of one part of the screw clasp over the jump ring, then add a washer, and close the ring with the pliers so it's two ends meet perfectly. Open another jump ring.*

2 *Slip the jump jump ring through the first washer, then add another washer before closing. Continue linking the washers until they are long enough to fit your wrist. Add another jump ring to the last washer, and attach the screw clasp.*

Ironware items

Use a little imagination, and turn ordinary bits and pieces into dazzling jewelry.

Take a ball of string

Y OU WILL BE AMAZED AT THE VARIETY OF stylish jewelry you can make with a simple ball of string. String can be braided, crocheted, and worked in macramé style to make unusual necklaces and bracelets. Glued to cardboard bases, it can be transformed into earrings and brooches. To give your string jewelry a special finish, decorate it with metallic paints or beads.

▲ *Glue a spiral of string to a large circle of cardboard to make a brooch to match the earrings opposite.*

STRING PENDANT

This pendant is really easy to make. The string is wound into a spiral around a central wooden bead, then hung from a length of leather thong

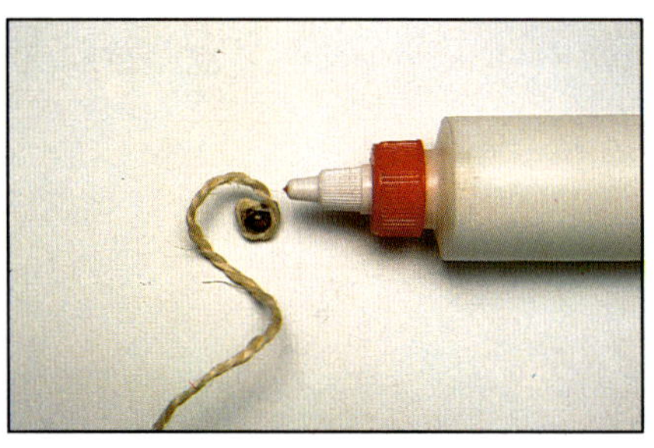

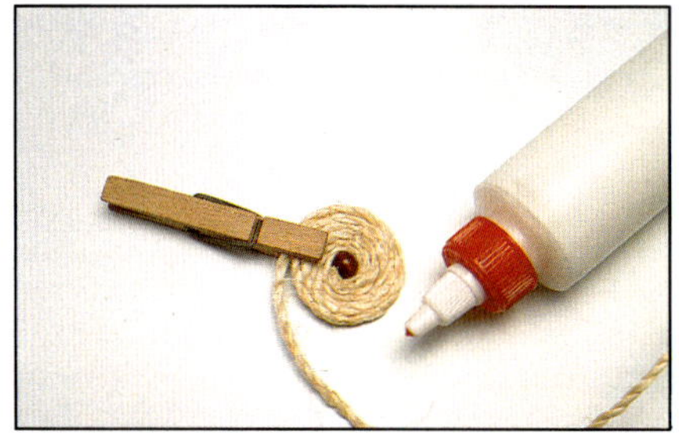

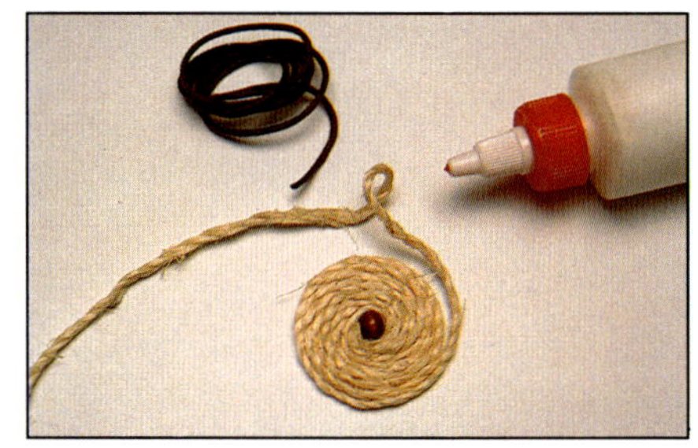

1 *Take the length of string and dab a small blob of adhesive on one end. Insert this end through the hole in the bead. Hold until it sets, then leave to dry. When dry, start winding the string around itself in a flat spiral.*

2 *As you wind the spiral, add blobs of adhesive along the string's length. Work one or two rounds at a time, then leave the adhesive to set. Keep the string in place while it dries with a peg. Continue until the spiral is almost the size you want.*

3 *At the start of the last round make a loop. Glue the loop, then leave to dry with a peg holding it in position. Finish the last round, adding a blob of adhesive to secure. When dry, thread the thong through the string loop, and knot the ends.*

STRIKING STRING SUNDRIES

Just look around at all the different thicknesses and colors of string available and you'll find lots of inspiration for unique designs of your own. A book on knots is also a good source of ideas.

▲ *Braiding is a simple way to make a string necklace. This one has been decorated with beads and simple tassels. To make the tassels, fold a length of string in half. Push the looped end through the braid from the wrong side, and then insert the end through the loop, and pull up quite tightly.*

▶*Wind string around a wooden or plastic bangle, gluing as you go along. Finish by decorating with metallic paint.*

▲ *Cut small circles of cardboard, and use glue a long length of string to each one in a spiral effect.*

Clever ideas for curtain rings

Wooden curtains rings are easy to transform into items of jewelry, such as hoop earrings, or pendant necklaces. They usually have a ready-made brass loop screwed into the top that makes it simple to attach to thong, cord, or ear hooks. Brass curtain rings can quickly be turned into hoop earrings, and make really stylish bracelets when linked together with jump rings.

Brass curtain rings make pretty chain bracelets.

CURTAIN RING EARRINGS

Ricrac braid is zigzag-shaped material often used as a trimming on clothing. You can use it in jewelry to give a new look to curtain rings, transforming them into attractive drop earrings.

2 wooden curtain rings

Ricrac braid

Acrylic paint in colors that co-ordinate

with the braid

Paintbrush

Strong, clear-drying multi-purpose adhesive

Jewel stone

Jump rings

Pliers

Ear hooks

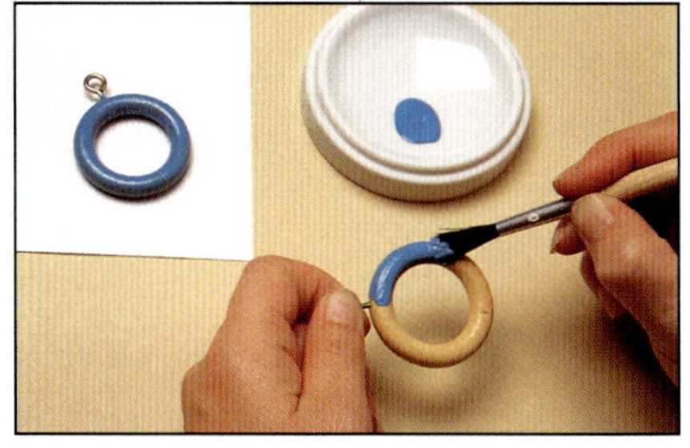

1 *Paint the curtain rings, so that they are covered completely. This may take at least two coats.*

2 *Glue end of braid to ring. Wrap braid over ring, gluing it in place where it touches the ring. When covered, glue the end.*

3 *Open up a jump ring using pliers, and slip through the brass loop on the curtain ring, and the loop on the earring hook. Close so its ends meet perfectly.*

▶ *Paint wooden curtain rings in white with black dots, and join earring wires to the loops at the top.*

RADICAL RINGS

Curtains rings can be painted, wrapped with braid, dressed up with glittery jewel stones, or simply linked together to make totally original jewelry.

▲ *Ricrac braid comes in a wide range of different colors, so experiment with different combinations.*

▼ *Glue tiny glass embroidery beads to a brass ring to give it a jewel encrusted finish, and thread with a decorative metallic cord.*

Use ribbon if you have no metallic cord.

If the curtain ring has no bass loop, a leather thong can simply be looped on.

Wooden curtain rings come in a range of different sizes.

◀ *Use metallic pens to add a decorative finish to a simple wooden ring. Loop through a length of leather thong to make into a pendant.*

Pliable plastic tubing

CLEAR PLASTIC TUBING IS READILY AVAILABLE FROM stores that sell wine-making equipment, and is a versatile material for making modern-looking jewelry. It's easy to cut and shape with scissors, and can be filled with anything — from tiny beads, to the brightly colored "hundreds and thousands" used to decorate cakes. Use tubing with a wider diameter to join the ends together.

TUBE NECKLACE

Cut ordinary plastic tubing into spirals to create an unusual-looking necklace.

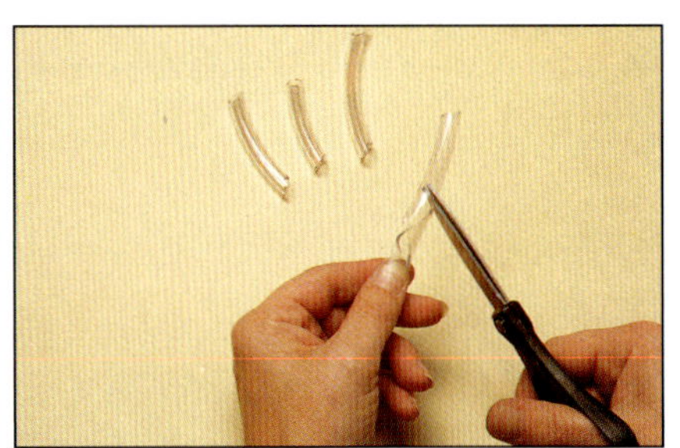

1 *Cut the tube into a range of different lengths. Cut each length diagonally around it's circumference, and up the length, to make spirals.*

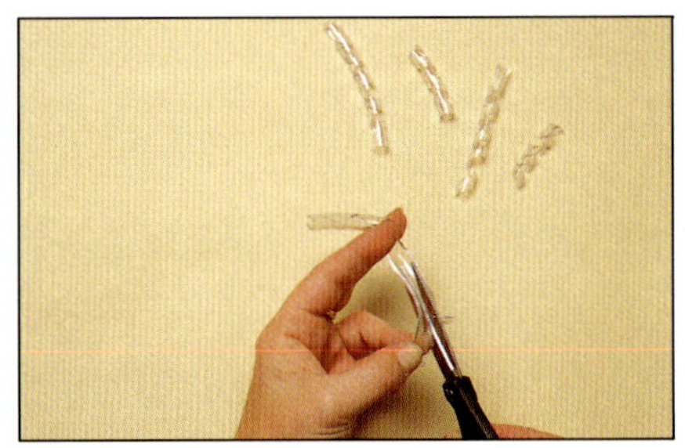

2 *Open each spiral section out, and cut up the middle to form two narrower spirals. Don't worry if they aren't all the same width.*

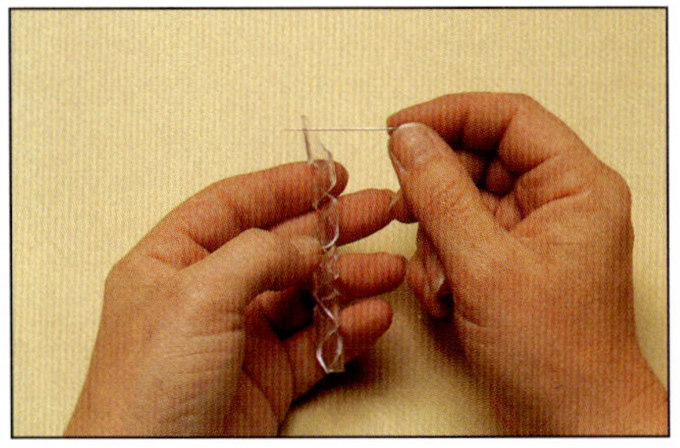

3 *Taper one end of each spiral, and pierce with a needle. Cut a length of wire, long enough to take the plastic spirals and beads, with space to make loops in either end to attach the chain.*

4 *Loop one end of the wire. Use the pliers to open up the center link in the chain. Discard this, and attach one end of the chain to the wire loop. Thread the wire through a bead, followed with a spiral.*

5 *Repeat until you've threaded on all the spirals, and beads you need for your design. Attach the rest of the chain to the other end of the wire, and loop it over with pliers to secure.*

Here are a few more ideas for jewelry to make from plastic tubing, but once you've experimented, you'll come up with all kinds of different ideas of your own.

▲ *Use small pieces of wider tube to make these earring. Cut small lengths, and slice them up the middle. Add a jewel stone for extra sparkle.*

▶*Lengths of chain can be brought from jewelry specialists, or you can use an old necklace you don't want any more.*

▼ *Twist a longer length of tube around itself to make a different bangle. Join the two ends together with a piece of wider tubing, and clear-drying adhesive.*

Fill tubes with tiny beads, or anything else you fancy.

Wrapped with style

ONE WAY TO DISPLAY A BEAUTIFUL OBJECT THAT doesn't have a pre-drilled hole is to wrap it decoratively with wire. This simple technique, provides lots of scope for experimenting with different effects. Jeweler's wire is available in gold and silver, and in a variety of thicknesses. The finest is the easiest to work with, but more interesting finishes can be achieved with the thicker ones, which need pliers and a little practice to bend and shape.

SPIRAL EARRINGS

Wrap fine jeweler's wire around a pair of snipe-nosed pliers to make a loose coil, and link to a glittering crystal bead to make a dazzling pair of earrings.

MAKING SPIRAL EARRINGS

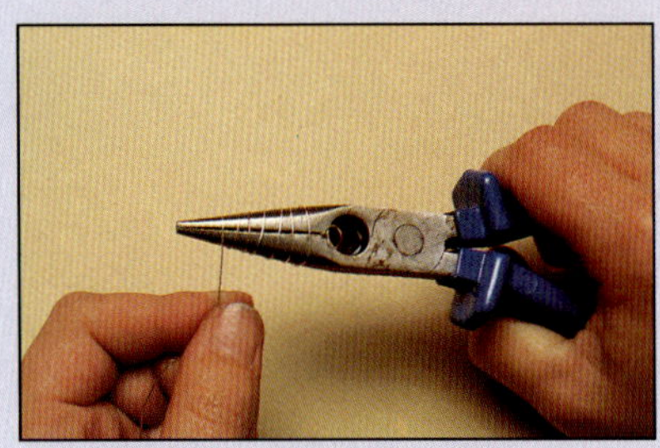

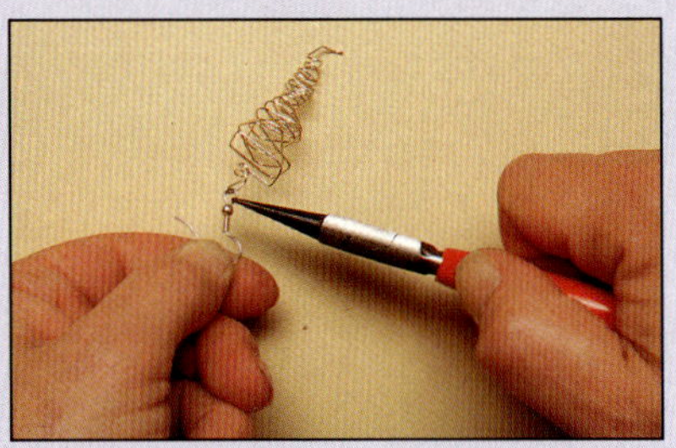

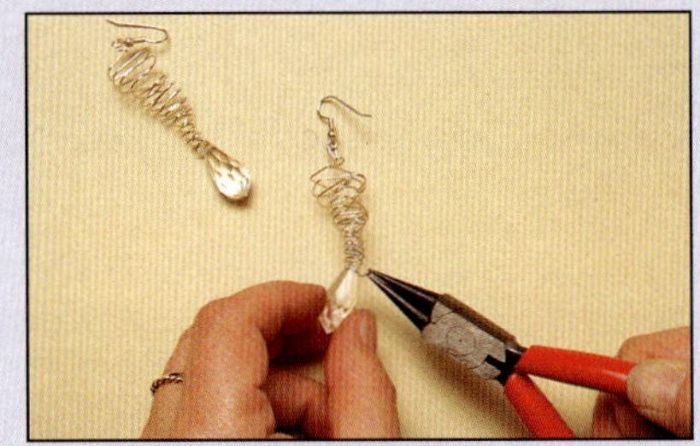

1 *Make a loop in one end of a length of wire. Grip this between the jaws of the pliers at the widest end. Wrap the wire tightly along the length. Trim any excess wire with scissors.*

2 *Using pliers, open the loop on the ear hook, and slip over the loop on the wire spiral you have just made. Close securely with pliers. Repeat the whole process for the other earring.*

3 *Slip the other end of the wire spiral through the hole of a drop bead, and make a loop with pliers to secure it in position. You can stretch the earring spiral, to make it looser if you wish.*

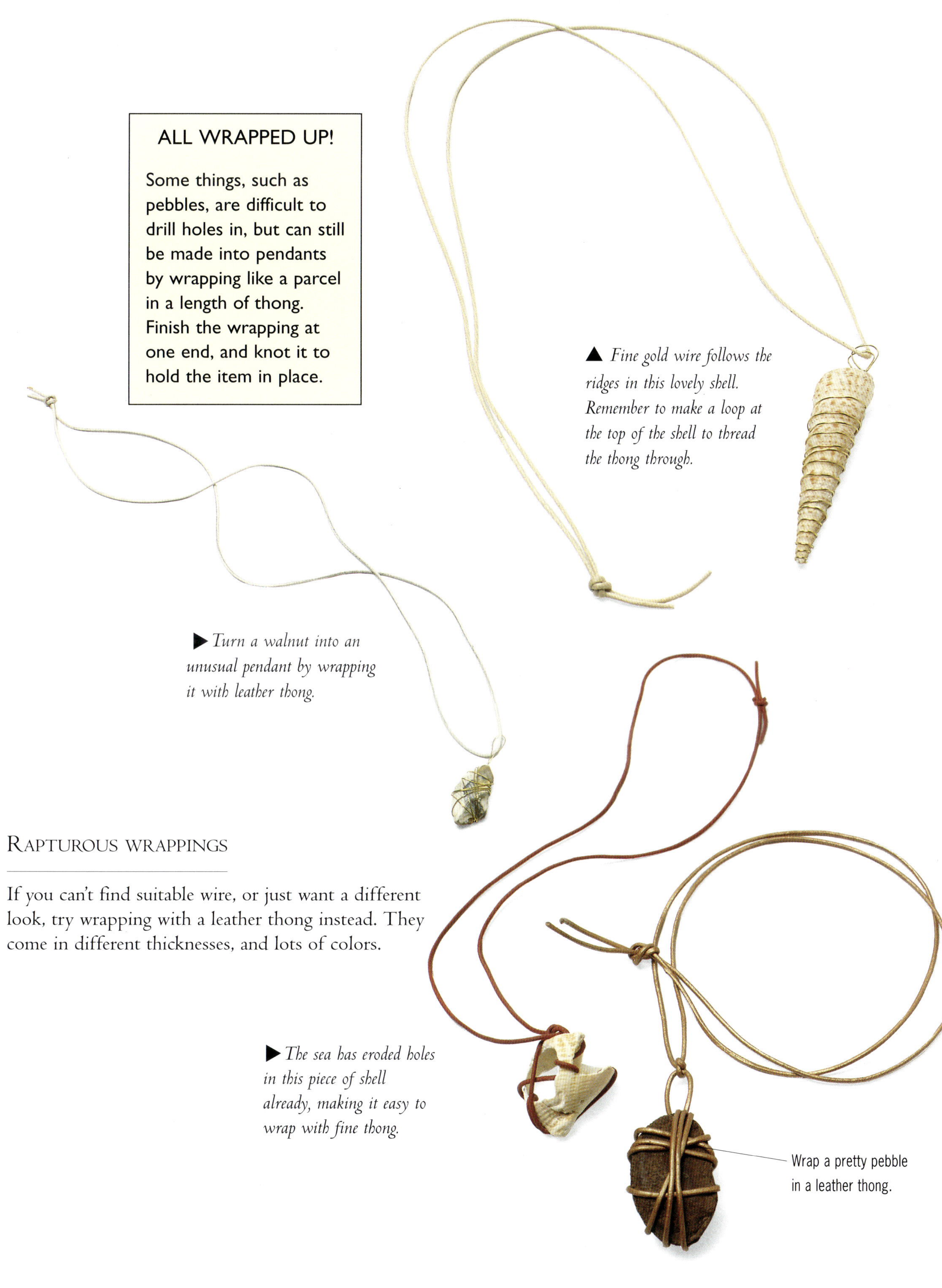

▲ *Fine gold wire follows the
ridges in this lovely shell.
Remember to make a loop at
the top of the shell to thread
the thong through.*

▶ *Turn a walnut into an
unusual pendant by wrapping
it with leather thong.*

Rapturous wrappings

If you can't find suitable wire, or just want a different
look, try wrapping with a leather thong instead. They
come in different thicknesses, and lots of colors.

▶ *The sea has eroded holes
in this piece of shell
already, making it easy to
wrap with fine thong.*

Wrap a pretty pebble
in a leather thong.

Sensational safety pins

SAFETY PIN JEWELRY WAS MADE FAMOUS MOST recently by punk rockers back in the seventies. Decorated with small glass rocailles, bugle beads, or other small beads, it is easy to disguise their appearance, and make absolutely stunning jewelry. You can get all kinds of different effects by varying the beads, and mixing assorted sizes of pins together.

SAFETY PIN BRACELET

Decorated with small beads, the safety pins are almost unrecognisable as the base for this bracelet.

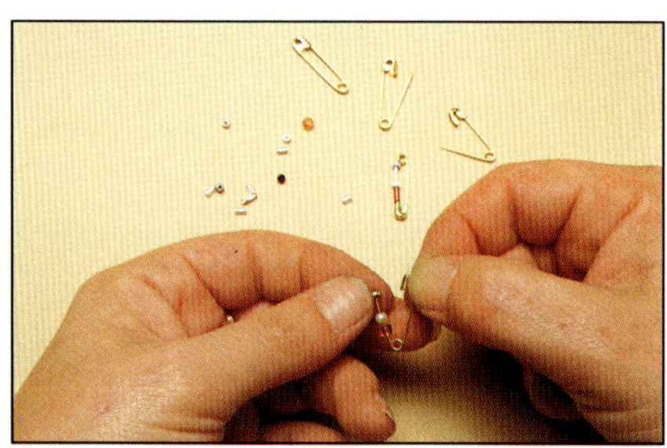

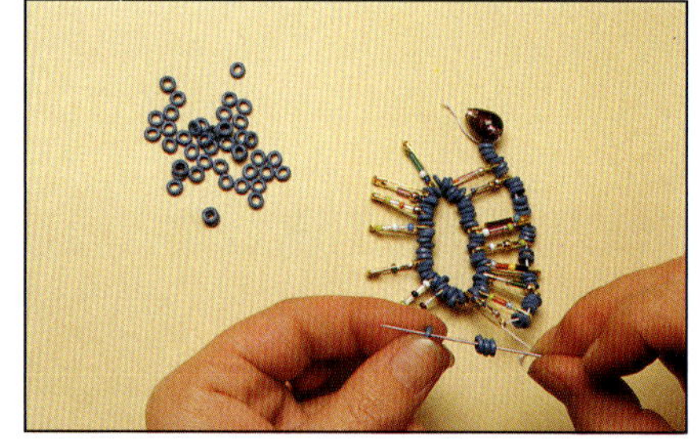

1 *Open up a safety pin, and thread on a random selection of rocailles, bugle beads, and other small beads. Close the pin, and squeeze the head with pliers to make sure it stays closed. Decorate the rest of the safety pins in the same way. Thread the needle with elastic, long enough to fit your wrist comfortably when stretched, plus a little extra. Tie the loose end to a large bead to stop the pins falling off.*

2 *Thread the pins on to the shirring elastic, with the beaded edges facing the same way, and alternating them — take the needle through the head of one pin, through a few small beads, and then through the base hole of the next pin. Continue until all the pins have been strung. Knot the ends together securely. Work the bottom thread in the same way, adding the same number of beads between each pin.*

▼ *Thread different sized beads on to safety pin, and join several together to make fun earrings.*

▼ *Glass rocaille beads always look pretty, but can be a bit fiddly to thread. Bigger beads or bulge beads take less time.*

◀ *Link different sized safety pins together, and hang as a pendant from a length of chain, leather thong, or string of beads.*

SPLENDID SAFETY PINS

Once you start making safety pin jewelry, you'll find it an addictive hobby, and you may begin collecting all the safety pins you can.

Happy halloween

Make some ghoulish jewelry to wear when trick or treating, or to a special Halloween party. Spiders are always creepy, and really easy to sculpt in modeling clay, and turn into spooky earrings, or brooches. Bright orange clay in perfect for pumpkins – make them look ghoulish by adding spooky features. Make a large pumpkin for a brooch, and two smaller ones for matching earrings.

SPIDER SET

Spooky spiders are perfect for trick or treating. These earrings are made out of modeling clay, and can be finished with an earring hook, or clip-on back. The spider pendant is wonderfully simple to make using a pressed cotton ball, pipe cleaners, and stick on eyes – all available from craft stores.

I *Break off a small piece of black modeling clay, and knead with your fingers until soft. Roll two balls, and squash each flat with your thumb to make the earring bases.*

2 *Roll out tiny black sausages. Lay across the base, curving the ends downward to make legs. Make two for each earring, making the bottom one shorter than the top one. Press firmly in place.*

3 *Wash your hands, then roll two tiny balls from the white clay. Squash flat, and press in position for the eyes, on the opposite side to the legs. Add black pupils, and a tiny red strip for the mouth.*

4 *Insert the eye pin through the top of the spider before baking. Harden in a low temperature oven, following the instructions on page 122. Leave to cool, then attach earring hooks.*

5 *To make the spider pendant, paint the cotton ball black, and glue eyes in place. Insert pipe cleaners as legs, and glue to secure. Insert the eye pin, and glue. Loop through a length of leather thong.*

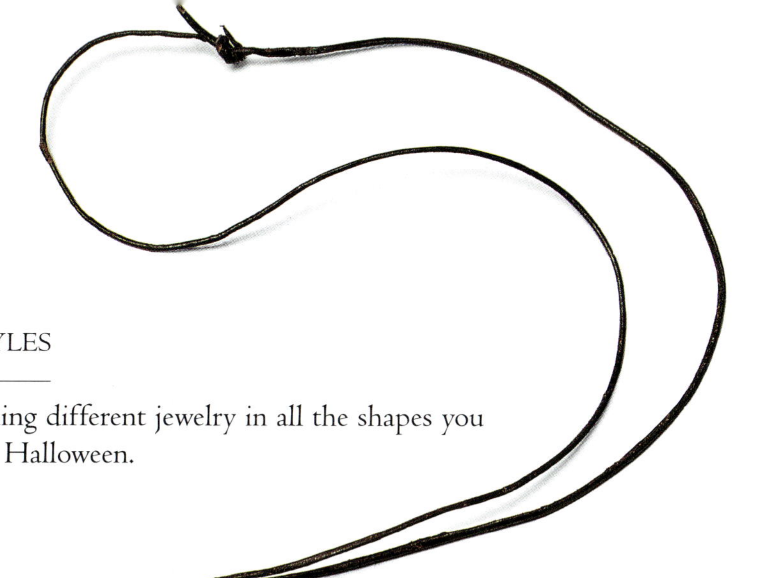

SPOOKY STYLES

Have fun making different jewelry in all the shapes you associate with Halloween.

▼ *This wonderfully wicked witch is made from a pressed cotton ball. She has been given some wool hair, and a card hat and nose. Make a loop from jeweler's wire and insert into the hat to hang her from a length of thong.*

WHAT YOU NEED

Earrings:
Black, white and red modeling clay
Eye pins
Pliers
Ear hooks

Pendant:
Cotton ball
Black paint
Paintbrush
Stick on eyes (from craft stores)
Black pipe cleaners
PVA adhesive
Long eye pin
Black leather thong

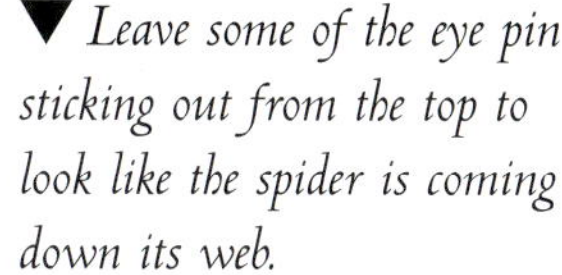

Trim the eye pins to fit.

▼ *Leave some of the eye pin sticking out from the top to look like the spider is coming down its web.*

Festive fun

Christmas is a time for dressing up, and you can add the perfect finishing touch to a favorite outfit by making your own festive jewelry. Modeling clay is easy to mold into shapes that can then be decorated. Give it a glittery finish by brushing on a special powder before baking, or simply mix a little varnish with glitter.

Mold a jolly snowman.

Christmas tree earrings

Glittering Christmas tree earrings add the perfect finishing touch to a festive outfit.

Green modeling clay
Brown modeling clay
Round-bladed kitchen knife
Modeling clay glitter powder
Paintbrush
2 eye pins
Pliers
2 Jump rings
2 Ear hooks

CHRISTMAS TREE EARRINGS

1 Break off a small piece of green modeling clay, and knead with your fingers until soft. Roll out into a sausage that tapers. Starting from the point of the sausage, cut off five discs, each about 0.1 inch in depth.

2 Place the discs on top of each other, and press gently together. Break off a tiny ball of green clay, and add to the top of the tree. Break off a small ball of the brown clay, and mold to make the trunk. Press into place.

3 Brush with glitter powder, and insert an eye pin, trimmed to fit, through each tree top. Bake in a low temperature oven, following the instructions on page 122. (Ask an adult to supervise this stage.)

4 Use pliers to open up the jump rings, and push through the eye pins on each baked tree. Close the rings. Open up the loops on the ear hooks, and slip through the jump rings. Close the loops again securely.

Enjoy making your own fun jewelry to wear throughout the festive season, or to give to family, and friends as presents.

▲ *These plumb puddings earrings are so realistic you could almost eat them. Make them out of modeling clay and wear them of Christmas day.*

▼ *Ready-made foil parcel decoration make great earrings — simple glue on a stud, or clip-on back.*

▼ *Decorate a plain hair comb with festive tinsel. Wrap around the top bar, taking the tinsel in, and out of the comb's teeth.*

▼ *These festive earrings would make an ideal Christmas present.*

Easter holidays jewelry

COLORFUL BROOCHES, EARRINGS, AND HAIR SLIDES ADD a touch of fun to Easter holiday outfits, and make great presents, too. Use the simple ideas shown here to inspire your own designs. Clay or cardboard can be cut, shaped, and decorated in endless ways, and the craft foam used to make the bunny hair slide is very versatile.

BIRD'S NEST SET

A fun bird's nest, complete with colorful eggs, has been made into a brooch and earring set that will brighten up the holiday.

1 Roll out balls of brown modeling clay, and squash flat with your thumb to make the bases — make the base for the brooch bigger than those for the earrings. Roll more brown clay into tiny sausage shapes of different lengths, and use to build up a nest shape on the base.

3 Wash your hands to remove any traces of brown modeling clay, and then mold small egg shapes in different colors. Position these inside the nest, pressing gently in place. Bake in a low temperature oven, following the instructions on page 122. (Ask an adult to supervise this stage.)

2 When the nest is the right size, add a few more shorter "sticks" to the middle, for the eggs to sit on.

4 Glue a brooch back to the base of the larger nest, and earring findings to the smaller nests.

Paint

Set your creativity free and you will find you can produce a whole host of original and exciting prints and gifts.

Introduction

Using paint is fun, and we have chosen plenty of projects to help you explore its qualities of color and texture. You will find lots of different experiments and ways of applying color, and we have included ways to use your results in things to make, with clear, step-by-step pictures for you to follow. It is nice to enjoy making things. To be able to give the things you have made to your family and friends makes it even better.

Read through each project before you start, so that you see what you will need and what is involved. To highlight safety, some of the photographs are bordered with red warning triangles, and the instructions are written in bold underlined text. You should make sure there is an adult present as **these steps involve the use of sharp knives, hot surfaces, or other things which could easily harm you**. There are a few safety rules and methods of working you should know. Read the next few pages before you get to work.

You will find that painting can give you hours of pleasure and become an interest for life.

SAFETY FIRST

The only rules that apply are safety rules. Some of the projects involve materials or processes that could be dangerous if they are misused. We have highlighted them throughout the book.

Be sure to:-
- follow the instructions found on the packaging of materials.
- be very careful when using scissors, craft knives, or other sharp items of equipment.
- be very careful if matches, an oven, or hot water are needed. Be sure the oven is switched off after use and that matches are fully extinguished.
- be very careful with liquids. Some can be dangerous. Read the precautions on the container. Avoid spillages. Wash any splashes off the skin immediately with water.
- keep your working surface neat and uncluttered.

ABOUT THE PROJECTS

See these projects as just beginnings. All of them can be taken further. Once you have found out how to do a particular technique, then use your own ideas for subjects. Always choose things that you are interested in.

These projects were selected because they do not rely too much on drawing skills, although of course they all contain an element of drawing. It is a good idea to get yourself a sketchbook. It does not need to be large, but a bound one is best. Use it to note down your own ideas and thoughts (they are easily forgotten) and to draw from nature, the world about you, your friends, your home. Anything and everything is useful to help you learn and to feed and inspire your imagination. See what other artists are doing. Talk with your friends and swap ideas. Go to local art galleries. Take out books about famous painters from the library.

Young artists often have expectations of their work and they become disheartened when the results fail to match up. It is nice to be surprised by your own work. See the projects as experiments that can be developed. The more projects you do, the better you will get, and so the more you will enjoy doing them.

Set your own creativity free.

TOOLS AND EQUIPMENT

We have kept the materials used in the projects at a simple level. They can be bought at art and craft stores, or from art departments in large stores, stationery stores, or toy stores.

All the paints and inks, etc., are water soluble. You only need water to mix with your paint, wash your brushes, and clean your rollers and other equipment. But, even water-based materials can stain; after all, that is what they are for! So it is a good idea to wear an old shirt or an apron.

Acrylic paints, although soluble in water while still wet, become waterproof when dry. If the paint on your brushes dries out, they dry waterproof, too! So your brushes and equipment must be washed immediately.

Cover your table with pieces of newspaper, plastic cloth, or plastic sheeting taped down. It is a good idea to cover the floor, too, especially if there is a carpet.

Make sure you clean all your equipment afterward and clean up. Keep your work safe and clean, too.

ADHESIVES AND GLUES

COLD-WATER PASTES Wallpaper paste is good for gluing paper, making papier-mâché, and mixing with paint. It is cheap and easily mixed. The directions for mixing the paste will be on the package, but often the directions are for large amounts and may vary according to the make. As a general guide, use six heaping teaspoonfuls to a half pint of water. You can adjust this later if necessary. Pastes often contain fungicide. Cold-water pastes without fungicides can be obtained from art stores.

DOUBLE-SIDED TRANSPARENT TAPE Useful for immediate and invisible sticking together of two surfaces of paper, cardboard, etc.

GLUE STICK Good for sticking paper, cardboard, cloth, etc. It dries quickly and does not cause the paper to wrinkle.

MASKING OR DRAFTING TAPE Masking tape is useful for anchoring your work securely to a board or work surface as it peels off easily afterward.

CRAFT GLUE A white liquid glue. It is good for gluing wood, cloth, cardboard, paper, etc. It does not stick immediately, so you may have to leave your work under a weight, or secured temporarily with clothespins until the glue sets.

TRANSPARENT TAPE Useful for immediate joining of cardboard, paper, etc. when the seams will not be in view.

DYES

COLD-WATER DYE These are simple to use and are obtainable from hardware and department stores. They need water from the hot faucet and salt to mix with the setting ingredient.

FABRIC PAINT A variety of brands are available. The paints are usually packed in small jars. Simple to use, the colors are normally set by __ironing with a hot iron__. These directions may vary with different brands.

FABRIC PENS These are very similar to ordinary felt-tipped pens, but the colors can be set by __ironing with a hot iron__. These directions may vary with different kinds.

EQUIPMENT

BENCH HOOK Used in linocutting. One end hooks over the worktable edge, the other provides a surface to push the linoleum against and prevent it from slipping. It allows you to keep your fingers out of the way of the cutters. It is very simply made from scraps of wood.

A piece of wood
or chipboard   6 x 9 x ¾ inches
Two pieces of wood   6 x 1 x 1 inches
Four wood screws   1¼ or 1½ inch

Simply screw the pieces of the 1-inch-square wood to the front

and back of the larger piece of wood, but at opposite ends. This will make a Z-shape when seen from the side. See illustration above.

BRUSHES Both bristle and soft hair brushes are useful and available in a variety of sizes and shapes. A medium-sized bristle brush, flat or round shape, is ideal for general use. Change to a different size when you need to; a large brush if you have a large area to cover, a small brush if there are small shapes and detail to paint.

Cheap soft brushes can be too floppy and blunt-ended, and will be irritating and hard to use. Sable brushes are best, but are extremely expensive. There are, however, many soft brushes made with synthetic fibers at more reasonable prices. Stenciling brushes are made from bristles put together to make a flat-ended, round shaped brush. They are available in different sizes.

Keep all your brushes clean. Be especially careful when using acrylic paints. Never leave brushes standing in a jar of water, as this will bend the hair.

CRAFT KNIFE There are many designs of craft knife available. If you need to use one, look for its safety qualities. Get one with a retractable blade. Make sure the knife is not thin and flexible. Always keep the knife closed when it is not in use, and in a safe place.

<u>**Keep your fingers out of the way when you are cutting.**</u> You will need a surface to cut on, a piece of hardboard for instance, to prevent cuts on your table or floor. Special cutting mats and boards are available.

INKING PLATE This is the name given to a flat sheet of plastic, thick glass, or metal that is used for rolling printing ink on.

LINOLEUM The linoleum used in linocuts is of a particular kind. It can be bought from art and craft stores already cut into small rectangles. A thick vinyl is also available as an alternative.

LINOLEUM CUTTERS A set of different shaped cutters, together with a handle, comes in a box, usually with instructions for use. They are available from art and craft stores. They are sharp and should be used with care.

PAINT ROLLERS AND SPONGES Use them with ready-mixed paints, particularly for large-scale work. They can be used for simple printing with paint.

PALETTES Use them for putting out small amounts of paint, diluting paint, and mixing new colors. Those with nine large wells are very useful, especially for ready-mixed paint. Remember that acrylic paint dries hard and will not wash off. You can often use empty plastic food containers as palettes which can be thrown away when they are no longer useful.

PRINT ROLLERS Used particularly for inking linoleum print blocks, but are also used in relief printing and mono printing. They spread the ink out evenly on the printing surface. The roller has a hard rubber surface. Keep the roller clean and do not let the surface become damaged. When the roller is inked up, but not in use, rest it on its back, so that the roller itself is not left in contact with the inking plate.

RAGS, PAPER TOWELS Always have paper towels or lint-free rags at hand. Use them for wiping your brushes and equipment, and also in case they are needed for mopping up spills.

SCISSORS Use a pair of scissors that feel comfortable, not too large or small. There are safety scissors available, but it is important to get ones that cut. Avoid those with very sharp points. Never walk around holding an opened pair of scissors.

INKS

COLORED DRAWING INKS

These are made with dyes and are transparent but strongly colored. They can be diluted with water, and the brushes used can be washed in water, but the ink dries waterproof.

INDIA INK A black waterproof ink. It can be diluted with water, and the brushes used can be washed in water. It dries waterproof.

INK PAD These are obtainable from stationery stores. They are used for stamping, etc.

WATER-SOLUBLE PRINTING INK This looks more like paint than ink. It is used with a roller and an inking plate in relief printing, particularly linocuts. It is also useful for mono printing. They can be diluted with water and the equipment cleaned with water. They do not dry waterproof.

PAINTS

ACRYLIC PAINT Acrylics generally have a better choice of colors than ready-mixed paints and are more expensive. Dilute them with water and wash your brushes in water. Acrylics dry waterproof and quickly. These are very useful qualities, but you must be careful to keep your brushes and equipment washed clean.

READY-MIXED PAINT Brightly colored and water-soluble, these paints are cheap and easily available. They are useful for painting on paper, cardboard, etc.

SILK VINYL PAINT A paint made for interior decorating. It is very similar in character to acrylic. White silk vinyl can be used for printing nonmetal surfaces. It dilutes in water, and brushes and equipment are washed in water. It dries waterproof.

PAPER AND CARDBOARD

CARDBOARD Available in a great variety of thicknesses, colors, and finishes. Thin cardboard is most suitable for constructing boxes, printing greeting cards, and making frames or mats for your pictures. Cardboard from cereal boxes, etc., is very useful. Use it for making combs and spreaders for use with paint. Glue materials to it when making relief printing blocks, and use it for making templates.

CARTRIDGE PAPER A general-purpose white paper for drawing and painting. It is available in different-sized sheets or pads and in different weights. The heavier weight indicates a thicker paper.

LINING PAPER Produced for lining walls prior to painting or wallpapering. It is sold in rolls, is cheap, and is particularly useful if you need a good length of paper, for a frieze, for instance.

NEWSPRINT Newsprint is available from art and craft stores by the sheet. Many cheap drawing pads are made with it. However, it is useful for large-scale work if you can get the end of a roll from a newspaper office or wastepaper merchant. They usually make a small charge for it.

CONSTRUCTION PAPER A thin but strong paper, it is available in intense, bright colors from stationery stores and art and craft stores. Useful for printing on and using as wrapping.

VARNISH

INTERIOR QUICK-DRYING VARNISH Used for giving a final gloss or satin coat to craftwork. It dries in thirty minutes, is low odor, and brushes are cleaned simply in water.

WAX CRAYONS

WAX CRAYONS Sold in sets of bright colors. The thick ones are the easiest to handle and less likely to break. They are available in long and short sizes.

TECHNIQUES

RELIEF PRINTING

This term applies to all the printing processes where ink is applied to the top surface of a printing block and then printed onto paper. The printing block may be made from many things. Traditionally, it was wood or metal, but it can also be made from linoleum or thick cardboard. You can also print directly from objects by rolling printing ink or paint over them and pressing onto paper.

INKING UP

For relief printing with a roller and printing ink, you need to roll some ink on an inking plate first. Squeeze out an inch or so of ink onto the plate. You can spread it out with a plastic knife if you have one. Use your roller to distribute the ink evenly over the inking plate by rolling back and forth. Try to keep the ink in a rectangle and not spread all over the plate. Roll in

one direction and then at right angles to it, until you have no lumps or holes in the ink surface.

Listen to the sound of the roller on the ink. If it is making a loud, tearing kind of sound, it is too thick. You should spread it out a bit more, until it makes more of a hissing sound when you roll it. If the ink itself is too thick, or the plate is drying up, the ink can be diluted with a little water.

When the roller is inked, you then transfer it to your block and roll over the surface several times in each direction until the ink is evenly distributed over the surface.

MONO PRINTING

This term applies to those printing processes where the print is more or less unique. The simplest way is perhaps to paint directly onto a flat surface, such as an inking plate. Then place a sheet of paper over it and press down. You will produce

"Love Letters," make sure that you complete "A Basic Linocut Print" project on page 256, so that you learn the techniques properly.

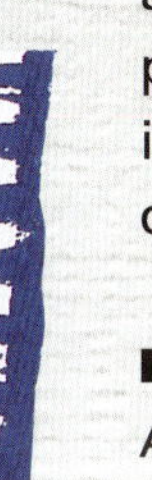

a mirror-image print of your painting. The process imparts interesting textural and chance qualities of its own.

LINO PRINTING

A lino print is a relief print. You make your own printing block by cutting the design into a piece of linoleum with special cutting tools. It is very similar to the much older craft of woodcut printing. You can print a virtually unlimited number of identical prints. The simplest method of making a print is to use one color. Multicolored prints can be made by cutting and printing at different stages, or by using more than one block. Before you try to make the "Cut-out Clown" or the

PAINTING

Painting is the most direct and expressive way to apply color. There are a number of different kinds of paint that can be mixed with water, and they each have their own qualities of handling. They can all be thinned down to a transparent quality with water, and to a certain extent, all can be used opaquely, too. Acrylic paint can be used very thickly, but ready-mixed paint (and gouache or poster paint) will crack and come away if used too thickly. Those paints called watercolors are designed to be used transparently.

Glue such as craft glue or wallpaper paste, which has been mixed with water, can be added to ready-mixed paint to give it more texture.

All these paints will work on most absorbent surfaces such as wood, cardboard, paper, or cloth. On shiny or plastic surfaces it is useful sometimes to add dish washing detergent to your paint to help it spread and adhere.

STENCILING

Stenciling is a particular way of painting that allows you to produce an unlimited amount of identical images. Using a stencil brush, you dab color through holes cut in thin cardboard or plastic. Hold the brush upright to achieve the best results, and lift the stencil off carefully. There are many different stencils available in art and craft stores; patterns, animals, flowers, people, etc. They are very useful as a way of decorating all kinds of surfaces; wooden boxes, walls, and furniture as well as paper. You can also combine them to make pictures. It is sometimes necessary to hold a stencil in place with masking tape. You can buy stencil paper and cut your own designed stencil, or use "found" or ready-made objects, such as paper doilies, as stencils.

MIXING COLORS

All of the paints used in *Arts for Children* can be mixed to make new colors.

Red plus yellow makes orange
Red plus blue makes purple
Blue plus yellow makes green

Red, blue, and yellow are called primary colors. Green, purple, and orange are called secondary colors. You may find that your mixing does not make the expected result. For instance, if you want to make purple, you need red and blue. If the red you use is an orange sort of red, you will get a brownish color because you are adding yellow to the mixture. You can experiment and see just how many different colors are possible by mixing the colors you have.

MAKING A FRAME

It often helps to display your work by mounting it in a cardboard frame. Cut a "window" in a piece of cardboard, allowing a couple of inches all around as a border. Remember to cut the hole in the cardboard smaller than your picture. If your picture comes right up to the edge of the paper it is on, you can only overlap the frame by a quarter-inch or so. If there is a lot of space around your picture, you can cut a smaller hole, bringing the frame edge closer into your picture.

Decide how big your window is going to be and measure it carefully on the cardboard. With thin cardboard you can cut the hole out with scissors. Hold the picture in place behind the hole with tape.

SCORING

When you are making things from paper or cardboard, you will often need to make folds. To make a neat fold, it is useful to score along the fold line first. Run the back edge of a pair of scissors along the line of the fold, thus making an impression along the line. Make sure to do it on what will be the inside of the fold. You may find another implement that works well; a letter opener or a plastic modeling tool, perhaps.

Painting

Think Ink

Try these three ways of playing with color.
See what effects and forms you can create with ink.

YOU WILL NEED

- Masking tape
- Board or newspaper
- Sponge roller
- Large plastic tray
- Water
- Eye droppers
- Colored inks (blue, purple, yellow, red)
- Containers for inks
- Drinking straws
- Plain white paper towels
- Paper

Experiment 1

1 Tape your paper onto a board or newspaper with masking tape. Dampen the paper using the sponge roller.

2 Use the eye dropper to drop a few drops of colored ink onto the damp paper. Watch the way it spreads.

3 Clean the dropper if you only have one. (Some colored inks have droppers already in their lids.) Drop another color onto the paper. Watch how the colors blend. Try dropping on some spots of water, too.

Experiment 2

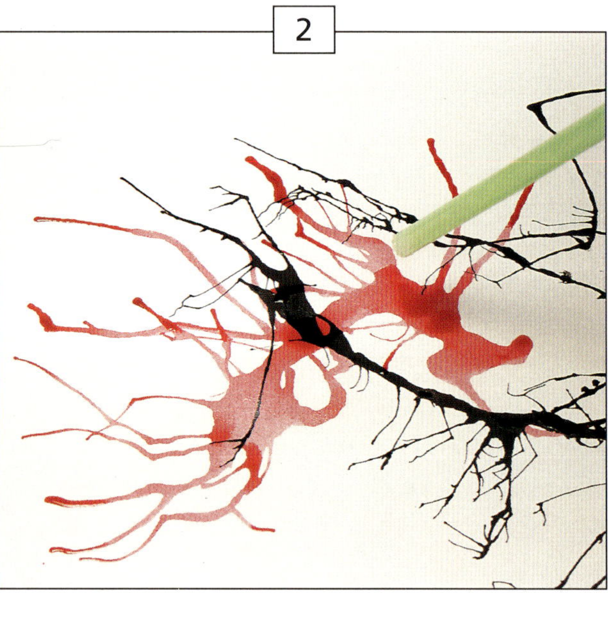

1 Take a sheet of dry paper. Drop some ink on it.

2 Blow the ink through your straw. You can chase it across the paper. See how it splits like a tree's branches. Try some more colors. Turn the paper around. Wave the straw around while you are blowing.

Experiment 3

1 Put a few drops of colored ink into separate containers. Dilute them with a little water. Take a white paper towel and fold it into eight.

2 Dip a corner into one of the colors. Then dip another corner into a different colored ink. Continue with the other corners.

3 Unfold and let it dry.

TIP

☛ Now try folding the paper in different ways – diagonally perhaps – and dipping it differently.

2
3
TIP
☛ Try combining two of
the experiments.

Wax and Wash

Wax naturally resists water and so provides the process
for this visually dramatic technique.

- Wax crayons
- Paper
- Palette
- Ready-mixed paint (black)
- Water
- Paintbrushes
- Plain white candle (optional)

Painting 1

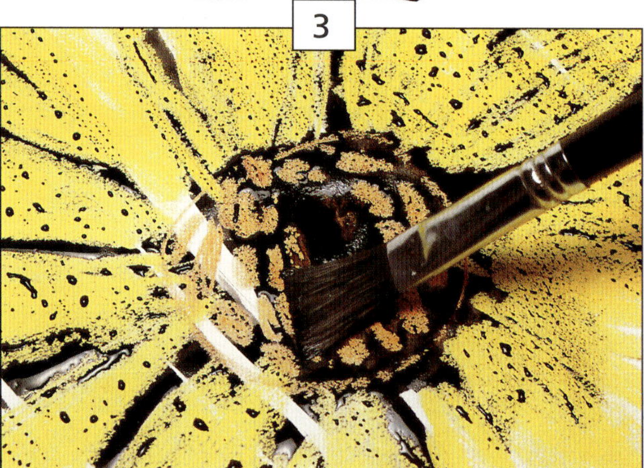

1 Draw firmly on your paper with the wax crayons.

2 Thin a dark-colored paint with some water. Now brush a wash of the paint over your wax-crayon drawing.

3 The wax resists the water paint and shows through.

4 Put the paint on lightly, without rubbing it too hard.

Painting 2

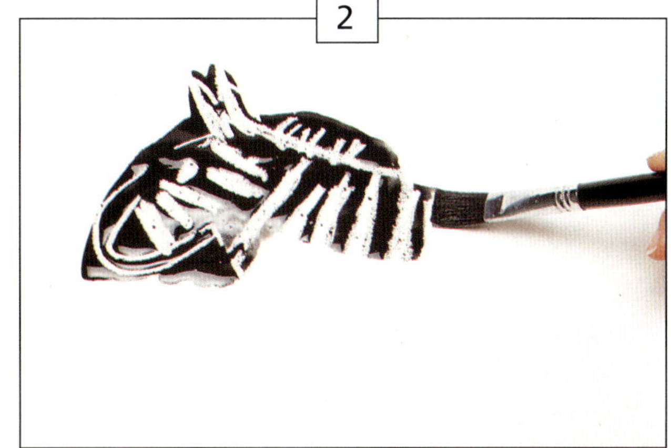

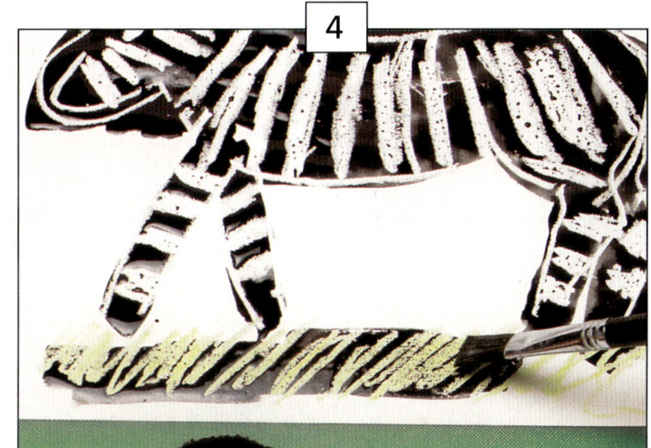

1 Try drawing with a candle or white wax crayon. It is hard to see what you have drawn, but if you tilt the paper toward the light, you can just see it.

2 Paint over the drawing with black paint. Your picture will begin to appear.

3 Paint only where you have drawn with the crayon.

4 When you have painted over all the white crayon, your picture will be revealed.

Wash Away

When you put your painting under running water, watch your picture gradually appear. The unexpected qualities and textures that result are always a surprise and visually exciting.

YOU WILL NEED

- Ready-mixed paint (not acrylic) (white)
- Containers for paint
- Paintbrushes
- Cartridge paper
- India ink or waterproof black ink

1 Using the white paint, paint all the parts of your picture that you want to remain white. Make sure the paint is fairly thick. Leave gaps where you want black lines.

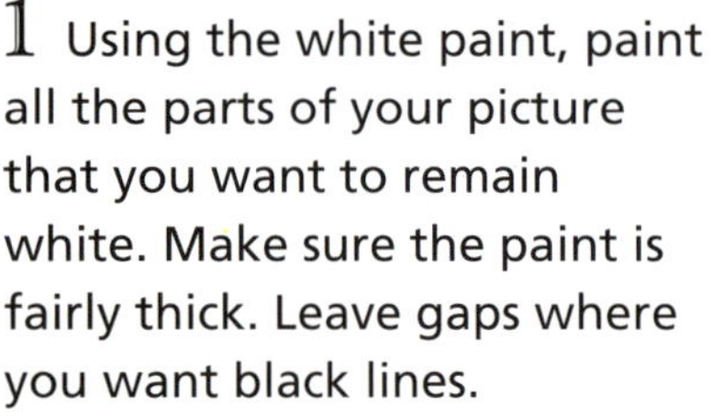

2 When your painting is dry, paint over the whole paper with black ink.

3 When the ink is dry, hold your painting under cold running water. The ink will wash away where the white paint was and leave that paper exposed.

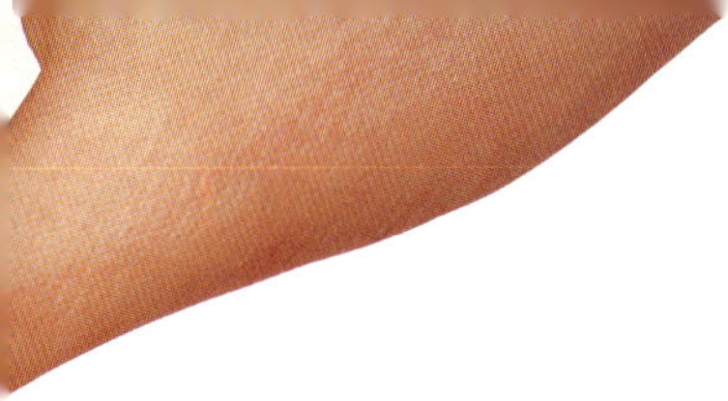

4 You may need to rub gently with your fingertips to remove all the ink from the painted areas, but take care not to rip the paper. Leave it to dry.

TIP

☛ Try the process with a different-colored waterproof ink.

Paint a Pot

Brighten up your windowsill by transforming your flowerpots
with these colorful designs.

- Terracotta flowerpots
- Acrylic paints (black, white, orange, red)
- Paintbrushes
- Water
- Pencil

1 Make sure the flowerpots are clean. You may have to scrub them if they are old. Give the pot a coat of white paint first where you want to paint your patterns. Hold the pot sideways by the rim. Turn the pot as you go. Allow the paint to dry.

2 You can draw your chosen design on with a pencil if you want to.

3 Use strong bright colors. Keep the paint thick. Paint patterns around the pot.

4 Let the paint dry before painting another color on top of it. You can add diagonal stripes, dots, or crosses, for example. Leave the black stripes until last.

TIP

☞ These Mexican-looking designs will go well with a collection of cacti.

Play and Paint

Get together with your friends and work on a painting big enough for you all to have a turn . . . where anything goes.

YOU WILL NEED

- Ready-mixed paint (green, red, black, brown, blue, yellow)
- Flat trays for paint
- Water
- Sponge rollers/sponges
  A large sheet of paper (perhaps you can tape sheets of newsprint or lining paper together)

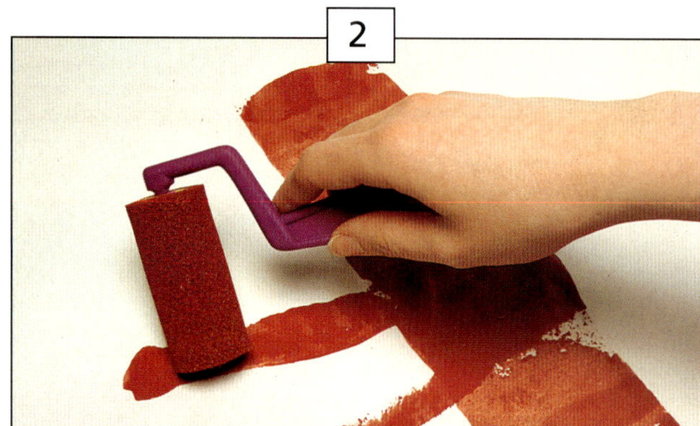

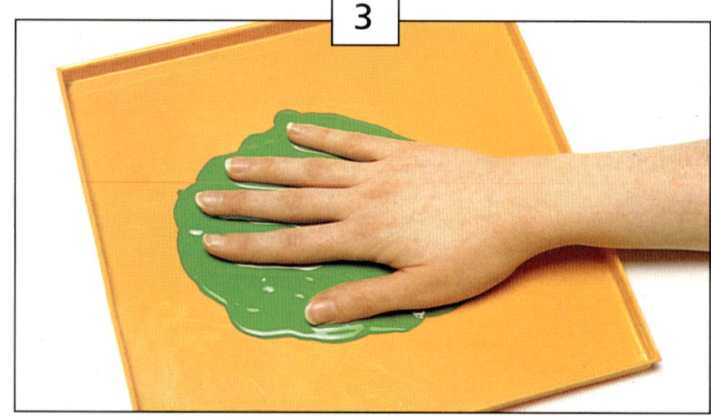

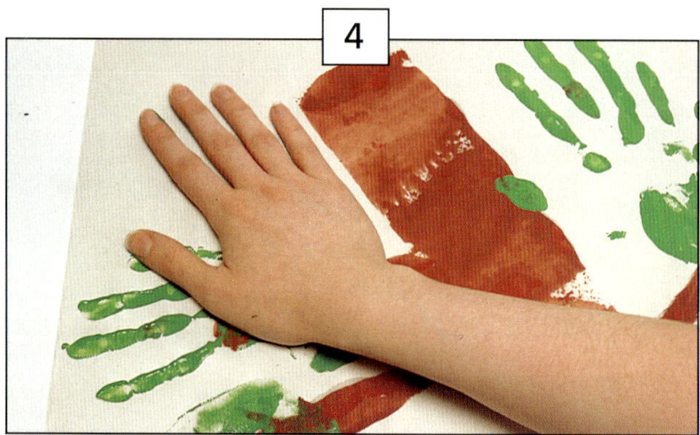

1 Three basic shapes are used in this painting. Put some paint in a tray and dilute with a little water. Use the sponge rollers to draw tree trunks, branches, and landscape.

2 You can use the edge of the roller for thinner lines.

3 Spread out some green paint in a large, flat tray. Put one of your hands into the paint.

4 Spread out your fingers and print leaves on the trees.

5 Use sponges to print bricks for the buildings.

TIP

☞ Tape the paper to a wall if you can. Put some newspaper along the bottom to catch any drips. On a nice day you can work outside in the yard or in the garage.

6 With your friends, work together to paint the picture.

Petal Paperweight

First catch your stone! This project shows you how to make a paperweight. However, if you find a large stone, you can make it into a doorstop in exactly the same way!

- Your chosen stone
- Acrylic or ready-mixed paints (white, blue, yellow, orange, brown)
- Paintbrushes
- Pencil
- Paper
- Scrap of cardboard
- Scissors
- Felt
- Craft glue
- Clear varnish

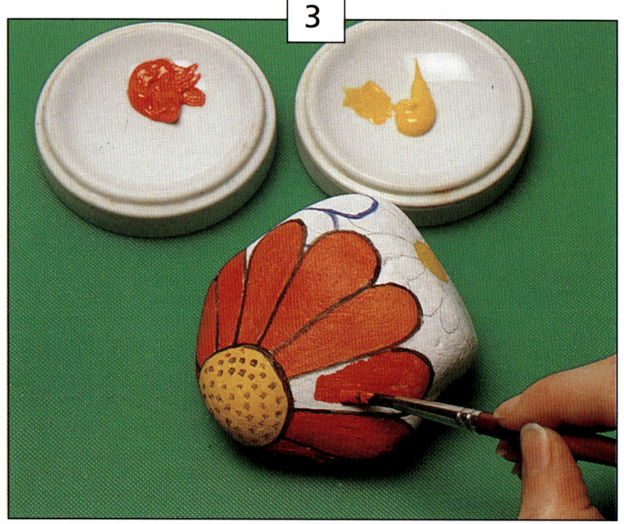

1 Wash your stone well and let it dry. Its shape can give you an idea of what to paint on it. Find which is the best way to stand it. Give the stone a coat of white paint. This will seal the surface and make the colors brighter, especially if you have a dark stone.

2 Draw your design on the stone in pencil.

3 When you are completely satisfied with your design, paint the stone.

4 When you have finished painting the stone, let it dry. Stand it on a piece of paper and draw around it to make a template to fit the base of the stone.

5 <u>**Use the template to cut out the piece of felt.**</u>

6 Glue the felt shape to the base of the stone with craft glue.

7 Finally, give your stone a coat of varnish.

Bright Light

Make these simple, but attractive candle holders, by recycling jars.

YOU WILL NEED

- Glass jars
- Scissors
- Black felt-tipped pen
- Paper
- Soft paintbrushes
- Acrylic paints (yellow, orange, white)
- Shallow containers
- Night lights or short candles

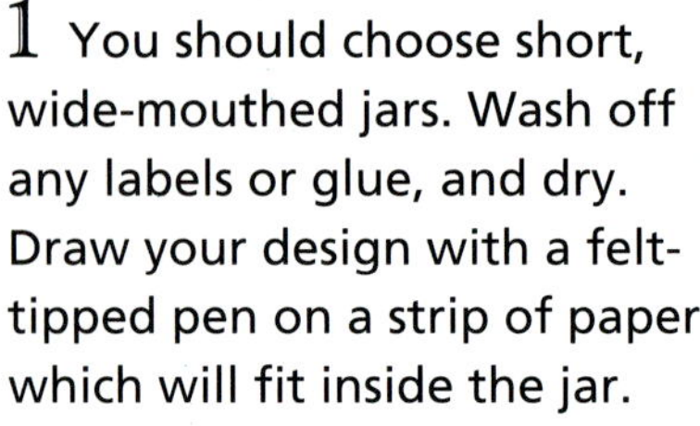

1 You should choose short, wide-mouthed jars. Wash off any labels or glue, and dry. Draw your design with a felt-tipped pen on a strip of paper which will fit inside the jar.

2 Put the design in the jar. Position the drawing where you want the design to be.

3 Try to paint on the glass jar with single brush strokes. Don't let the paint get too watery or it will run.

4 Gradually build up your design using different colors.

5 Slide the paper around in the jar, bringing the next part of your design into its correct position.

6 Now paint the next element of your design.

7 Remove your paper design. Stand your night lights or candles in the middle of your jars. Adults have longer fingers than you do, **they can use long matches to light the candles.**

Deep Sea Frieze

Use thick paint and combs to create a frieze of underwater life.

YOU WILL NEED

- Wallpaper paste
- Plastic bowl
- Plastic containers
- Ready-mixed paint (orange, green, brown, blue)
- Scissors
- Scrap cardboard
- Paintbrush
- A long sheet of paper (lining paper – or the back of some old wallpaper)

1 Mix some wallpaper paste to a very thick consistency. See page 180.

2 Put some paste into your containers with a different color paint in each and mix.

3 Cut up cardboard to paint with. Cut notches along the edge on some of them to make combs of different sizes.

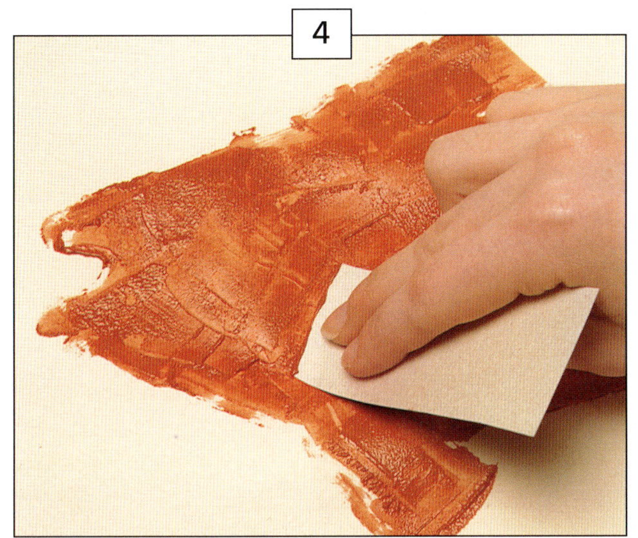

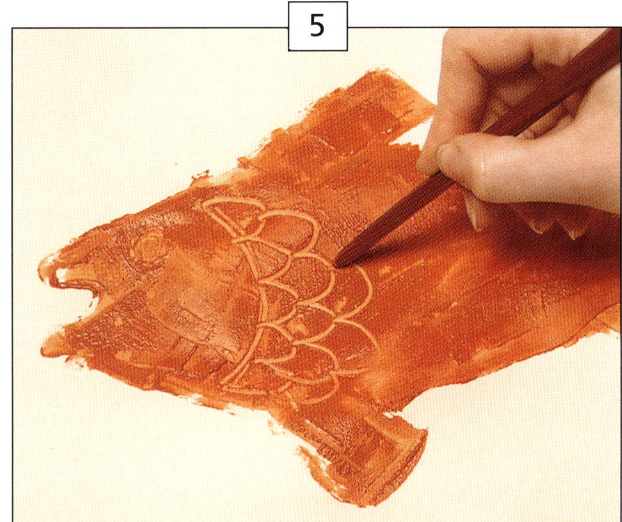

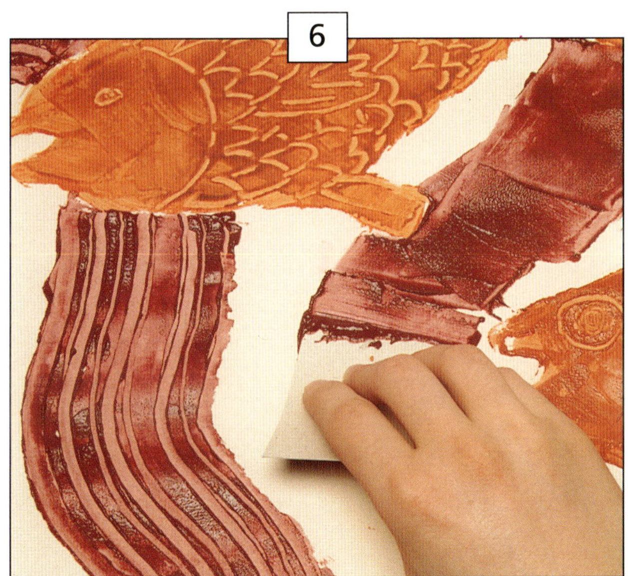

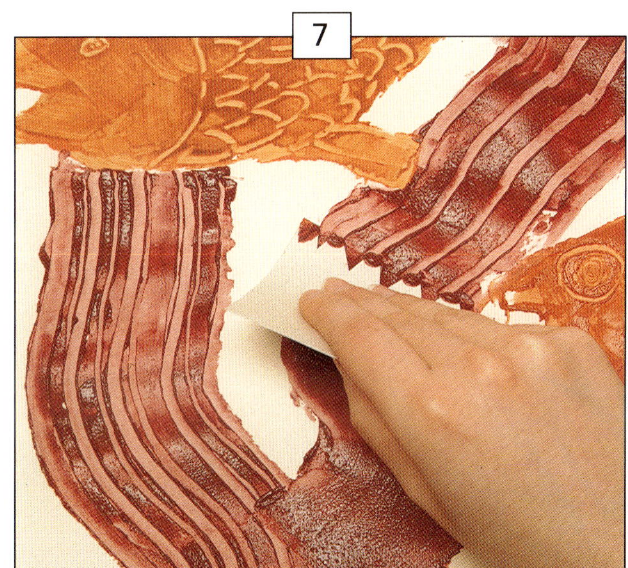

4 Paint the big fish with a flat piece of cardboard.

5 Draw into the paint with the end of a paintbrush handle to make the scales.

6 Now paint the seaweed using flat pieces of cardboard to spread the paint.

7 Scrape through it with the notched combs, so that the paint shows up in lines.

8 Now paint the sea by spreading the paint on with flat cardboard.

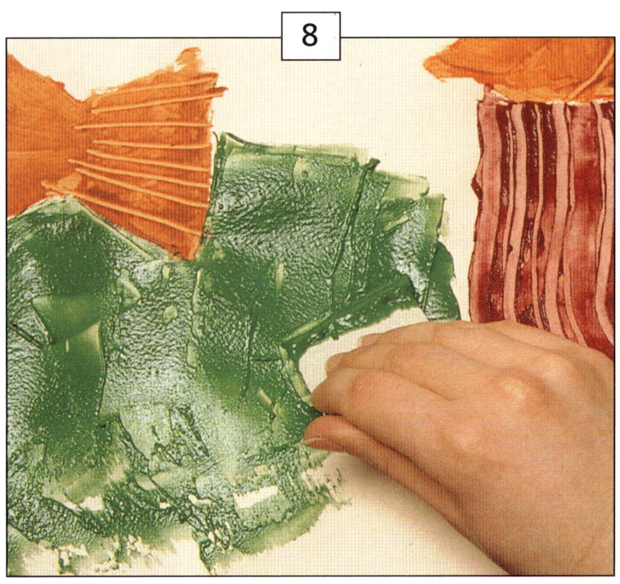

9

10

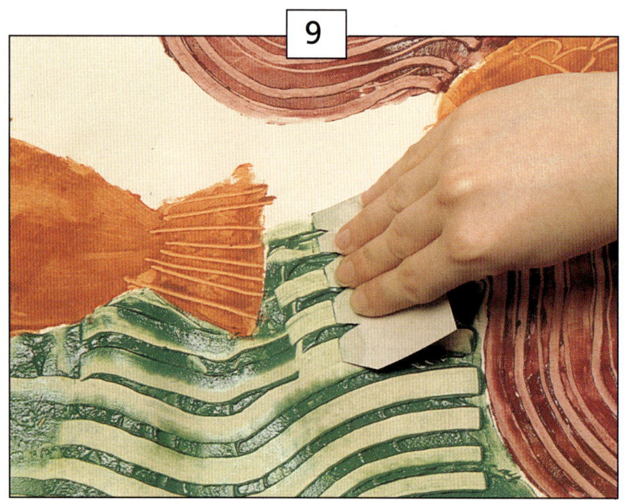

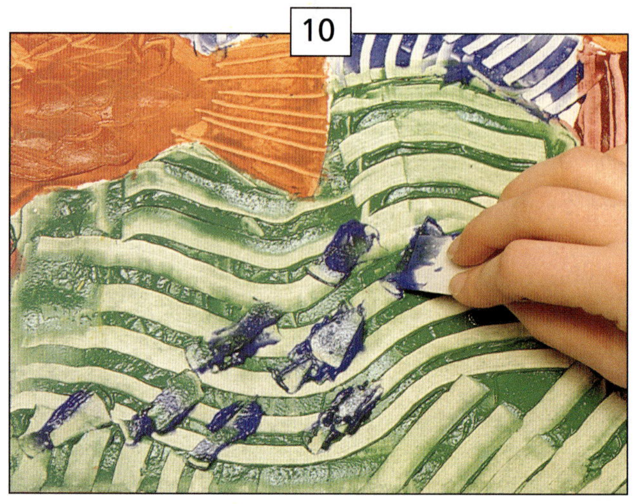

9 Make the water swirl and flow. Make the seaweed wave in the movement.

TIP

☛ Join the lengths of your underwater scenes together to form a frieze which you could put around the room.

10 Little fish swim in groups that flow and spiral like water. Put the fishes in using narrow pieces of cardboard.

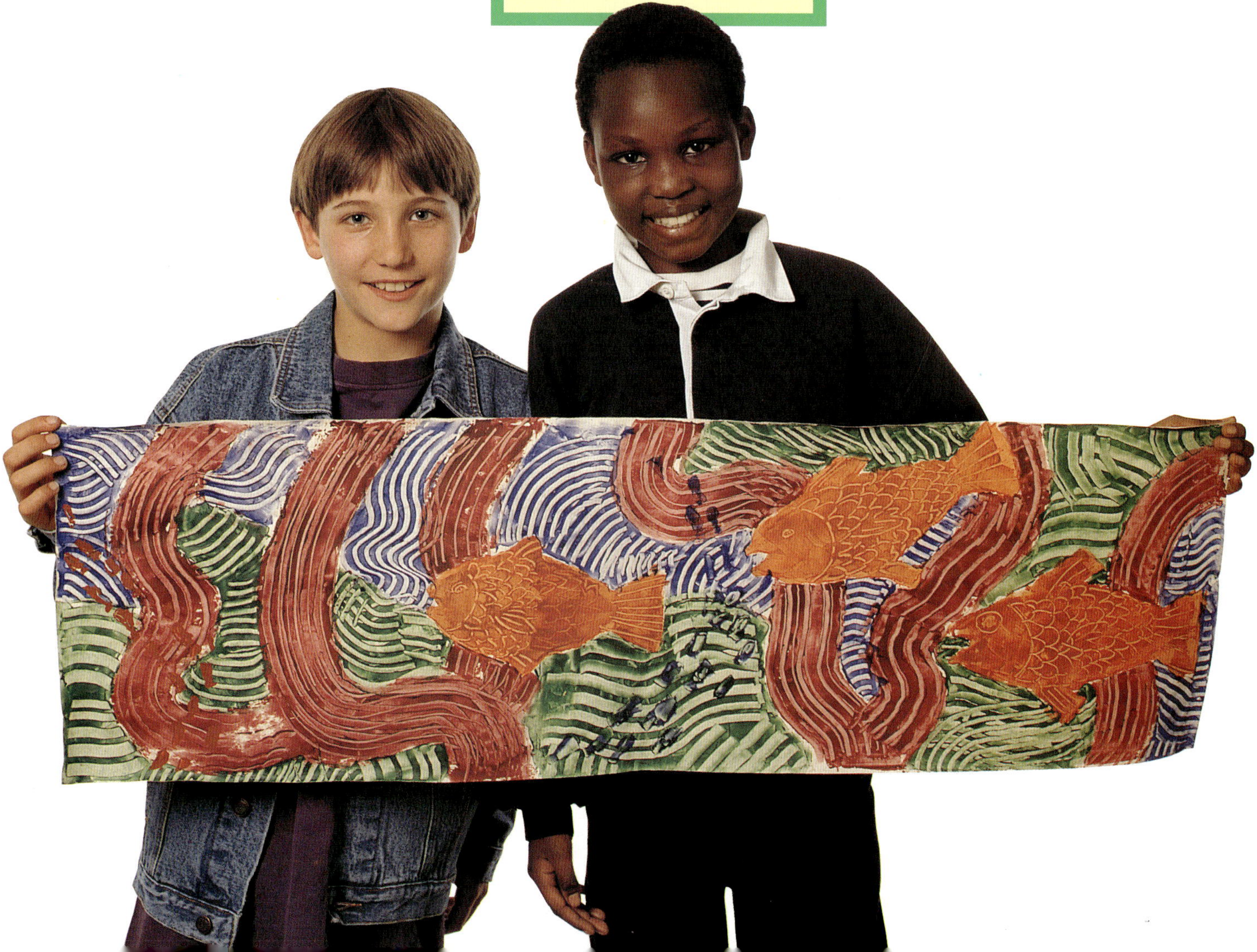

Stripes and Circles

Change your own boring leggings into these far-out striped ones.

YOU WILL NEED

- String
- Washed cotton leggings
- Dishwashing bowl
- Water
- Rubber gloves
- Cold-water dye (purple)
- Pitcher
- Salt
- Cold dye fixative
- Wooden spoon or stick
- Laundry detergent

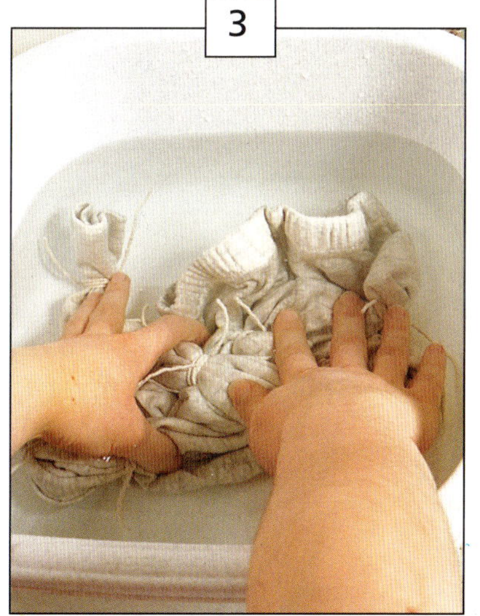

1 Wind the string around one of the legs and tie tightly. Continue tying along both legs, about 2–3 inches apart.

2 As you get near the top of the legs, you can bunch up the cloth and tie around it with the string. These will come out as circles.

3 Fill a dishwashing bowl with water and push the leggings under the water. Make sure they are wet all over. Then remove them and squeeze out any excess water.

4 Fill the bowl again with enough cold water to cover the leggings. **Wear the rubber gloves now and for the next 4 steps. Dissolve the dye in 1 pint hottest tap water in the pitcher. Stir well and add to bowl. Dissolve 4 ounces salt and one sachet of cold dye fixative in about ½ pint hottest tap water and add to bowl.**

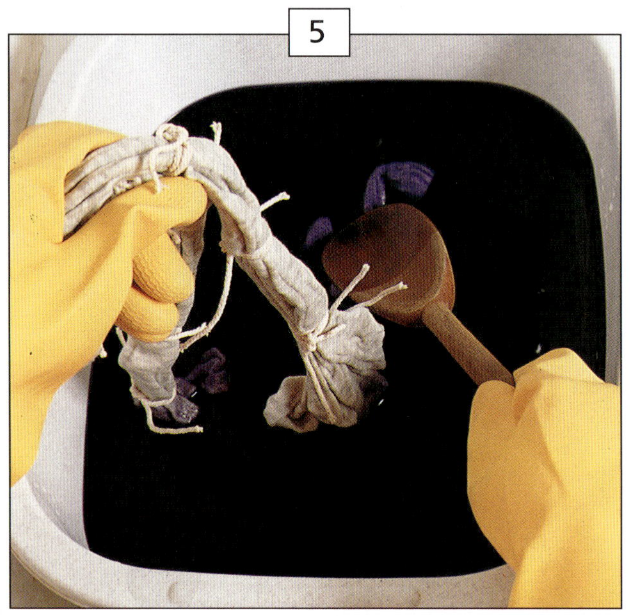

5 Put the damp leggings into the colored dye. Leave in for one hour.

6 Use the wooden spoon/stick to stir the leggings around for the first ten minutes. After that, stir occasionally. Make sure they stay under water.

7 Remove leggings from the dye – squeeze out excess dye.

8 Rinse under cold water until the water runs clear. **Wash in hot water with your usual washing detergent.**

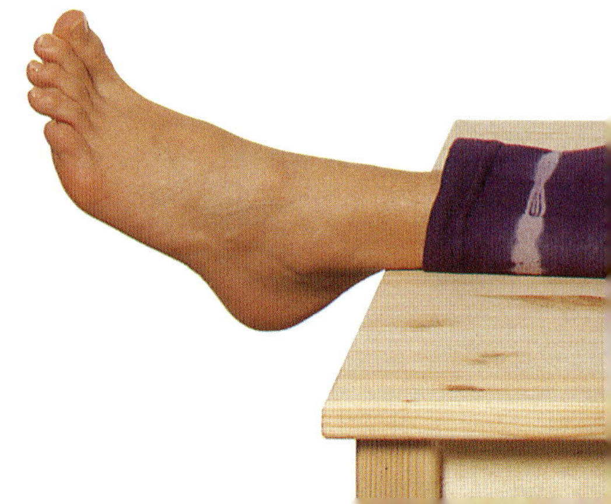

9 Undo the strings.

10 The stripes and circles will be revealed as you untie the string. Dry leggings as usual.

TIP

☛ You can use this technique on any cotton garment such as a shirt or T-shirt. Lighter colored garments dye best.

Make Friends

You will need someone else to work with you on this project.
Your companion can be whoever you want.

YOU WILL NEED

- Newsprint
- Black felt-tipped pen
- Palette
- Ready-mixed paint
- Paintbrushes
- Scissors
- Craft knife
- Craft glue
- Large cardboard box or sheets of cardboard
- Glue stick
- Pieces of wood

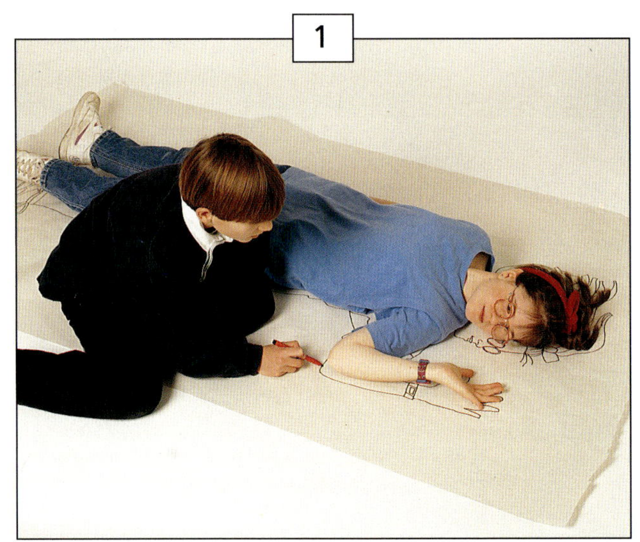

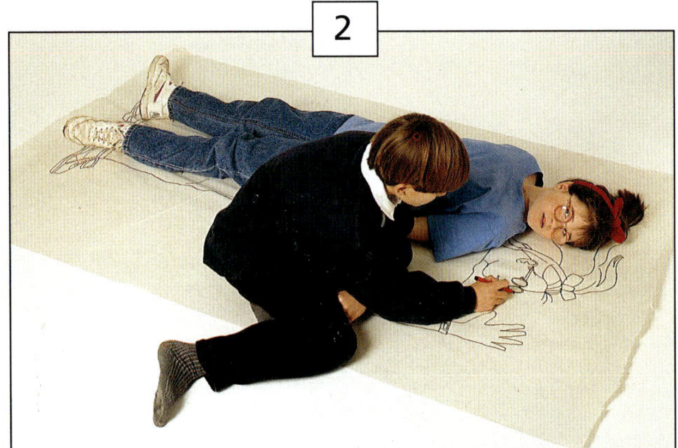

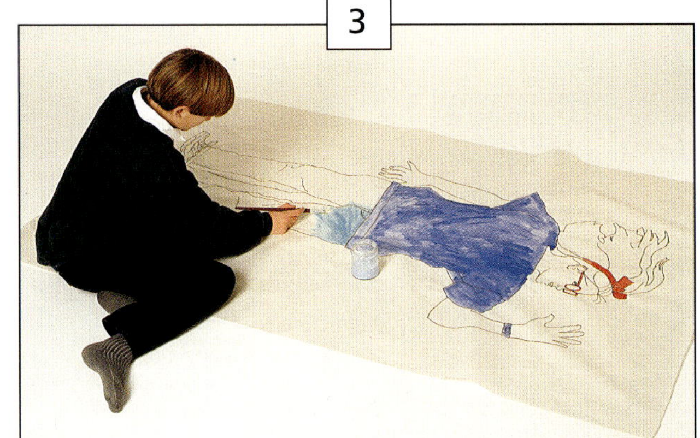

1 Lay the newsprint on the floor. It is best if you lie on a hard surface. Lie down on the newsprint and take a pose. Ask your partner to draw around you with a felt-tipped pen. Keep the pen vertical.

2 Be sure to try to get all the details. Move over to one side, in the same pose, so that your partner can draw in your features, clothes, etc.

3 Paint your figure.

4 **Then cut out your figure.** You could hang it on your bedroom door at this stage.

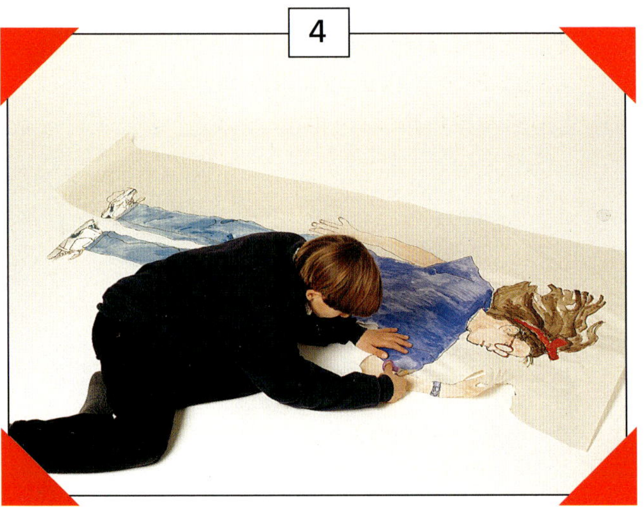

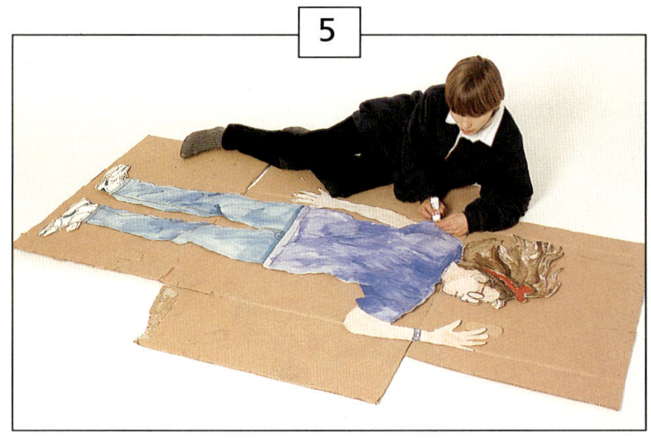

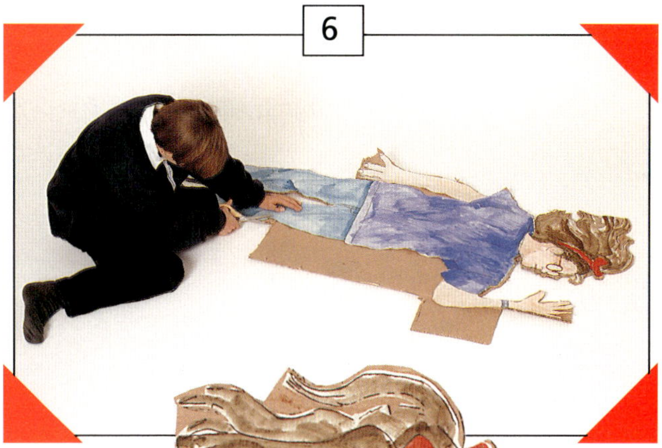

5 If you want your figure to be sturdier, you could open out a large cardboard box or glue some sheets of cardboard together and glue your painting on it.

6 **You can then cut your figure out using scissors or a craft knife**.

7 You may need to glue some sticks on the back to make your figure rigid. Use craft glue for this. Stand your figure up using a bamboo pole or a long stick as a prop.

TIP

☛ If your figure is a superhero, it could be flying and suspended from the ceiling.

Sunflower T-shirt

Turn a plain white T-shirt into this sunny-looking design using fabric paints and pens.

YOU WILL NEED

- White cotton T-shirt
- Tracing paper
- Pencil
- Scrap cardboard
- Scissors
- Black felt-tipped pen
- Paper
- Fabric color pen (purple, black)
- Thumbtacks
- Board
- Clean cloth
- Iron
- Ironing board
- Fabric paints (green, yellow, orange)
- Paintbrushes

1 If you use a new T-shirt, you must wash it first to get rid of the dressing. If it is not new, you must still make sure it is clean and flat. Trace the templates on page 263. Transfer the tracings to cardboard and **cut them out.**

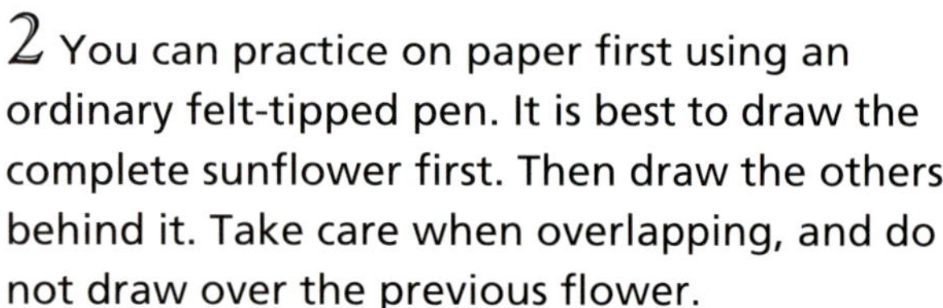

2 You can practice on paper first using an ordinary felt-tipped pen. It is best to draw the complete sunflower first. Then draw the others behind it. Take care when overlapping, and do not draw over the previous flower.

3 Pin the T-shirt onto a board. When you are happy with your design on paper, you are ready to print the T-shirt.

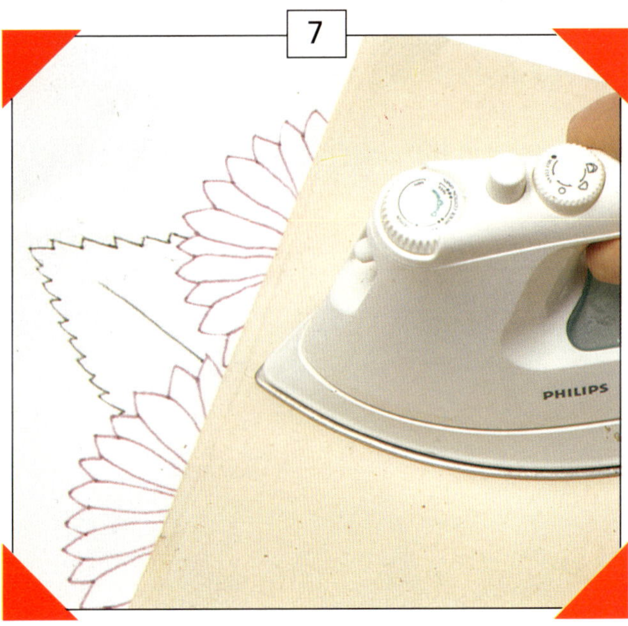

4 Put a sheet of cardboard or layers of paper inside the T-shirt to stop the colors from soaking through.

5 Draw around the flower templates using a fabric pen. Use a different-color pen to draw around the leaf template. Overlap the flowers, and add the leaves.

6 You will need to draw in the lines for the petals for the sunflower. When you have drawn the sunflowers and leaves onto your T-shirt, let the design dry for five minutes.

7 Then cover the T-shirt with a clean cloth. **Ask an adult to help you iron the design for 1–2 minutes on a cotton setting to seal the ink.**

TIP

☛ Different paints and pens might have slightly different directions. Follow the instructions on the pack.

8 Use the fabric paint to fill in the drawing. It may be necessary to mix red and yellow paints together for the orange in the sunflower. Use a small-bristle brush for the main parts and a small soft brush for details.

9 Allow the paint to dry for four hours. **Then ask an adult to help you iron the reverse side of the design for 2 minutes. The iron should be set on cotton.** This will set the fabric paint.

It's My Party

Use stencils to brighten up paper tableware for a party with your friends.

YOU WILL NEED

- Acrylic paints (orange, green)
- Water
- Shallow containers
- Stencil brushes
- Stencils
- Paper
- Paper tablecloth and napkins
- White paper plates, cups
- Folded cards
- Envelopes

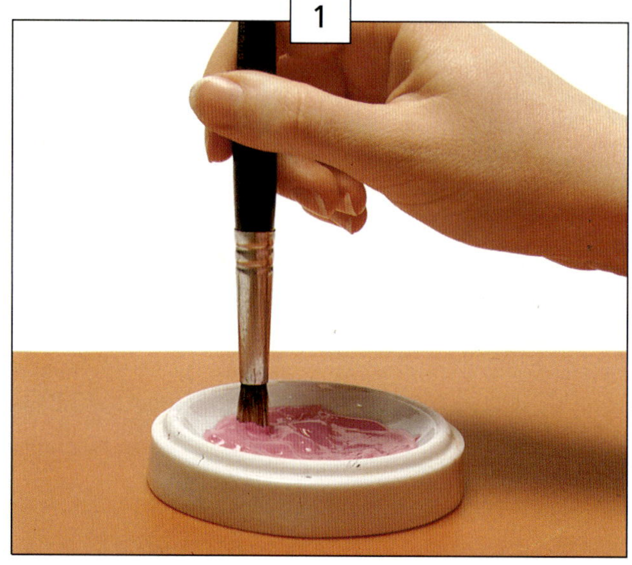

1 Put a little color in a shallow container. First, try stenciling on some paper. Hold your stencil brush vertically and dab it into the paint.

2 Try out a few different stencils first. Hold the stencil down on your paper. Now dab your brush vertically on the stencil until the space is covered. If the paint is too watery or you have too much on your brush, it may run under the edges of the stencil.

3 If you use two colors, allow the first to dry. Take care when you lift the stencil off. Do not drag it.

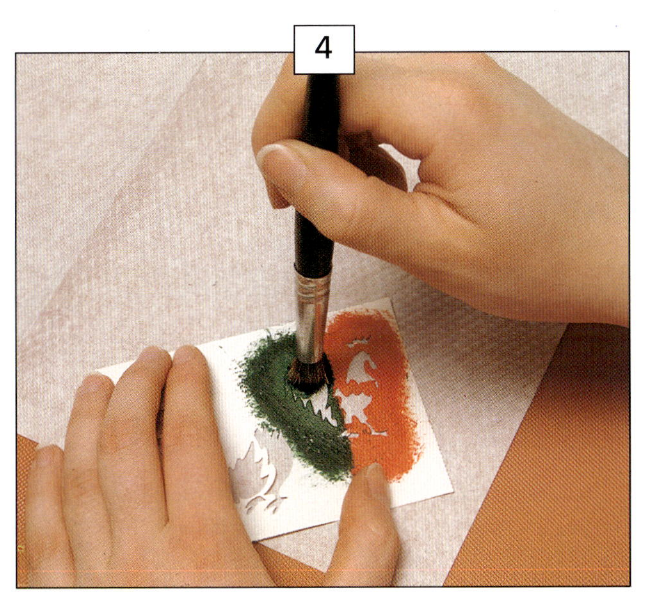

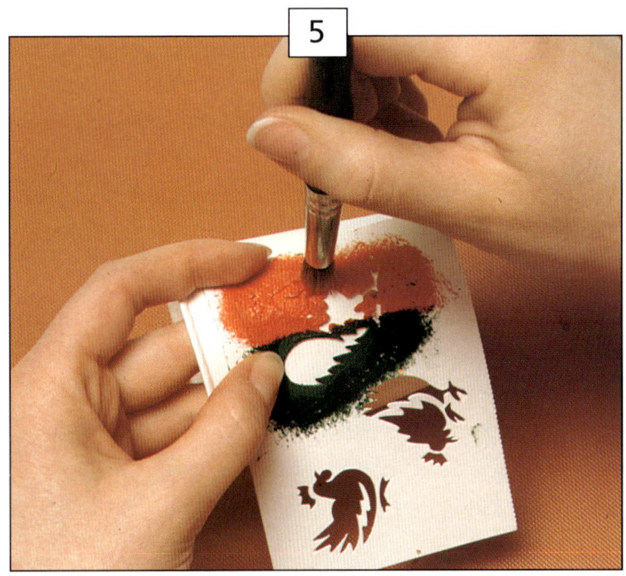

4 When you've got the hang of it, select your stencil. Stencil the napkins and the rest of your objects.

5 When you stencil the cup or anything similar, hold it carefully with one hand, using the thumb and index finger to hold the stencil in place.

TIP

☛ Protect your stenciled design and only use your plates for wrapped or dry food.

Fancy Gift Box

Spray with a toothbrush! – and recycle any box into a gift box.

YOU WILL NEED

- Colored inks (red, purple)
- Shallow containers
- Eye dropper
- Ivy leaves
- Two old toothbrushes
- Paper
- Pieces of scrap cardboard
- Paper doilies
- Cardboard box
- Glue stick
- Clothespins
- Scissors

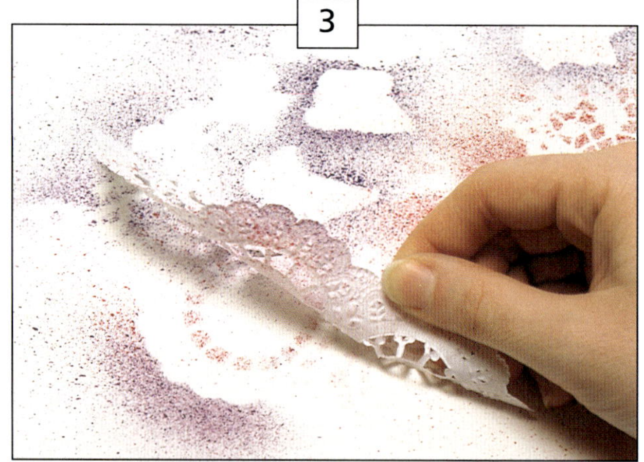

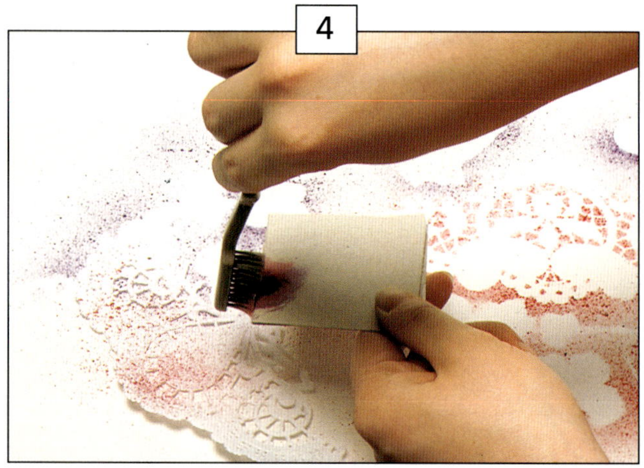

1 Put some different colored inks into shallow containers with an eye dropper.

2 Try out your pattern on some scrap paper first. Lay some ivy across your paper. Dip a toothbrush in one of the inks. Hold the toothbrush over your paper and push it across the edge of a piece of cardboard so that it sprays the ink across the ivy.

3 Now try using a paper doily the same way. Lift it to check what is happening. If there is too much ink on your brush, it will make blobs. It is better to be patient. Experiment until you get it right.

4 Now spray the paper you will use for your box. Use the other toothbrush with the other color ink. Move your ivy and lace across the paper. Change the colors for different parts of your picture. Move the objects and spray again until the paper is covered.

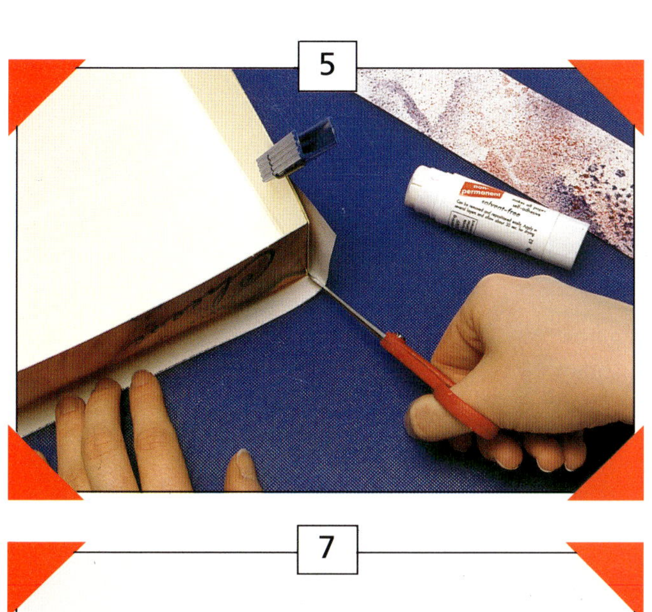

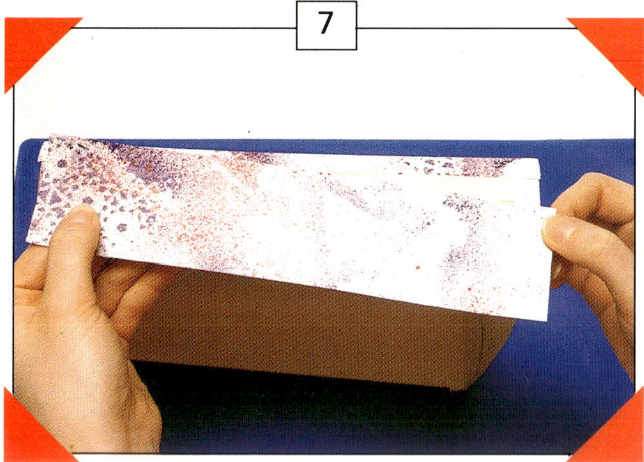

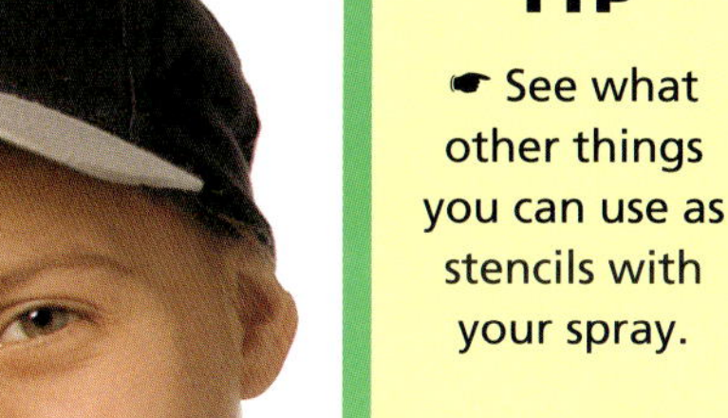

5 Now cover the box lid with the paper. Glue it to the top and over two sides. Cut off the excess paper carefully and put to one side. Hold the paper in place with clothespins while the glue dries. **Snip the corners of the paper where it overlaps the other two sides.**

6 Fold the edges over and glue them down. Hold them together with clothespins while they dry.

7 **Cut the extra paper into strips to cover the remaining two sides.**

Papier-Mâché Dish

Use waste paper to make this dish with a stenciled decoration.

- Plastic bowl as mold
- Petroleum jelly
- Old newspapers
- Water
- Wallpaper paste
- Plastic mixing bowl
- Teaspoons
- Large paintbrush for paste
- Clean newsprint
- Ready-mixed paint (blue, red)
- Shallow containers
- Stencil brush
- Stencils
- Brush for varnish
- Varnish

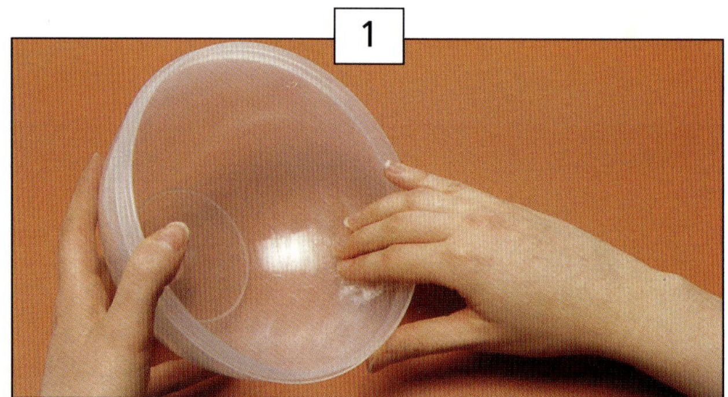

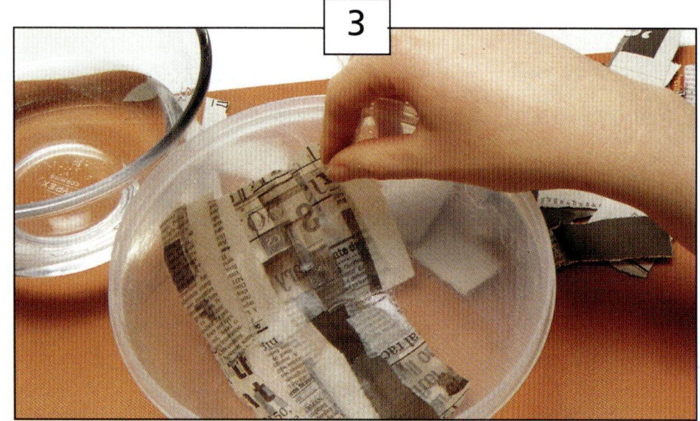

1 Give the inside of the plastic bowl a fine coating of petroleum jelly. This is so that your dish will come away easily when your papier-mâché dish is finished.

2 Tear the newspaper into long thin strips about 1 inch wide. You will find it tears more easily in one direction than the other. Then tear these long strips into 3-inch strips so that you have small pieces of newspaper.

3 Dip the individual strips in water. Shake the excess water off them. Lay them around the inside of the bowl, overlapping them, until it is completely covered.

4 Mix the wallpaper paste in a bowl with water according to directions. See page 180.

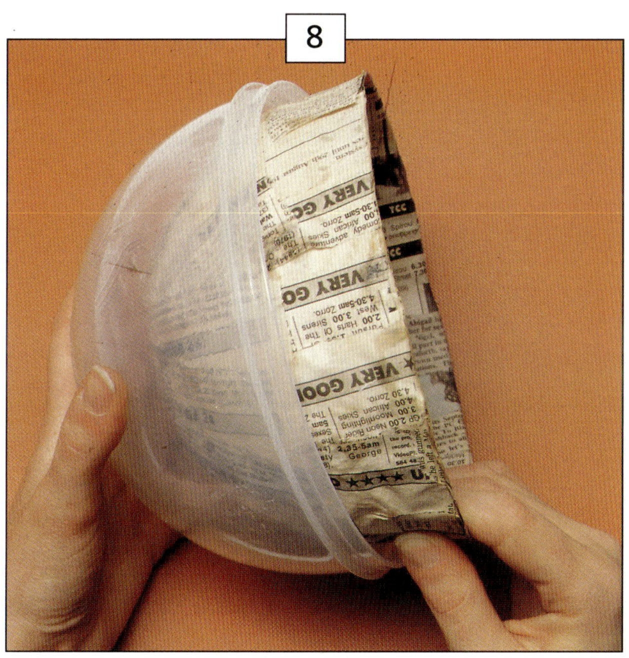

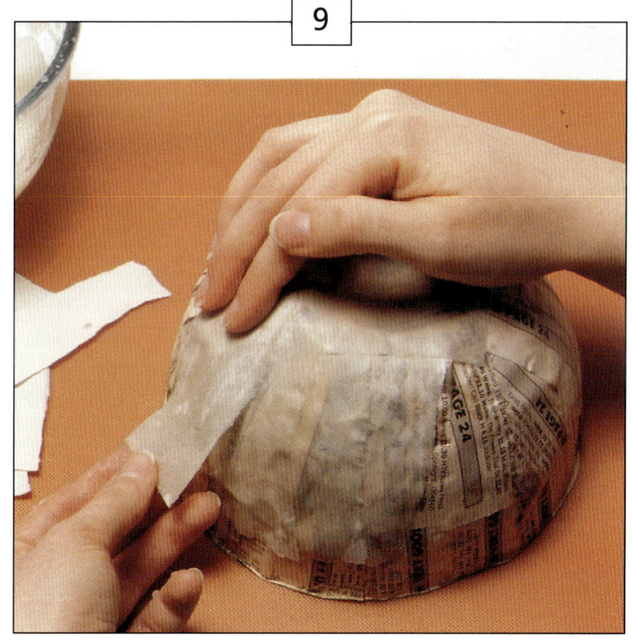

5 Stir well and leave it to form a paste.

6 Paste strips of newspaper with the brush or your hands and lay them around the inside of your bowl.

7 For the second layer, lay the newspaper strips in the opposite direction. Continue layering for four or five layers. Remember to alternate the direction of each layer. Let the paper dry between layers. You can put it on a radiator, or out in the sun, depending on the time of year.

8 When your papier-mâché bowl is dry, take it out of the bowl. To do this, get hold of the edges of the papier-mâché bowl and twist to remove from bowl.

9 Now paste a layer of clean newsprint on your bowl. Tear strips as before and put a single layer on the inside and outside of your bowl.

TIP

☞ You can build up papier-mâché on all sorts of objects if you cover them with petroleum jelly first. You may need to cut it in half to get it off, but you can paste it together again with more strips. (Be sure to ask an adult if you can use an object.)

10 Overlap the strips in the same way, but this time take the pieces over the rim of the bowl to make a neat edge.

11 Stencil a number of motifs onto a piece of newsprint and let them dry.

12 Tear these motifs out. Make sure there are torn edges all around the motif and not sharp edges. The torn edges blend in more easily.

13 Paste these motifs onto the inside and the outside of your bowl.

14 Use a brush to dab them down. Let these stencils dry.

15 Finally – give your bowl one or two coats of varnish.

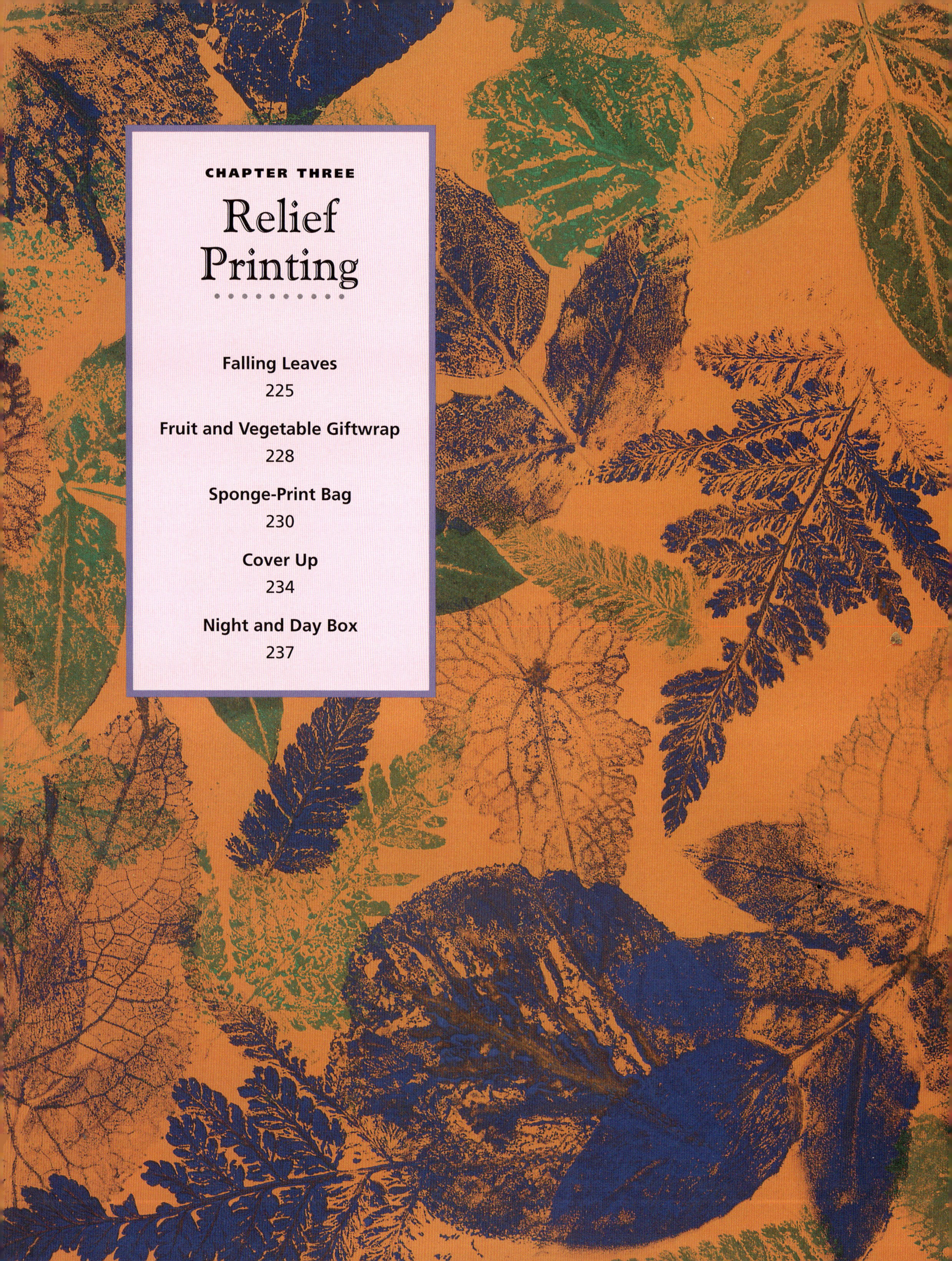

CHAPTER THREE

Relief
Printing

Falling Leaves
225

Fruit and Vegetable Giftwrap
228

Sponge-Print Bag
230

Cover Up
234

Night and Day Box
237

Falling Leaves

Explore your neighborhood. Discover and collect a variety of interesting shaped leaves for your print.

YOU WILL NEED

- Printing inks (blue, green)
- Sheet of glass or plastic (inking plate)
- Printing roller(s)
- Newsprint
- A variety of leaves
- Colored paper
- Cardboard frame
- Scissors
- Craft glue

1 Put some ink on your inking plate and ink your roller.

2 Roll over a leaf with the inked roller. Make sure you put enough ink on.

3 Practice on newsprint. Place the leaf ink side down on your paper. Cover it with another piece of paper.

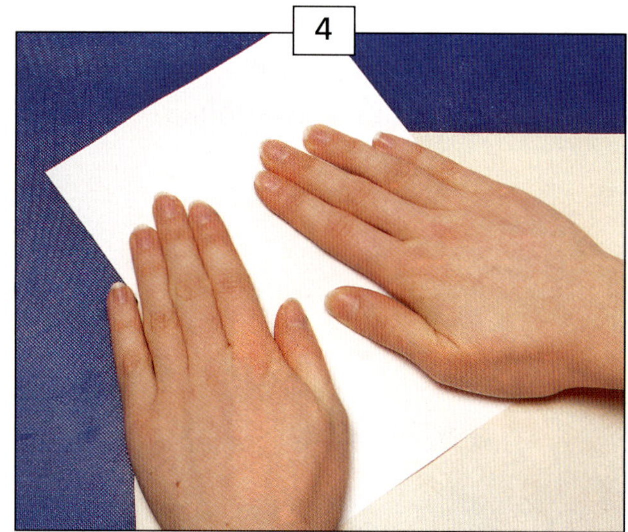

4 Press down on the paper with both hands. You could roll over it with a roller if you have another clean one.

5 Carefully peel off the leaf to leave a print behind.

6 When you are ready, you can print the leaves onto your colored paper. Use another color as well and print until your paper is covered with leaves.

7 **To make a frame, cut a rectangle in a piece of cardboard the size you want your finished picture to be.** Use your frame to select the part you think is best.

8 **<u>Cut the picture out</u>** and glue it behind the frame.

TIP

☞ Print from some other flat things such as squashed soda cans.

Fruit and Vegetable Giftwrap

Make your own wrapping paper by printing with fruit and vegetables. It will make your gift more exciting to look at and more personal to receive.

YOU WILL NEED

- Kitchen knife
- Various fruit and vegetables: e.g. cucumber, apples, lemon, bell pepper, cabbage, onion, leek, celery, tomato, carrots
- Paper towels
- Ready-mixed paint (green, blue, red, brown)
- Plastic lids
- Pieces of cardboard
- Paintbrush
- Newsprint
- Colored paper (yellow)

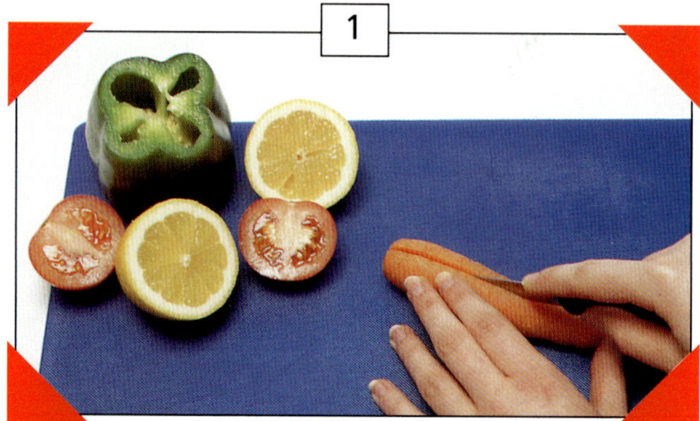

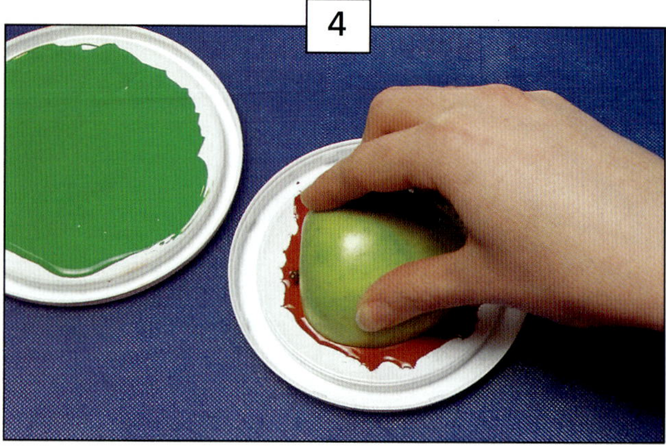

1 __Cut your fruit and vegetables in half. Cut lemons and similar fruit across the middle. Cut apples or similar through the ends.__

2 Some of them may need drying. Stand them on their cut end on some paper towels.

3 Put small amounts of paint onto plastic lids. Spread the paint with pieces of cardboard.

4 Press your cut fruit or vegetables into the paint.

5 Use a brush to put the paint on, if necessary, if the object is too large for your paint container.

6 Experiment on newsprint to see what shapes you can make. Press the fruit or vegetable onto the paper.

7 Then print onto the colored paper.

8 Combine shapes and colors to make patterns for your wrapping paper.

Sponge-Print Bag

Print your own cloth and make a bag for keeping all kinds of things in.
You will enjoy using it simply because you have made it.
It can also be a great gift.

YOU WILL NEED

- Scissors
- Pieces of sponge (not the real sort)
- Black felt-tipped pen
- Shallow containers
- Acrylic paint (we used iridescent colors, but any acrylic will do)
- Paper
- Iron
- Ironing board
- A piece of muslin or other cotton cloth 12 x 28 inches
- Needle and thread
- Clothespins
- Safety pin
- Two pieces of cord or fabric tape, 30 inches long
- Scraps of fabric

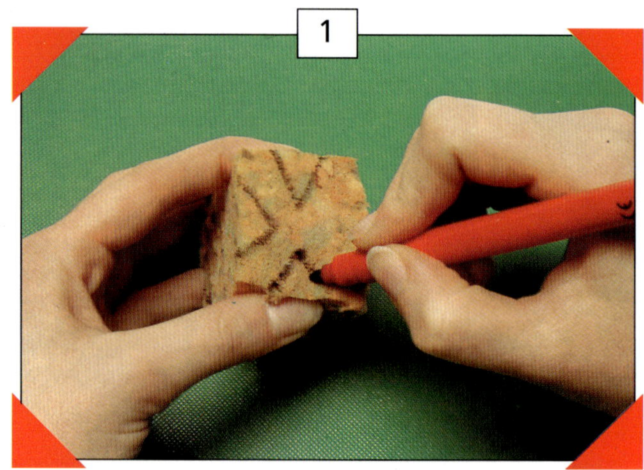

1 <u>Cut the sponge into 2-inch squares.</u> Draw the shape you want onto the top of the square with a felt-tipped pen. Keep the shapes simple.

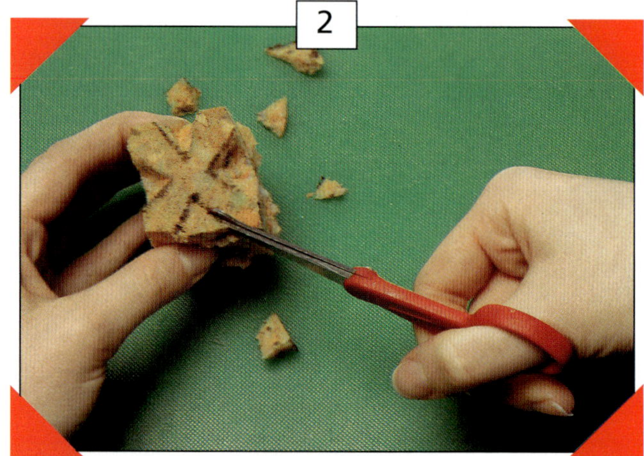

2 <u>Cut the shape out with scissors by carefully snipping the sponge.</u>

3 Pour some paint into the shallow containers and stamp the cut shape into the paint and print it on some paper. Try out each of your shapes. Combine them to make different patterns.

4 <u>Set the iron to a cotton setting. Iron the piece of cloth flat (with an adult present). Fold the cloth in half and iron flat</u>. Then open out the cloth so that you can see where both sides are.

TIP

☞ You can try printing on other fabrics. Make a scarf perhaps. Use some fabric paints.

5 Now that you have decided on a pattern, you can print your cloth. Put some paper underneath to stop the color from damaging your working surface. Leave a margin of at least ¾ inch down each of the long sides. Leave at least 1½ inches at the top and bottom. Allow the paint to dry.

6 Fold the cloth in half again, with the printed side facing in. <u>Sew up the sides ¾ inch from the edge.</u>

7 Fold the top edges over ½ inch and <u>iron flat</u>.

8 Then fold them over ¾ inch and <u>iron flat</u>. Sew along the bottom edge of these folds. You can use clothespins to hold the cloth in place.

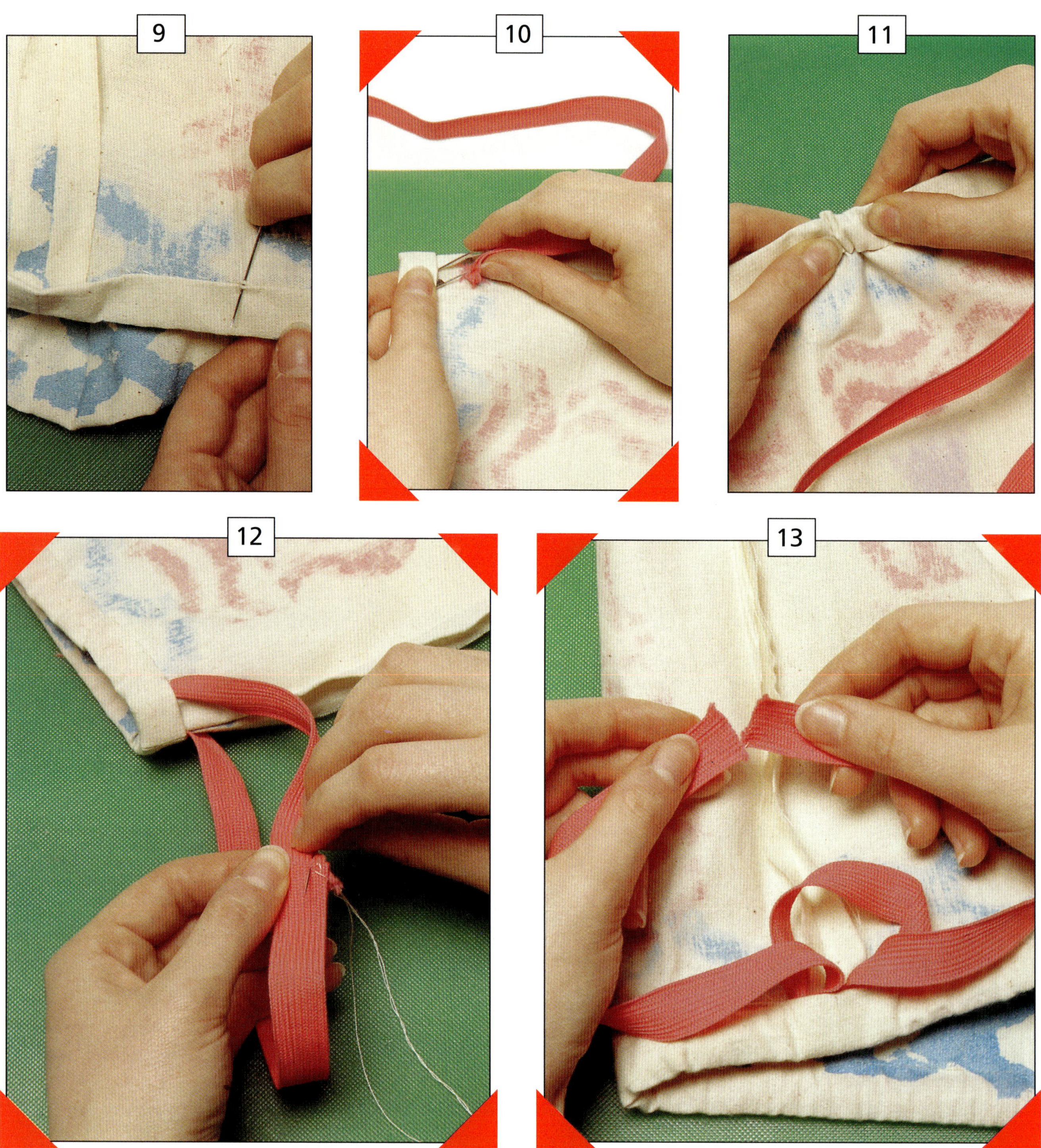

9 Leave a 1½-inch gap at each side edge. This is where the cord or tape will go.

10 <u>**Fasten a safety pin onto the end of one of the pieces of cord or tape.**</u>

11 Thread it through all the way around the top.

12 <u>**Sew or tie the two ends together.**</u>

13 Now thread your other piece of cord or tape through, so that the ends come out at the opposite side. <u>**Sew or tie these ends.**</u>

14

15

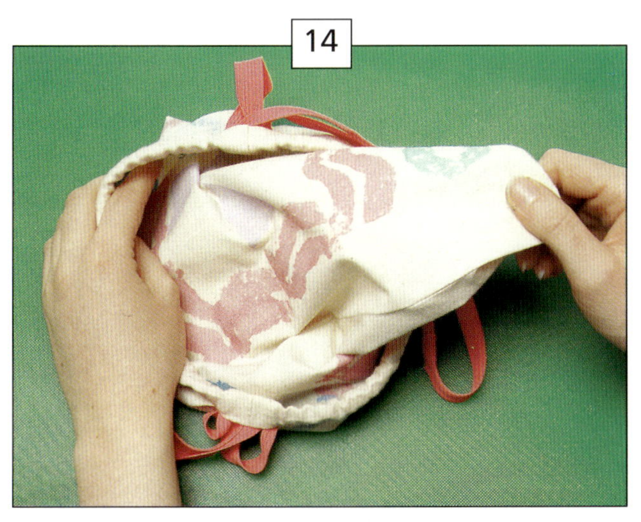

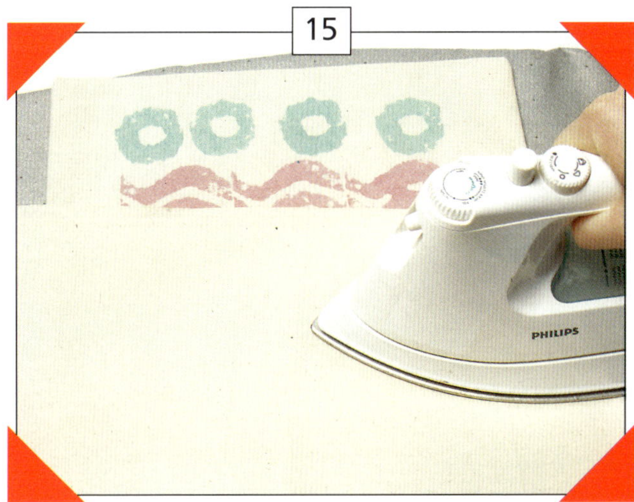

14 Turn the bag so that the pattern is on the outside.

15 Cover the bag with a scrap of material and **iron flat**. When you pull the tapes, the bag will close.

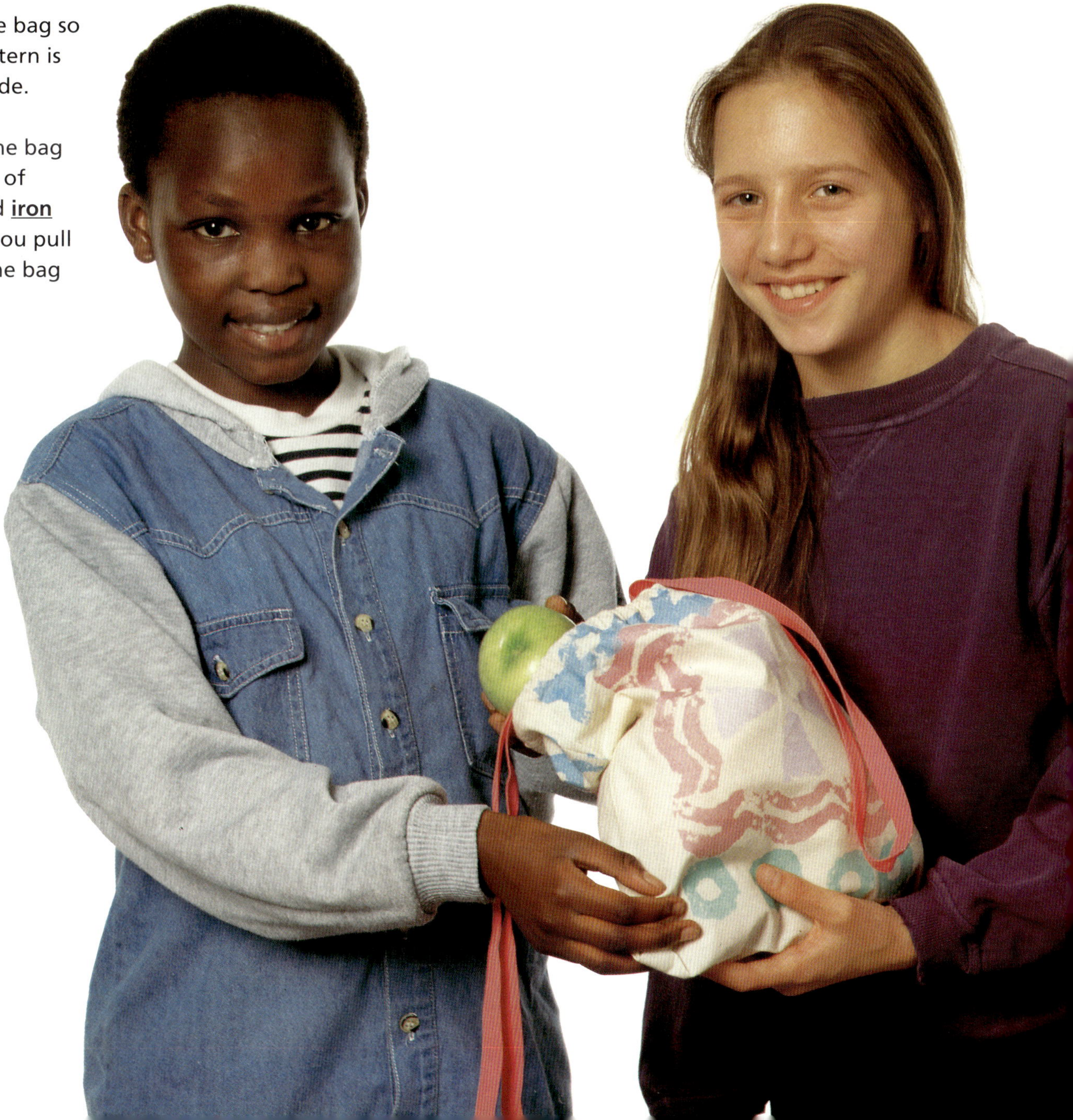

Cover Up

Make your own printing block from string to print a book cover.
Not only will you enjoy making it, your favorite books will be kept clean,
and be just yours.

YOU WILL NEED

- Craft glue
- String
- Scrap cardboard
- Scissors
- Printing ink (blue)
- Sheet of glass or plastic (inking plate)
- Printing roller
- White paper
- Ruler and pencil

1 Use craft glue to stick your string on a 2-inch square of cardboard. You can draw your pattern on first as a guide. Make continuous spiral shapes, **or cut the string into short lengths for straight lines.** Leave the glue to dry.

2 Squeeze some printing ink onto your inking plate. Roll the ink with your roller until it is spread evenly.

3 Roll the ink over your string printing block until it is completely covered.

4 Now try printing on some paper. Place the block face down on the paper and press down evenly all over. Inspect your print. You may need to use more or less ink. As you take more prints, the color will get stronger.

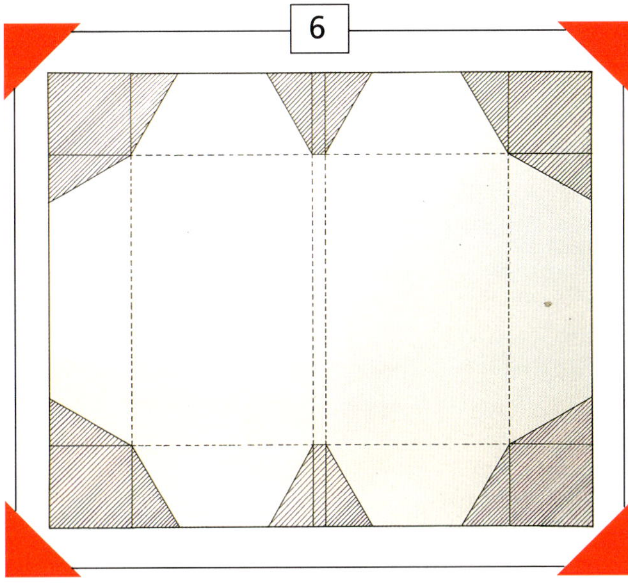

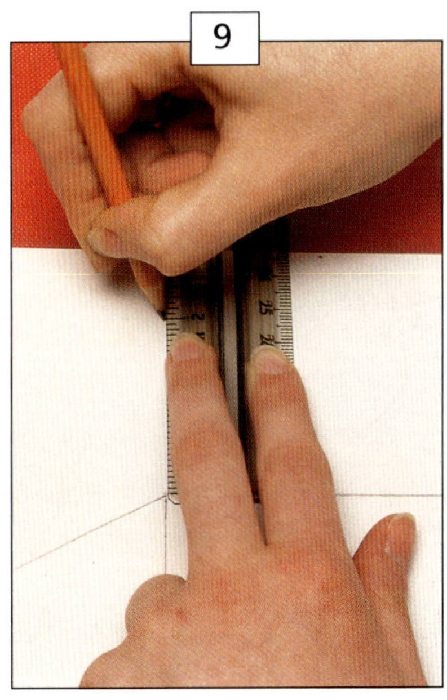

5 When your block is printing well, you can print the paper for your book cover. Your piece of paper needs to be at least 2 inches bigger than your open book. Don't forget to add the width of the spine in your measurements.

6 This diagram shows what your book cover should look like. **The shaded areas on the diagram show which pieces should be cut away, leaving the flaps.**

7 When the printing ink is dry, turn the paper over. Place the spine of the book in the center of the paper. Draw around one side of the book.

8 Then carefully turn the book over and draw around the other side. Remember to allow for the width of the spine of the book.

9 Measure 2-inch flaps using the diagram as a guide.

10 <u>**Begin to cut out your book cover.**</u>

11 <u>**Cut away the areas which are shaded.**</u>

12 <u>**Score along the lines which are shown dotted in the diagram.**</u>

13 Fold the printed cover over your book.

TIP

☛ Make another string block and overprint on your cover with a contrasting color.

Night and Day Box

Open your box of moon and stars to see the sunshine inside. Keep your precious things in there, or use it to make a gift extra-special.

YOU WILL NEED

- Black felt-tipped pen
- Corrugated cardboard
- Craft knife
- Craft glue
- Empty cereal box
- Sheet of thin white cardboard 10 x 12½ inches
- Pencil and ruler
- Scissors
- Printing roller
- Sheet of glass or plastic (inking plate)
- Printing ink (blue, orange)
- Clothespins

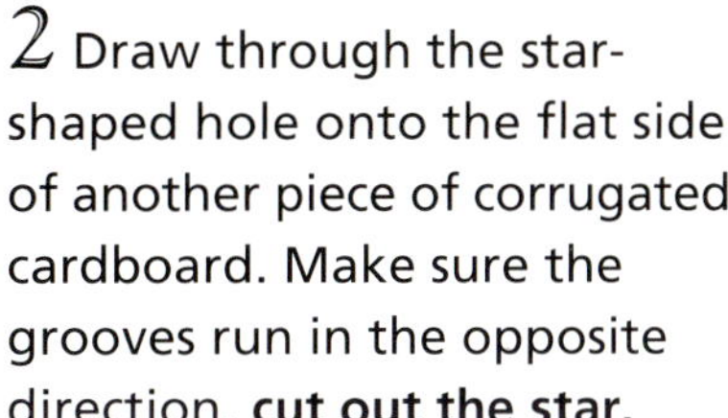

1 Draw a star shape on the flat side of a 3-inch square of corrugated cardboard. **Cut out the star with a craft knife** to leave a star-shaped hole.

2 Draw through the star-shaped hole onto the flat side of another piece of corrugated cardboard. Make sure the grooves run in the opposite direction, **cut out the star.**

3 Glue the cardboard with the star-shaped hole onto a 3-inch square of cereal box, and glue the star into the empty shape.

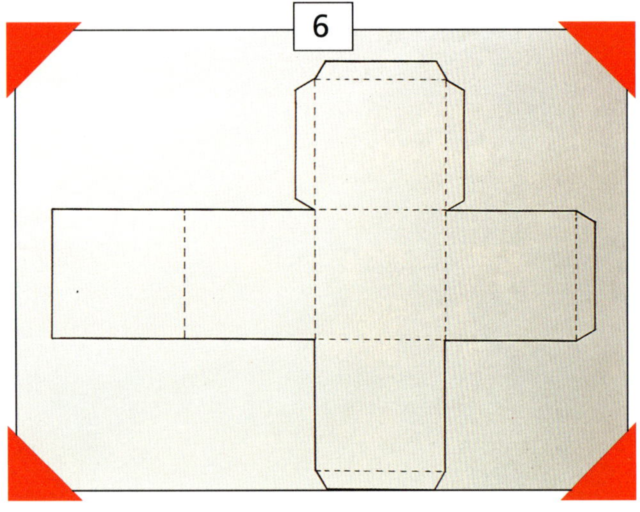

4 **Repeat the first three stages, but this time with a moon shape.**

5 **Cut out a 2-inch diameter circle** to represent the sun and glue it onto a flat piece of cardboard.

6 This diagram shows the shape you need to **cut out of your thin white cardboard**.

7 Draw on the cardboard the six 3-inch squares with 1½-inch flaps. You can use the template on page 262. **Cut out the shape.**

8 Roll some yellow or orange ink onto your inking plate. Roll over the sun shape.

9 Place it in the center of a square of your cutout box. Repeat for each square on one side of your cutout box .

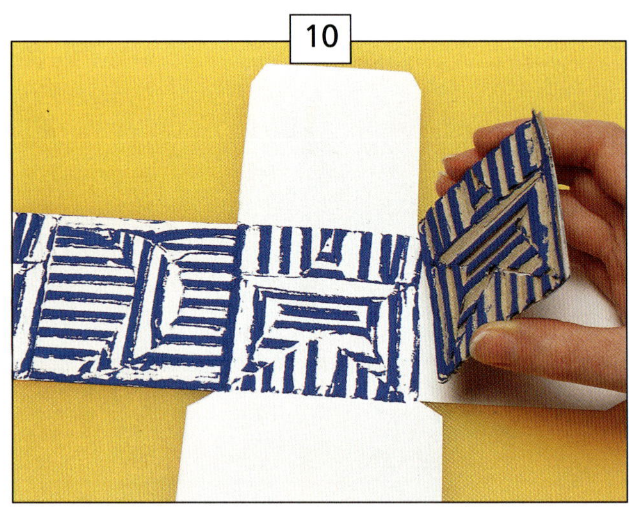

10 Roll over star and moon shapes with blue ink and print the other side of the box with the star and moon shapes, alternating the shapes.

11 When this is dry, <u>**score along the dotted lines in the diagram on the "day" side**</u> and fold up the box with the "night" on the outside.

12 Glue the side tab first, using clothespins to hold it together while the glue dries.

13 Glue the bottom tabs in place and tuck in the top one.

TIP

☞ Make other boxes using different shapes; hearts, clubs, diamonds, and spades, for example.

CHAPTER FOUR

Mono
Printing

Bug Masks

Use this intriguing technique to make these curiously insect-like masks.

YOU WILL NEED

- Paper approximately 9 x 11 inches
- Cotton thread 16 inches long
- Shallow containers
- Ready-mixed paint (red, blue, black)
- Paintbrush
- Water
- Scissors
- Stapler
- String 2 x 15 inches

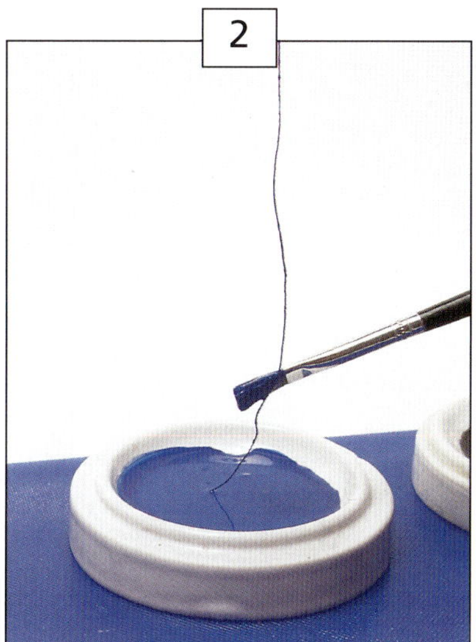

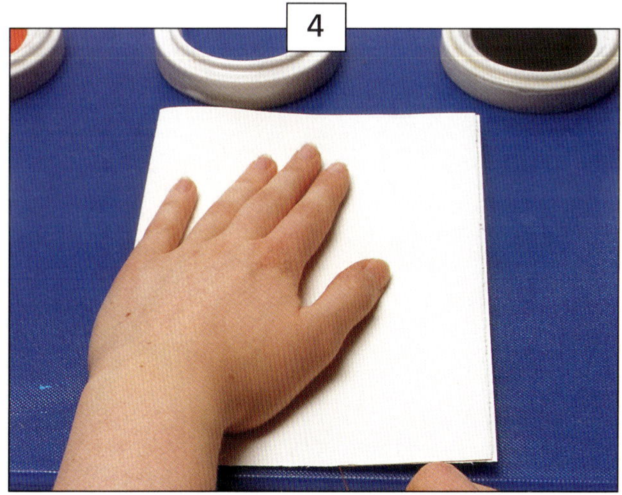

1 Fold the paper in half on the longest side then open it again. Put some different colored paints into the containers. The paint should be watered down just enough to make it runny. Hold one end of the thread and dip it in the paint. Push it under with a brush.

2 As you pull the thread out of the paint, let it run over the brush to remove any excess paint. This also straightens the thread.

3 Bring the thread out, fully covered with paint, and drop it onto one side of the folded paper. Hold one end and leave it hanging over the edge of the paper.

4 Fold the paper over and press down. Keep pressing with one hand and pull the thread out with the other. Pull toward the corner to make the shape wider.

5 Open your print.

6 Repeat the process with the other chosen colors.

7 **<u>Cut out a mask shape, leaving a gap around the edge of the print.</u>**

8 Tie a knot in one end of each length of string. Staple a string to each side of the mask.

TIP

☛ These would look good on your wall as decoration.

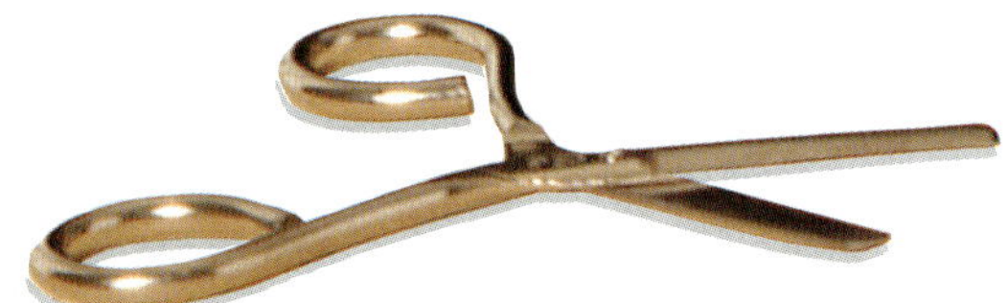

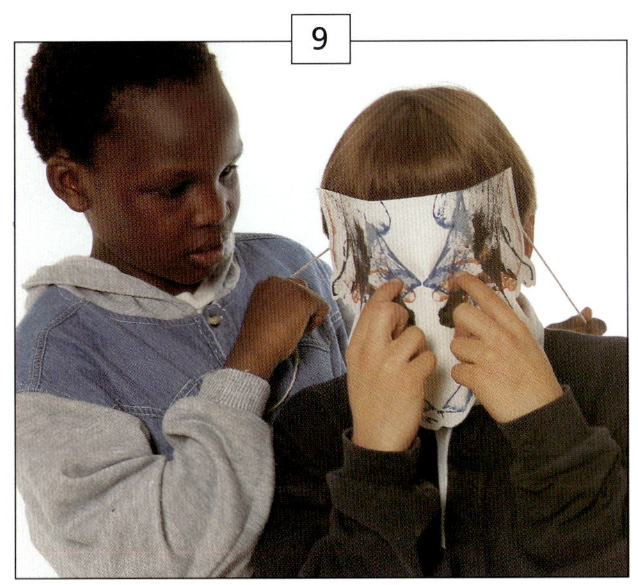

9 Try the mask on. Tie the strings at the back. Feel carefully where the eye holes need to be.

10 Remove the mask and mark with a pen where the eye holes need to be **and cut out small circles.**

Radical Robot

See what interesting odds and ends you can find
to build up this robot print.

YOU WILL NEED

- Various scrap objects: cardboard tubes, boxes, odds and ends
- Shallow tray for paint
- White acrylic paint (or silk vinyl latex)
- Black paper
- Paintbrushes
- Small container for inks
  Colored inks (blue, red)

1

2

3

4

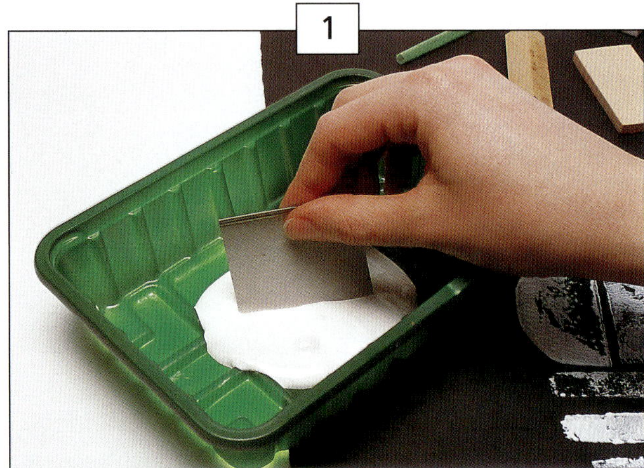

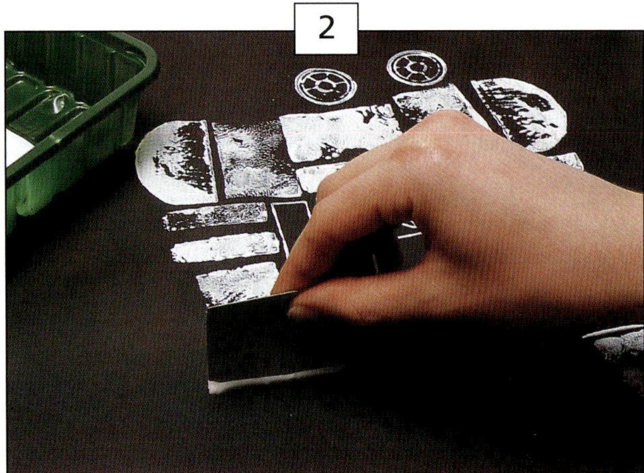

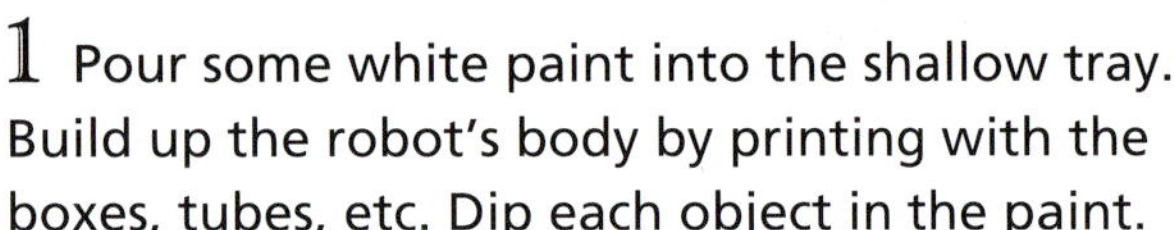

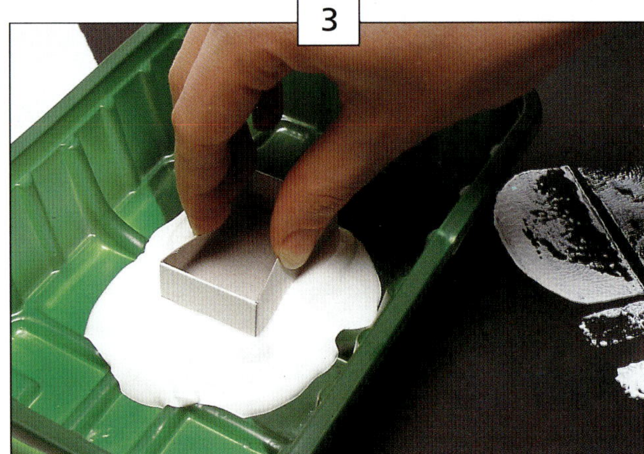

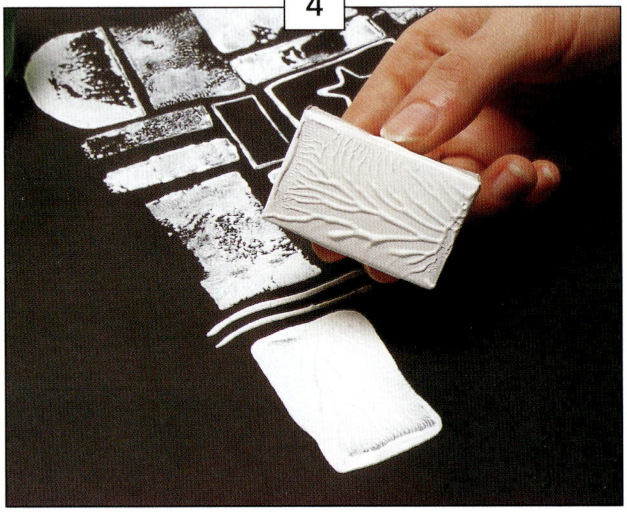

1 Pour some white paint into the shallow tray. Build up the robot's body by printing with the boxes, tubes, etc. Dip each object in the paint.

2 Press the object onto the paper. See what kind of shape it makes.

3 You can use small objects like keys, clothespins, a small box or empty spools for the robot's inner workings and use a slightly larger box for his legs. (You can wash the objects afterward.)

4 Gradually use more objects to build up your robot.

TIP

☛ You can make all kinds of pictures of machines or buildings like this.

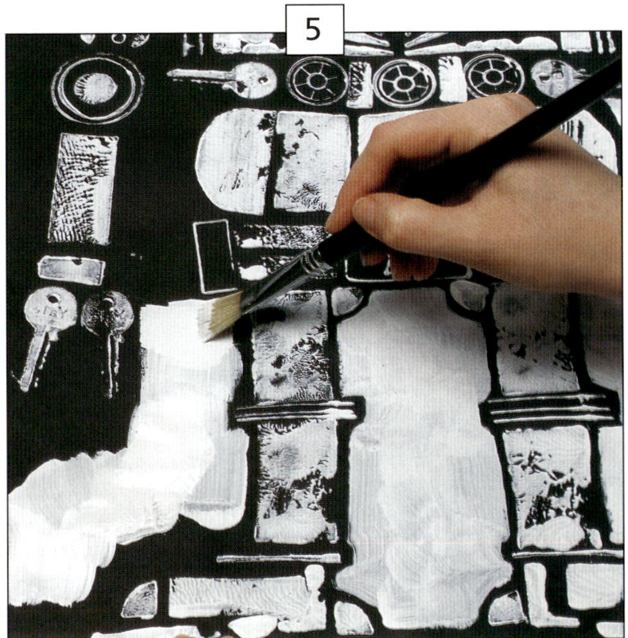

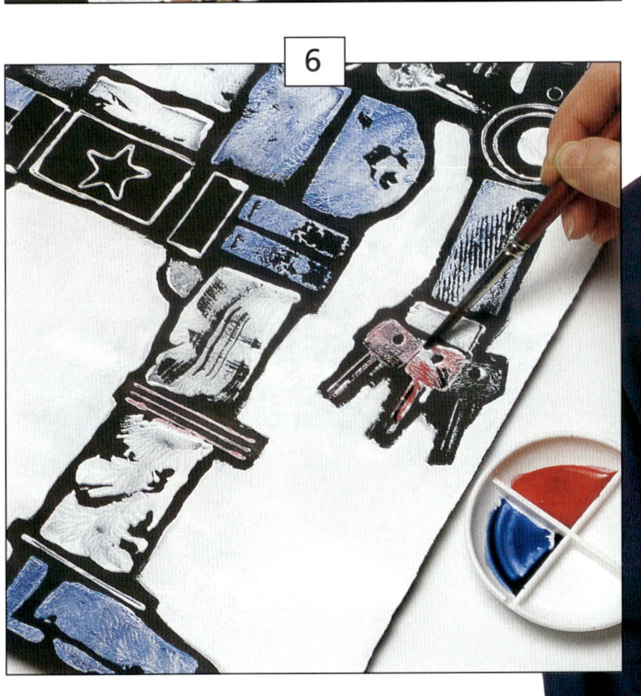

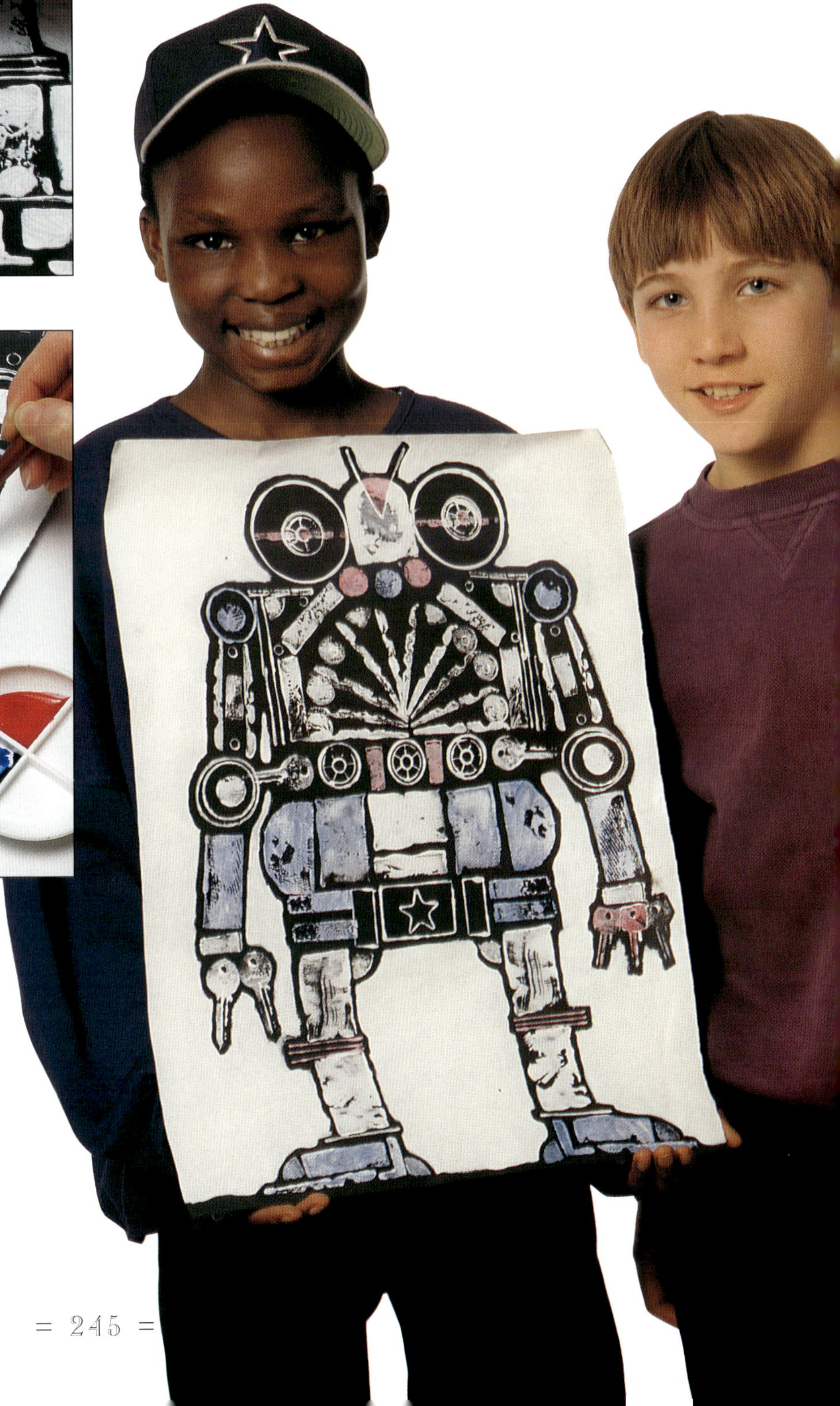

5 When you have finished printing, paint the background with white paint, leaving a black line around the robot.

6 When the white paint is dry, you can put thin washes of colored inks over the top where you feel it is needed.

Floating Butterfly

Enjoy squelching the colors in these big prints. Hang them on your bedroom wall as colorful decorations.

YOU WILL NEED

- Large sheets of newsprint
- Pencil
- Scissors
- Ready-mixed paint (yellow, black, red, white)
- Water
- Tape
- Thin garden stake
- Strong thread

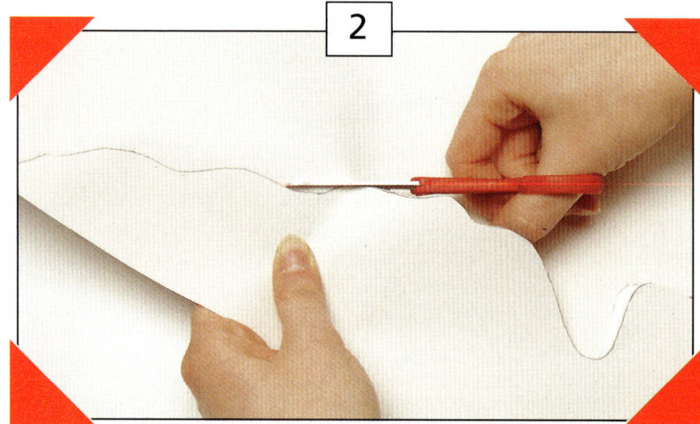

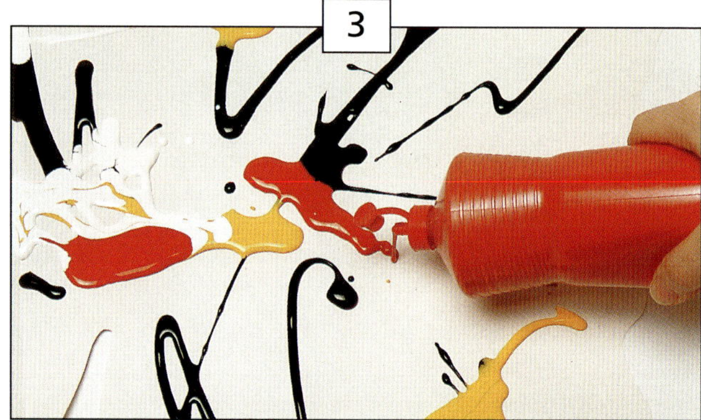

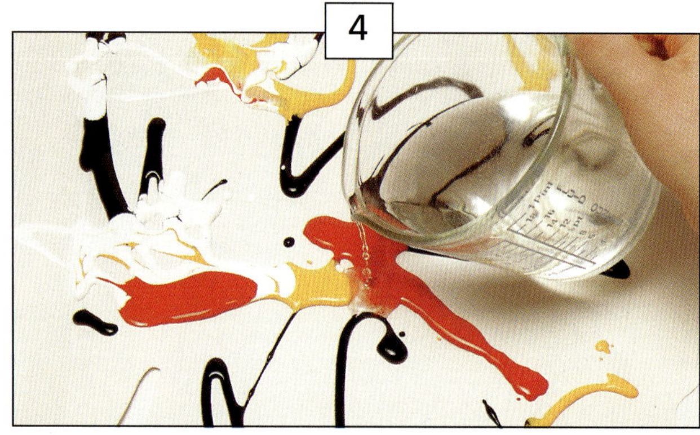

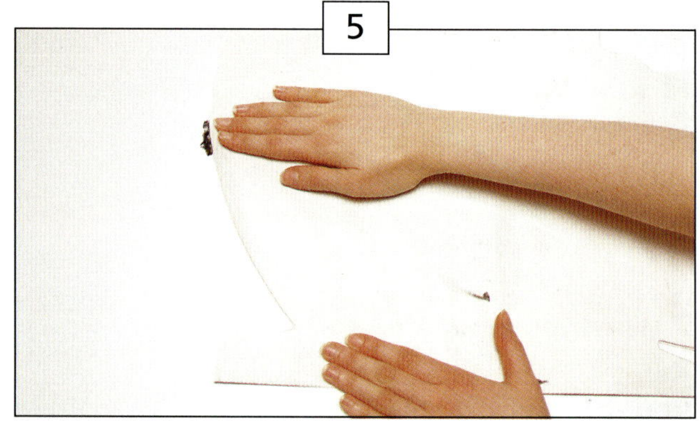

1 Fold a sheet of newsprint in half. Draw half a butterfly so that it fills the paper as much as possible. Make sure the center (the body) of the butterfly is on the fold.

2 **Cut out the shape and open up the paper.**

3 Squeeze some colors across one side and along the center of your butterfly.

4 Add some splashes of water, too.

5 Fold the paper over again.

TIP

☞ You could make a whole swarm of butterfly-sized prints.

6 Press it flat, pushing the paint along the fold and out toward the edges.

7 Unfold your print.

8 When the paint is dry, tape the stake across the back. Tie some thread to the stake and hang it on your wall like a Japanese kite.

Four Seasons Calendar

Use mono prints to illustrate the changing seasons. Hang the calendar at home or make it a New Year's gift.

- Pieces of paper approximately 5½ x 9 inches
- Sheet of glass or plastic (inking plate)
- Shallow containers
- Ready-mixed paint (assorted colors, red, brown, yellow, blue, green, orange, white)
- Paintbrushes
- Jar of water
- Paper towels
- Newsprint
- Paper (for frames)
- Pencil
- Scissors
- Glue stick
- Four sheets of black cardboard 9 x 11 inches
- Printed calendar
- Hole punch
- Ribbon

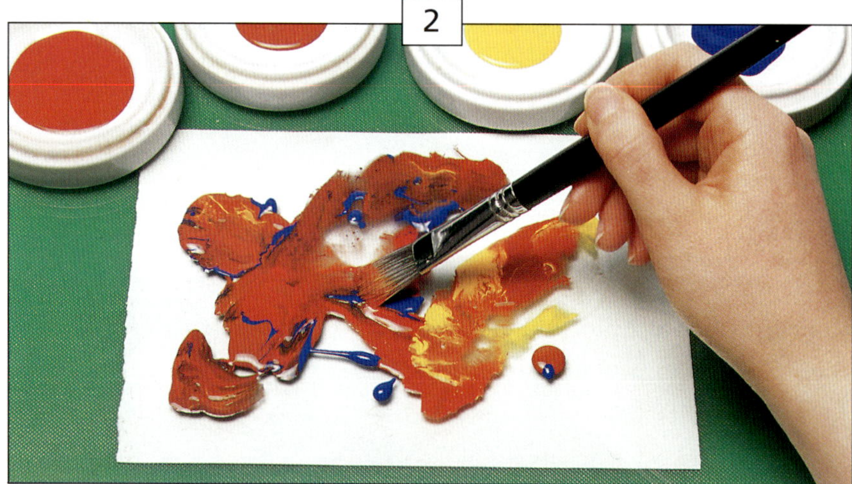

1 Begin with the picture for Fall. Put a piece of paper under your inking plate, so that you can see how big your picture is going to be. Paint some fall colors onto your inking plate.

2 Push the colors around with your brush until you think it looks about right.

3 You can also use paper towels, cardboard, or even your fingers to clear areas and to make different shapes.

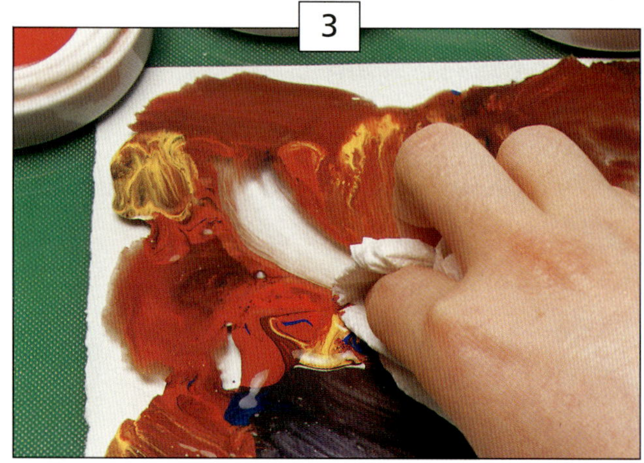

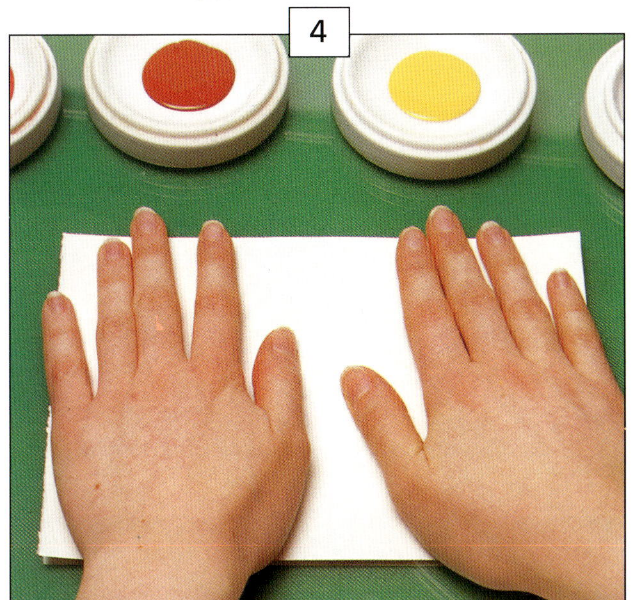

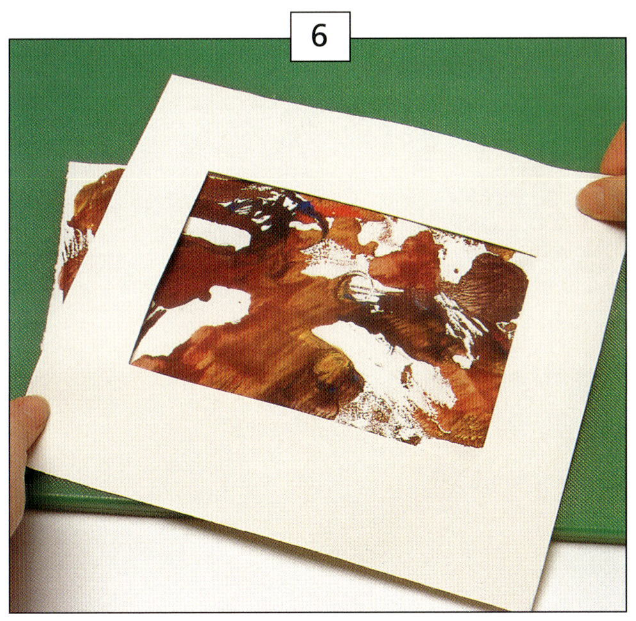

4 While the paint is still wet, lay a sheet of paper over it. Press down all over the paper.

5 Gently peel off your print from one side. You can make a number of different prints. Go on to make prints for the other seasons, choosing the most expressive colors. See pictures on page 251.

6 Choose your favorite print for each season. You can make a small frame to help you to select the best part of that print. Make the frame out of a piece of paper about 6 x 8 inches. Out of this, cut out a rectangle 4 x 6 inches.

7 Put the frame over your favorite part and draw around the inside rectangle.

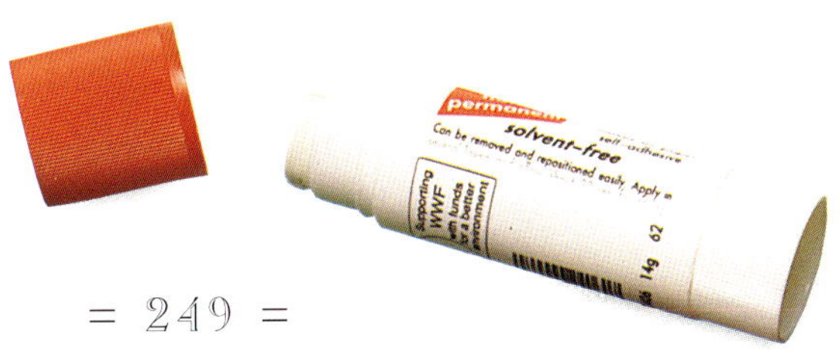

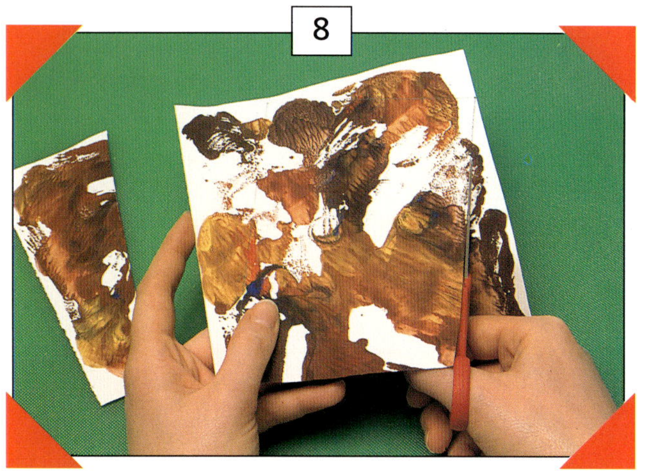

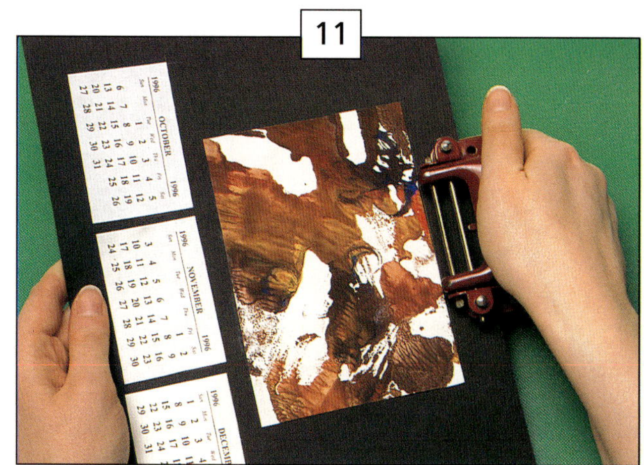

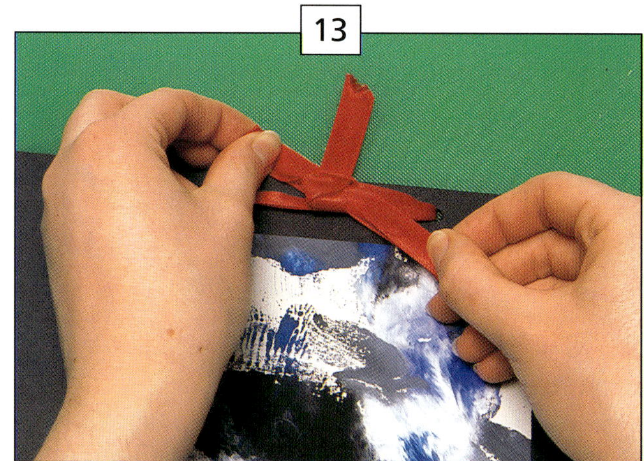

8 <u>Cut out the selected part.</u>

9 Glue each print onto a sheet of black cardboard, in the middle and about an inch from the top.

10 Place the appropriate three calendar months evenly underneath and stick down.

11 Punch holes in the center of the top of the four pieces of black cardboard.

12 Assemble them with the ribbon, in the right order, January to December.

13 Finish with a bow.

Bubble Bag

A fun method of printing that has fascinating results . . . and a way of making gift bags you can use again and again.

YOU WILL NEED

- Dishwashing detergent
- Ready-mixed paint (black)
- Water
- Plastic containers
- Paintbrush
- Drinking straws
- White paper
- Colored paper
  11½ x 16½ inches
- Pencil and ruler
- Double-sided tape
- Hole punch
- Cord

1 Mix some liquid detergent, ready-mixed paint, and a little water in a plastic container, and stir with a brush.

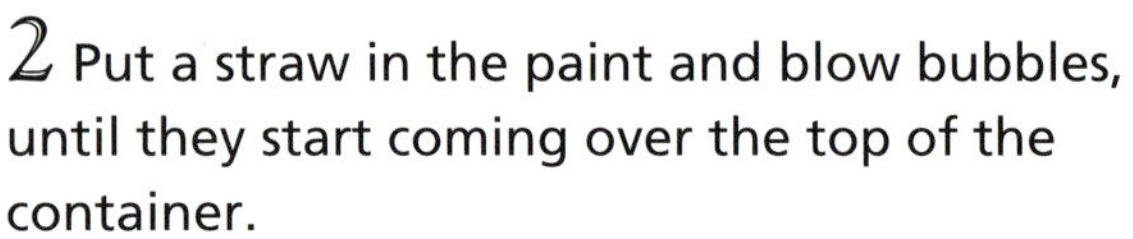

2 Put a straw in the paint and blow bubbles, until they start coming over the top of the container.

3 Practice the technique by holding a sheet of white paper with both hands and gently touch the bubbles with it.

4 Roll the paper around so that you catch all the bubbles. Let the bubbles burst on their own. When you have mastered the technique, print all over the colored paper.

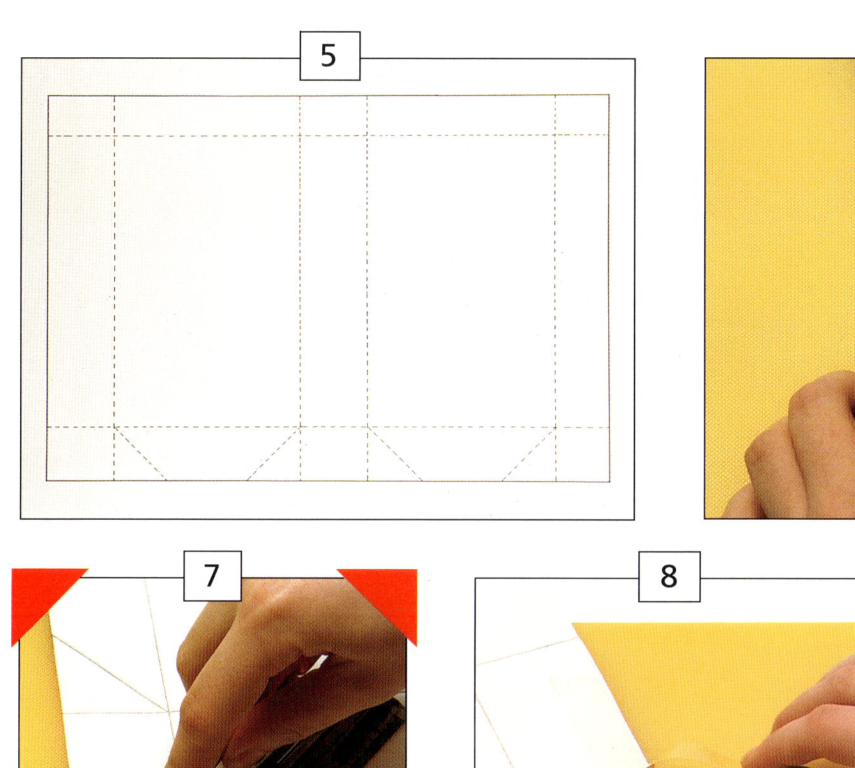

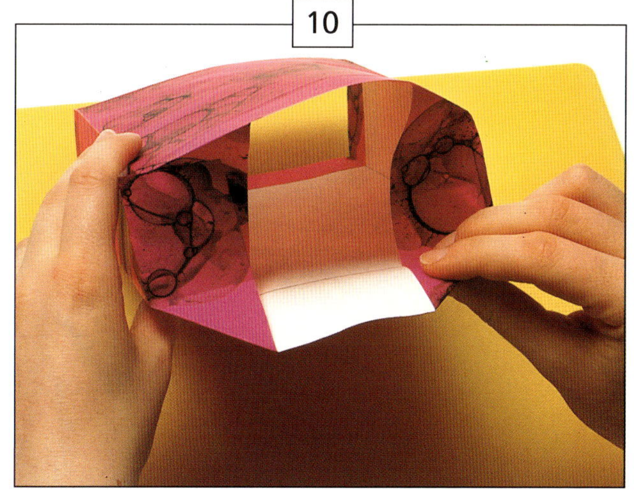

5 The diagram shows where the folds need to be to make the bag.

6 When the paper is dry, turn it over and draw lines as shown in the diagram, or trace the diagram from page 264.

7 **Score the dotted lines and fold them firmly.**

8 Fold along the bottom line and stick down with double-sided tape. Now put the double-sided tape along one side.

9 Stick the two sides together with double-sided tape.

10 Fold the bottom ends over along the scores.

11 Stick down, using double-sided tape.

12 Punch holes in the top edge on each side of the bag.

13 Tie the cord through the holes to make handles.

TIP

☛ Try combining a number of different colored paint mixtures on white paper.

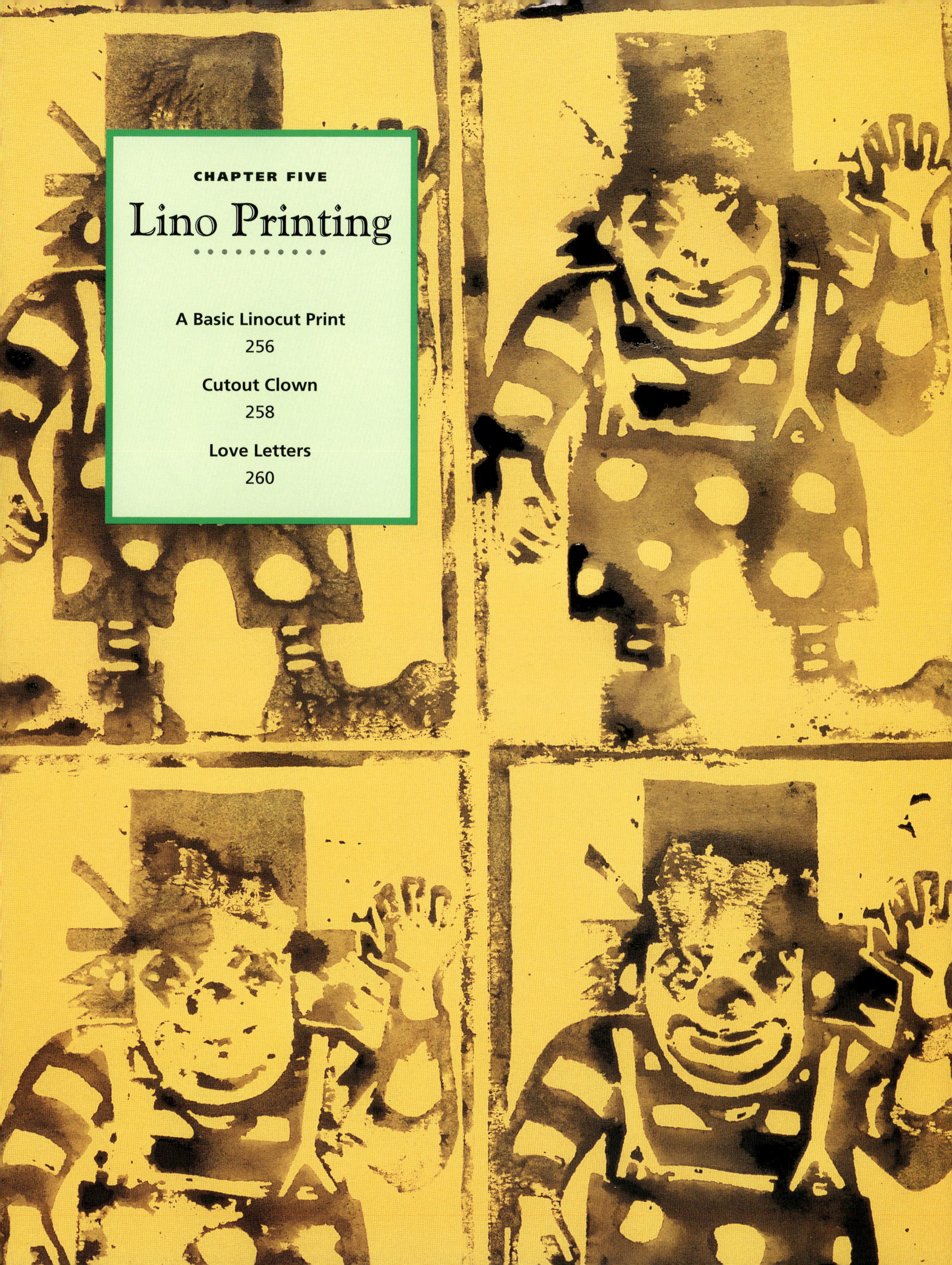

Lino Printing

A Basic Linocut Print

Follow the steps and you will learn a technique that will open up
all sorts of print possibilities.

YOU WILL NEED

- Pencil
- Linoleum for printing
- India ink
- Brush
- Bench hook
- Set of linoleum cutters
- Printing ink (green)
- Sheet of glass or plastic (inking plate)
- Printing rollers
- Water (optional)
- Newsprint
- Spoon

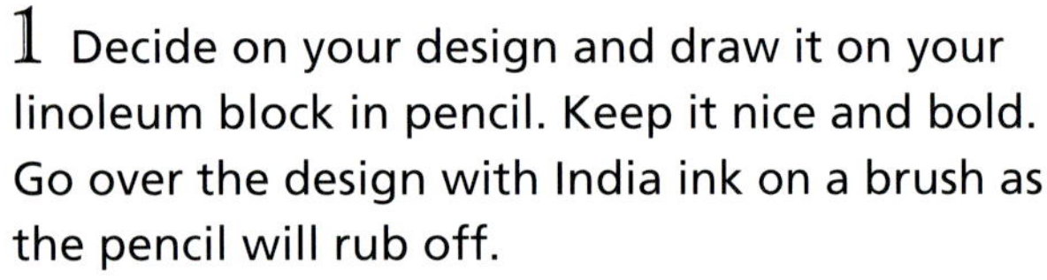

1 Decide on your design and draw it on your linoleum block in pencil. Keep it nice and bold. Go over the design with India ink on a brush as the pencil will rub off.

2 To stop your linoleum block from slipping, it's a good idea to make what is called a bench hook. It can be made from scraps of wood. It fits over the edge of your table and you push your linoleum block up against the top edge of it. See page 181. **In a linocut block, you must cut away all the parts you want to remain white in your print. Use the V-shaped tools to cut out lines and to cut around shapes.**

3 **The U-shaped tools are used to clear away large areas. Try not to dig into the linoleum. Turn the block as you cut, so that you always cut away from yourself. Keep the hand holding the linoleum close to you, and never in the path of the cutter.** Follow any instructions you received with your linoleum cutting tools.

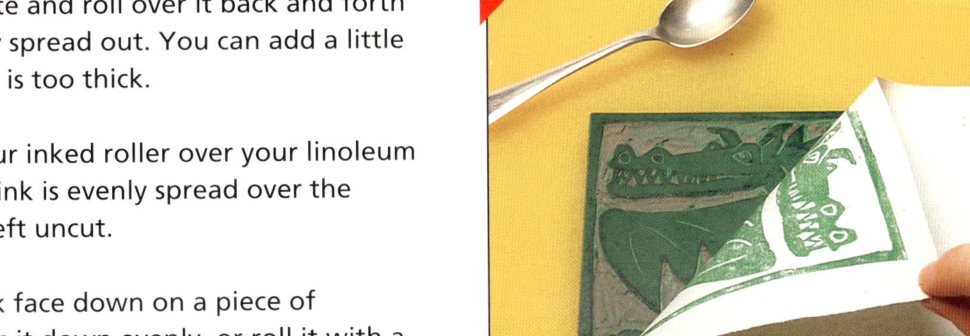

4 When you're ready to print, put some ink on your inking plate and roll over it back and forth until it is evenly spread out. You can add a little water if the ink is too thick.

5 Now, roll your inked roller over your linoleum block until the ink is evenly spread over the parts that are left uncut.

6 Lay the block face down on a piece of newsprint. Press it down evenly, or roll it with a clean roller.

7 Carefully turn over the paper and block. Holding the paper still, rub all over the paper with the back of a spoon in a circular motion. You can peel the print back from a corner to see how it is going.

8 When you have finished, peel the print off carefully. Inspect it to see if you need to adjust the ink or the rolling next time. **<u>Maybe you need to cut away some more linoleum.</u>**

Cutout Clown

Make your own greeting cards with your own personal message. There is a template you can use to help you.

- Scissors
- Thin cardboard
- Envelopes
- Tracing paper
- Carbon paper
- Linoleum blocks
- Linoleum cutters
- Printing rollers
- Printing inks (black, red)
- Gummed paper shapes

1 <u>Cut your cardboard into rectangles big enough for the clown on the template to fit.</u> Make sure that, when they are folded in half, they will fit in the envelopes.

2 Trace the template from page 263. Use carbon paper to transfer the tracing onto your linoleum block.

3 <u>Follow the instructions for cutting out your linoleum block on page 256.</u>

TIP

☞ Now draw your own design for your next greeting card.

4 Now draw and **cut out a block** for a greeting inside the card. Remember the letters and the word must be made back to front.

5 Fold your cards in half, then press them out flat again. Put some ink on the inking plate and roll it out as shown on page 257. Print the outside of the cards first.

6 When they are dry outside, print the insides with a different color.

7 Fold the cards again and stick on a gummed shape for the clown's flower.

Love Letters

Use a linocut to make your own personal stamp and make your stationery and envelopes your very own.

YOU WILL NEED

- India ink
- Paintbrush
- Linoleum
- Bench hook
- Linoleum cutters
- Scissors
- Craft glue
- Small block of wood
- Ink pad (from stationery stores) (red ink)
- Stationery
- Colored envelopes

1 Design a stamp based on your initials and a simple shape. Make your design about 1¼ x 1¼ inches.

2 Remember to write the letters backward. Draw the design on the linoleum with India ink. Refer to the previous project on page 258. It will be easier to cut out if you do it on the corner of a bigger piece of linoleum.

3 **Cut out your design with the linoleum cutters.**

4 **Then cut the square of linoleum off using the scissors.**

5 Spread some white craft glue across the back of the linoleum block.

6 Glue the square of linoleum to the block of wood.

7 With your ink pad, you can now stamp your stationery and envelopes with your own personal logo.

TIP

☞ Use your personal stamp on the inside cover of your books, too.

Templates

½"
Enlarge this template on a photocopier at A4 to A3 (141%) to trace at full size
½"
3"
3"
½"
12½"
½"
½"
10"
Night and Day Box

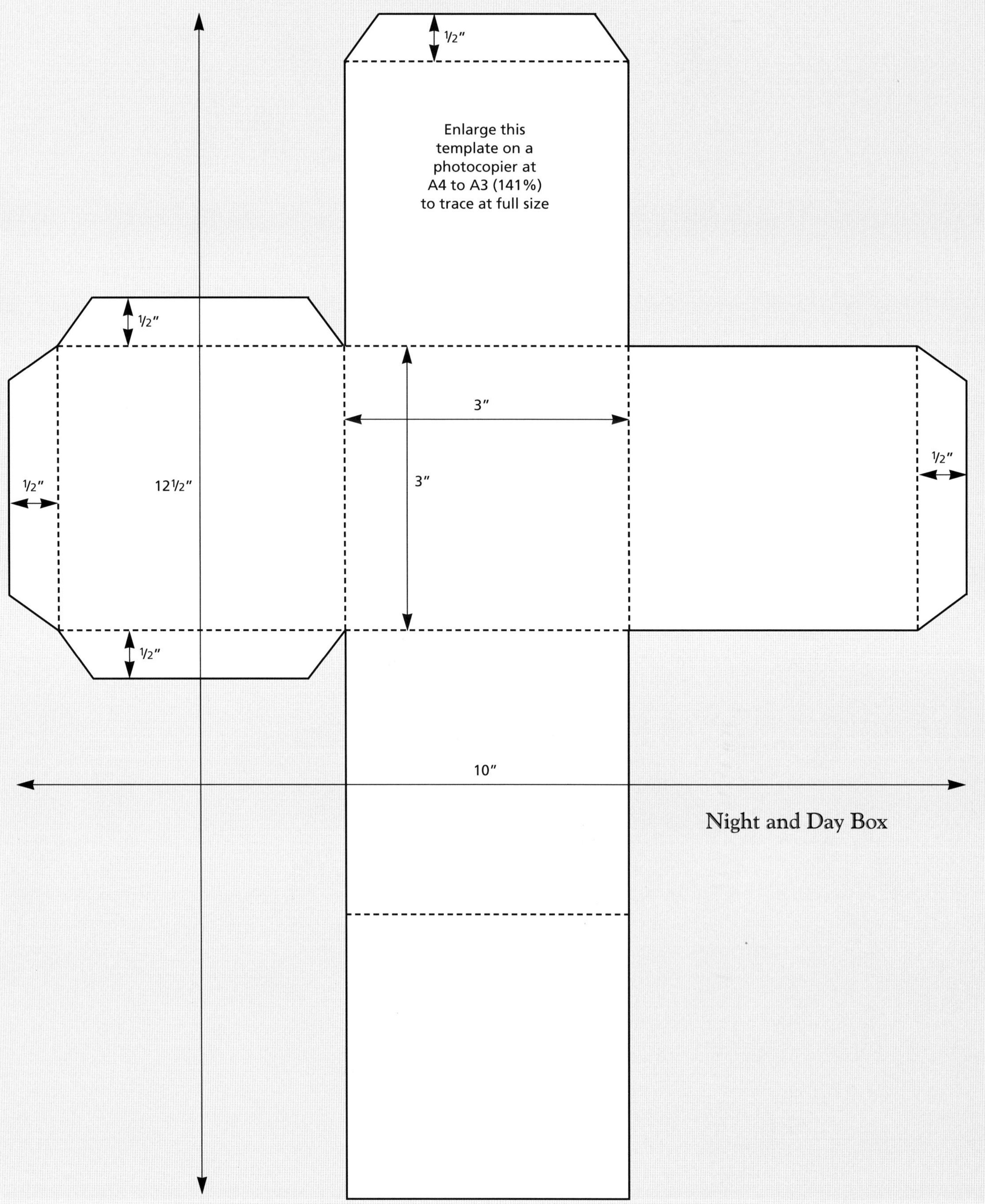

Sunflower T-shirt
Cutout Clown

1½"
1¼"
1½"
Enlarge this template on a photocopier at 200% to trace at full size
5½"
2"
16½"
5½"
2"
11½"

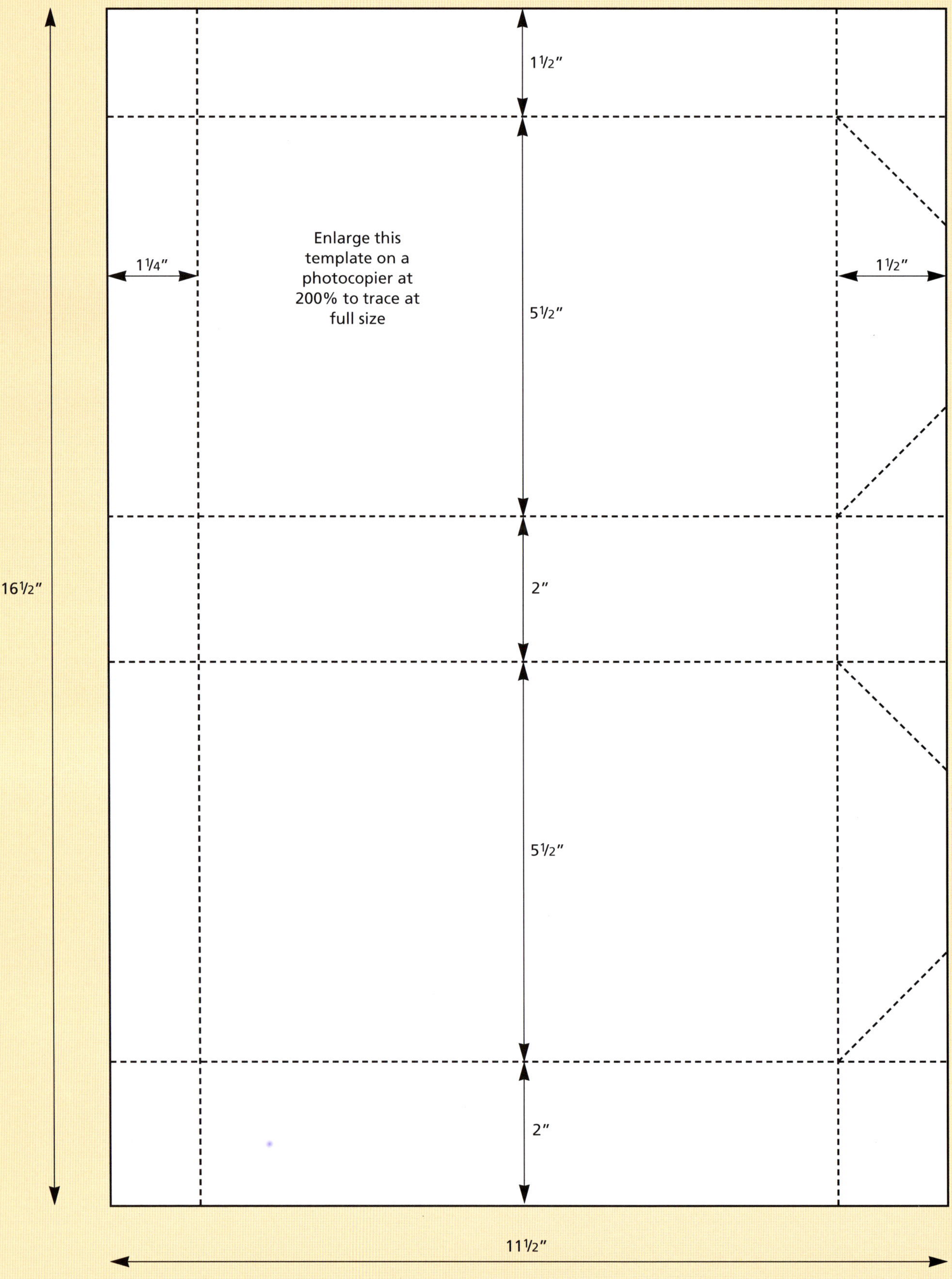

Bubble Bag